Grammar 6 Teacher's Book

Teaching grammar, spelling and punctuation with the
Grammar 6 Pupil Book

Written by

Sara Wernham and Sue Lloyd

Edited by Angela Hockley

Contents

PART 1: THE GRAMMAR PROGRAMME

    Introduction   3

    Teaching Ideas for Grammar   5

    Teaching Ideas for Spelling   24

    Spelling and Grammar Lessons   32

PART 2: LESSON PLANS

    Teaching with the Grammar 6 Pupil Book   35

PART 1

Introduction

For ease of use, this *Teacher's Book* has been divided into two distinct parts. The first part gives a comprehensive introduction, which explains the teaching method in detail. It is a good idea to read this part of the *Teacher's Book* before using the *Grammar 6 Pupil and Teacher's Books* in the classroom. The second part of the *Teacher's Book* provides a thorough and structured lesson plan for each day of teaching. The lesson plans in this part of the book are designed specifically for use with the corresponding pages in the *Grammar 6 Pupil Book*.

The *Grammar 6 Pupil and Teacher's Books* are designed to follow on from the *Grammar 1, 2, 3, 4* and *5 Pupil and Teacher's Books*. They are intended to:

- extend and refine the children's understanding of the grammar already taught,
- introduce new elements of grammar,
- teach new spelling patterns systematically,
- develop a greater understanding of sentence structure,
- improve vocabulary and comprehension,
- develop dictionary and thesaurus skills, and
- reinforce the teaching in the *Grammar 1* to *5 Pupil and Teacher's Books*.

Like the activities in the previous *Pupil Books*, the teaching in the *Grammar 6 Pupil Book* is multisensory and active. In the *Grammar 6 Pupil Book*, particular emphasis is placed on consolidating the children's learning and helping them to apply their new skills. As before in the *Grammar 1* to *5 Pupil Books*, each part of speech is taught with an accompanying action and colour. The actions not only enliven the teaching, but also make the parts of speech easier for the children to remember. The colours, which are useful when identifying and labelling parts of speech in sentences, are the same as those used in Montessori Schools. As in previous *Teacher's Books*, the *Grammar 6 Teacher's Book* explains all the essential teaching ideas.

Children's Achievement

The most dramatic improvements to result from using the *Grammar 6 Pupil and Teacher's Books* will be found in the children's writing. After completing the *Grammar 6 Pupil Book*, the children will spell and punctuate more accurately, use a wider vocabulary and have a clearer understanding of how language works.

In their first year at school, the *Phonics Pupil Books* taught the children to write independently by listening for the sounds in words and choosing letters to represent those sounds. This enables the children to write pages of news and stories. It is a joy to read their work and to see the great pride and confidence they derive from their newly acquired skills. It is important to build on this foundation in the following years.

The *Grammar Pupil and Teacher's Books* provide teaching ideas designed to develop the children's writing skills. The children become more aware that they are writing for a purpose: that their words are intended to be read and understood. They learn that their writing is easier to understand if it is grammatically correct, accurately spelt, well punctuated and neatly written. The children also learn that, if they use interesting words, their writing can give real pleasure. Even in the early stages, it is valuable for the children to have a simple understanding of this long-term goal.

The Format of the Pupil and Teacher's Books

The programme for *Grammar 6* consists of a *Teacher's Book*, offering detailed lesson plans, and a corresponding *Pupil Book*, with activities for each lesson. Enough material is provided in these books for 36 weeks' teaching, with two lessons for each week. The *Grammar 6 Pupil Book* is designed so that there is one activity page for each grammar lesson and two activity pages for each spelling lesson. Each lesson is intended to take up about one hour's teaching time.

Although it is referred to as the *Jolly Phonics Grammar Programme*, there are in fact two elements, namely spelling and grammar. The material in the *Pupil and Teacher's Books* is organised so that the first of the week's lessons concentrates on spelling and the second on grammar. However, the terms are used loosely and there is some overlap: parts of speech, punctuation and vocabulary development are among the areas covered in both spelling and grammar lessons. This is deliberate, as the two elements complement each other when combined.

INTRODUCTION

The overlap is particularly noticeable in the *Grammar 5* and *6 Pupil Books,* which have an extra activity page per spelling lesson. This page usually features one activity based on a related, or recently introduced, grammar point and another that looks at sentence structure within a grammar context.

The *Grammar 6* programme covers the more structured aspects of literacy, and is intended to take up only part of the teaching time set aside for literacy work. If two days' literacy lessons are devoted to grammar and spelling each week, this leaves three lessons that can be devoted to the areas not covered by *Grammar 6,* such as comprehension, group and individual reading, formal and creative writing and handwriting practice. The children should be shown how spelling and grammar relate to their other literacy work. For instance, if the children are studying a text that has an example of something they have recently learnt (such as a colon or semicolon, or the use of the passive voice), this should be pointed out. The children can then be encouraged to look, for example, at what goes before and after the punctuation, or identify the part of *to be* and the past participle used to form the passive verb.

For each activity page in the *Pupil Book* there is a corresponding page in the *Teacher's Book,* offering a detailed lesson plan and useful teaching guidance. More detailed explanations and advice are provided in the two following sections: 'Teaching Ideas for Grammar' and 'Teaching Ideas for Spelling'. Relevant material from the *Grammar 1* to *5 Teacher's Books* has also been included for easy reference.

To avoid confusion, the *Jolly Phonics* grammar materials follow the convention of using different parentheses to distinguish between letter names and letter sounds. Letter names are shown between these parentheses: ⟨ ⟩. For example, the word *ship* begins with the letter ⟨s⟩. By contrast, letter sounds are shown between these parentheses: / /. For example, the word *ship* begins with the /sh/ sound.

Teaching Ideas for Grammar

The benefits of learning grammar are cumulative. In the early stages, the children's grammar knowledge will help them to improve the clarity and quality of their writing. Later on, their grammar knowledge will help them to understand more complicated texts, learn foreign languages with greater ease, and use Standard English in their speech and writing.

The accents and dialects in spoken English vary from region to region. The grammar we learn first is picked up through our speech and varies accordingly. However, at times, there is a need for uniformity. If we all follow the same linguistic conventions, communication throughout the English-speaking world is greatly improved. An awareness of this fact helps those children who do not speak Standard English to understand that the way they speak is not wrong, but that it has not been chosen as the standard for the whole country. All children need to learn the standard form of English, as well as appreciating their own dialect.

In their first five years of *Grammar,* the children were introduced to the concepts of sentences, punctuation and parts of speech. In the *Grammar 1 Pupil Book,* they learnt about proper and common nouns, pronouns, verbs, adjectives and adverbs, and they learnt to use verbs to indicate whether something happened in the past, present or future. In the *Grammar 2 Pupil Book,* the children's knowledge was extended and their understanding deepened. Their knowledge of sentences was refined and they learnt to punctuate with greater variety and precision. They were also introduced to irregular verbs and to new parts of speech, namely possessive adjectives, conjunctions, prepositions and comparative and superlative adjectives.

In the *Grammar 3 Pupil Book,* the children's understanding was further refined. They learnt how to distinguish between a phrase and a sentence, how to identify the subject and object of a sentence and how to organise sentences into paragraphs. In dictation, they received regular practice in writing direct speech with the proper punctuation. The children also learnt how to form the continuous tenses and were introduced to new parts of speech, namely collective nouns, irregular plurals, possessive pronouns and object pronouns. They also had regular dictionary and parsing practice with the aim of building their dictionary skills, improving their vocabulary and reinforcing their grammar knowledge.

The *Grammar 4 Pupil Book* continued to build on the previous years' teaching. The children learnt the difference between simple and compound sentences, about how statements can be turned into questions and how to distinguish between a phrase, a clause and an independent clause. They had regular parsing practice, both at sentence and verb level, to secure their understanding of parts of speech and of grammatical person and tense. The children were also introduced to the idea of simple subject-verb agreement, seeing what happens to the words in a sentence when a singular subject is made plural or, for example, when a sentence in the first person singular is rewritten in the third person. They were also taught new parts of speech, namely infinitives, noun phrases and concrete, abstract and possessive nouns.

The *Grammar 5 Pupil Book* extended the children's understanding and reinforced their grammar knowledge. Their understanding of verbs was deepened as they learnt about transitive and intransitive verbs, phrasal verbs, past participles and how to form the perfect tenses. They learnt that verbs can be modified by prepositional phrases as well as adverbs, and that adverbs can modify other adverbs and adjectives. They looked in depth at how adverbs fall into the categories of manner, degree, place, time and frequency and how adjectives tend to be written in a certain order. They were shown how to use parentheses correctly and how to punctuate vertical lists using colons and bullet points. They also had regular practice working with sentence walls – a simplified form of sentence diagramming – with the aim of refining their knowledge of sentence structure and deepening their understanding of how different parts of a sentence relate to one another.

The later *Pupil Books* continued to work on improving the children's vocabulary and writing, with a particular focus on developing their knowledge of antonyms and synonyms, prefixes and suffixes, and commonly confused homophones. The children were also encouraged to use onomatopoeia and different forms of comparatives and superlatives in *Grammar 4* and were introduced to homographs, homonyms and heteronyms in *Grammar 5*. In *Grammar 6,* they learn about near homophones, alliteration, idioms, paragraph structure and cohesion. They also learn to recognise the different literary styles and vocabulary used in formal and informal writing.

The *Grammar 6 Pupil Book* extends, consolidates and refines the teaching of previous years. The children are introduced to many new parts of speech, namely countable and uncountable nouns, gerunds, relative pronouns, relative and modal adverbs, modal and linking verbs, coordinating and subordinating conjunctions, and adverbials. In addition, they learn that prepositional phrases, past participles and relative clauses can act as adjectives. Their knowledge of sentences and sentence structure is also refined. They learn to distinguish between the active voice (when the subject does the verb action) and the passive voice (when the subject receives the verb action), and are shown how a sentence with a direct object sometimes has an indirect object. They are taught that a complex sentence has a subordinate clause which gives us more information about the main clause, and learn how to use the verb *to do* as an auxiliary to add emphasis or to form a question or negative statement. The children are taught how to form imperatives, which usually end in a full stop but can be punctuated by an exclamation mark, and are introduced to semicolons, which can be used in compound sentences or as listing commas in complicated lists.

TEACHING IDEAS FOR GRAMMAR

They learn how colons can be used in sentences to introduce a list of examples, a single idea or an explanation and continue to parse sentences and put them into sentence walls on a regular basis.

The *Grammar 6 Pupil Book* builds upon the teaching in the *Grammar 1 to 5 Pupil Books,* so the children's understanding of this teaching must be secure before moving on. For this reason, it is important to go over anything the children are unsure of before introducing new concepts. The *Grammar Pupil Books* provide a systematic approach to revision. This enables even the slowest learners to keep up, while ensuring that more able children master their skills thoroughly and develop good grammatical habits. Every lesson should include some revision. Suggestions are provided in the lesson plans, but teachers should feel free to use their own judgment when deciding which areas their children need to revisit.

The term *grammar* is used broadly with children of this age. Definitions of the parts of speech, and of what constitutes a sentence, phrase and clause, have necessarily been simplified to age-appropriate working definitions. As the children grow older, these definitions can be expanded and refined.

Nouns

A noun denotes a person, place or thing. On the most basic level, nouns can be divided into proper nouns and common nouns.

Proper Nouns

Proper nouns were introduced in the *Grammar 1 Pupil Book* and revised in the subsequent levels. A proper noun starts with a capital letter, and is the particular name given to the following:

Action: The action for a **proper noun** is to touch one's forehead with the index and middle fingers. This is the same action as that used for *name* in British Sign Language.
Colour: The colour for all types of noun is black.

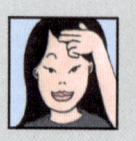

- a person, including that person's surname and title,
- a place, for example a river, mountain, park, street, town, country, continent or planet,
- a building, for example a school, house, library, swimming pool or cinema,
- a date, for example a day of the week, a month or a religious holiday.

In the early years, the focus was on people's names and then on the names of the months, including their correct spelling and sequence. In the *Grammar 3 Pupil Book* the focus moved to place names. The children learnt that in longer place names, such as *the Tower of London,* only the important words need a capital letter, not the short joining words.

Common Nouns

All nouns that are not specific names or titles are called common nouns. Common nouns can be further divided into concrete nouns (like *table* or *child),* abstract nouns (like *warmth* or *kindness)*

Action: The action for a **common noun** is to touch one's forehead with all the fingers of one hand.
Colour: The colour for all types of noun is black.

and collective nouns (like *the **group*** or *a **flock*** of birds). As abstract nouns and collective nouns are more difficult for young children to grasp, only concrete nouns were taught in the early *Pupil Books.* (The term *concrete nouns* was not introduced until *Grammar 4,* however.)

Everything we can see has a name by which we can refer to it: for example, *table, chair* and *pencil.* As these names are not specific to any one object, but refer to tables, chairs and so on in general, they are called common nouns and not proper nouns. At this stage the children find it useful to think of nouns as the names for things they can see and touch. A good way to help the children decide if a word is a noun is to encourage them to say *a, an* or *the* before the word and see whether it makes sense. For example, *a chair, an elephant* and *the table* make sense, whereas *a fell, an unhappy* and *the ran* do not. (The words *a, an* and *the* are the three articles, and are explained later.) In general, children understand the concept of nouns easily and have no trouble when asked to think of examples. Despite this, it can still be difficult for them to identify nouns in written sentences. This becomes easier with regular parsing practice, which is provided in the *Pupil Books* for *Grammar 3* onwards.

Collective Nouns

Collective nouns, which were introduced in the *Grammar 3 Pupil Book,* are words used to describe groups of people, animals or things: for example, *a **crowd** of people, a **herd** of cows* or *a **fleet** of ships.* They can also describe groups of abstract nouns: for example, *a **host** of ideas* or *a **wash** of emotions.* Abstract nouns are explained opposite. Collective nouns are usually singular (such as *a bunch, a band, a flock)* because they describe the group as a whole; whereas the nouns that make up the group are plural (as in *a bunch of **flowers**, a band of **robbers**, a flock of **birds***) because there are many of them. Collective nouns are a type of common noun, so they do not need a capital letter. Often, the same collective noun can be used to describe a number of different things: for example, *bunch* can be used to describe, among other things, flowers, keys and bananas. Sometimes more than one collective noun can be used to describe the same item: for example, a group of whales can be described as *a pod* or *a school*. Many collective nouns are used to describe groups of animals and birds. Some are very common (like *herd*, *flock* and *pride*), while others, particularly those used for birds, are quite obscure (like *a **murder** of crows*). Many new collective nouns, like *a **bounce** of kangaroos*, are not officially recognised, but are nevertheless entertaining for the children.

It is important not to confuse collective nouns with uncountable nouns. Nouns like *water* and *meat* are rarely used in the plural, while *furniture* and *traffic* never are; such nouns are considered uncountable and cannot be divided into smaller groups of one particular item. Collective nouns, on the other hand, can be plural when they describe more than one group of a particular type of object (as in *two **colonies** of ants*). The children are introduced to the idea of countable and uncountable nouns in the *Grammar 6 Pupil Book* (as explained below).

Concrete Nouns

In *Grammar 4*, the children learnt that the things they can see, hear, smell, taste or touch – that is, things that exist in a physical form – are called concrete nouns. The children were encouraged to think about different types of concrete noun and to categorise them according to the five senses.

> Action: The action for a **concrete noun** is to gently tap one's forehead twice with one hand.
> Colour: The colour for all types of noun is black.

Abstract Nouns

Once the children have learnt about concrete nouns, they can be introduced to the concept of abstract nouns. In *Grammar 4*, the children learnt that abstract nouns are things that cannot be experienced through the five senses. They are typically the names for things like ideas (like *justice* or *peace*), feelings (like *anger* or *love*), qualities (like *bravery* or *wisdom*), and actions and events (like a *walk* or a *meeting*). Children should be at the stage now where they are able to understand the concept of abstract nouns, at least in principle; with regular parsing practice they will find it easier to identify abstract nouns in their reading and writing.

> Action: The action for an **abstract noun** is to move one's hand away from the forehead in a spiral action.
> Colour: The colour for all types of noun is black.

Possessive Nouns

In the *Grammar 2 Pupil Book*, the children were taught that adding ‹'s› to a person's name shows possession, so that *Tiffany's bike* means *the bike belonging to Tiffany*. The apostrophe is used to show that the ‹s› is not there to make the proper noun plural. In the *Grammar 4 Pupil Book*, the children went on to learn that this is called a possessive noun. They learnt that common nouns, as well as proper nouns, can be possessive, as in *the **girl's** coat* and *the **kangaroo's** pouch*. The children were also taught that possessive nouns can be plural. Most plurals already end in ‹s›, in which case only the apostrophe is required, as in *the **girls'** coats* and *the **kangaroos'** pouches*. However, if the plural is irregular and does not end in ‹s›, both the apostrophe and the ‹s› are added, as in *the **men's** watches* or *some **mice's** tails*.

It is important the children do not confuse *it's*, which is a contraction of *it is* or *it has*, with the possessive adjective *its*. Possessive adjectives (explained in more detail on page 13) are used in place of possessive nouns, so that *the **girl's** coat* becomes **her** *coat* and *the **kangaroo's** pouch* becomes **its** *pouch*. Possessive adjectives already indicate possession, so they do not need ‹'s› at the end. With regular practice, the children will learn to distinguish between the homophones *it's* and *its* and use them correctly in their writing.

Despite its name, a possessive noun acts as an adjective in a sentence because it describes another noun. The children are already familiar with the idea that nouns can function as adjectives; in the *Grammar 3 Pupil Book* they learnt that nouns act as adjectives in compound words such as **apple** *pie* and **rabbit** *hutch*.

Countable and Uncountable Nouns

In the *Grammar 6 Pupil Book*, the children learn that while most common nouns can be counted – and therefore take a plural – some nouns in English very rarely take a plural and are usually considered uncountable. This is usually because they are words for substances (such as *dust, food, metal, mud, salt* and *water*) or abstract concepts (such as *intelligence, kindness, music, news* and *peace*), neither of which can be divided into discrete, countable units. However, a small number of uncountable nouns, such as *rice* and *sand*, for example, can be divided into discrete units (in this case, individual grains), but they are considered uncountable because it is not possible or practical to count such a great quantity.

Unlike countable nouns, uncountable nouns cannot follow an indefinite article *(a* or *an):* we do not ask for *an* advice or do *a* homework, for example. Neither can they be modified directly by a number: we do not buy, for instance, three *butters* or two *milks.* Instead, to indicate quantity we use general descriptions like *some, a lot of* or *more,* and if we want to express a specific quantity, we use noun phrases like *one slice of cheese, two teaspoons of sugar* or *a thick layer of dust.* Also, if we wish to know the quantity of an uncountable noun, we do not ask *how many?* as we would with a countable noun, but say *how much?* instead.

Uncountable nouns are singular and so they are always used with a singular verb, as in *The news **was** bad* and *Their luggage **is** in the car.* However, there are a few occasions when nouns that are normally considered uncountable become countable. This usually happens when we are referring to their different types, as in *a selection of soft cheeses* or *a plate of cold meats,* for example. Similarly, some nouns can be countable or uncountable depending on the context. For example, if we buy a couple of chocolate **cakes** now, we can eat some **cake** later, or we can have some **chicken** for lunch before feeding the **chickens**.

Other examples of uncountable nouns include the following: art, accommodation, blood, bread, education, equipment, flour, furniture, gas, gold, honey, information, jam, juice, lightning, liquid, money, pasta, rain, silver, snow, soil, thunder, traffic, transport, weather, wood. Uncountable nouns are also known as non-count or mass nouns.

Gerunds

The gerund, which is a verb form that functions as a noun, is introduced in the *Grammar 6 Pupil Book.* Rather than people or objects, gerunds name activities and they can do anything a noun can do. For example, they can function as the subject or object of a sentence (as in **Cycling** *keeps me fit* and *I love **reading**);* they can be the head of a noun phrase (as in *the **ticking** of the clock);* and they can function as the object of a preposition (as in *Before **jogging**, I always do some stretches).* Gerunds are not taught earlier because they are easily confused with the present participle. This is because gerunds and present participles are both formed by adding ‹-ing› to the root verb. Gerunds can also be used in gerund phrases, where the whole phrase acts as a noun (as in **Learning to cook** *is great fun* and *Dad likes **ironing his shirts**),* but the children can learn more about this when they are older.

Plurals

Most nouns change in the plural: that is, when they describe more than one of something. In the early *Grammar Pupil Books,* the two main ways of forming the plural were introduced: adding ‹-s› to the noun (as in *dogs* and *boys),* and adding ‹-es› to those nouns that end with ‹sh›, ‹ch›, ‹s›, ‹z› or ‹x› (as in *brushes, dresses* and *foxes).* These endings often sound like /z/ and /iz/, respectively, as in *girls* and *boxes.* Learning that these words are plurals help the children remember to spell the /z/ sound correctly.

In the *Grammar 2 Pupil Book,* the children also learnt to form the plural of nouns ending in ‹y›. If the letter immediately before the ‹y› is a vowel, the plural is simply made in the usual way by adding ‹-s› (as in *days, boys* and *monkeys).* However, if the letter immediately before the ‹y› is a consonant, ‹y› is replaced by ‹i› before adding ‹-es› (as in *flies, babies* and *puppies).* The children should already know that *shy* ‹i› does not like to be at the end of a word and is often replaced by *toughy* ‹y›. This helps them understand that while we would be unlikely to find *shy* ‹i› at the end of a word like *puppy,* we will find it in the plural, *puppies,* when *shy* ‹i› is no longer at the end of the word.

The *Grammar 2 Pupil Book* also introduced some common plurals in the weekly spelling lists that are irregular, or 'tricky', such as *children, women* and *mice (*from *child, woman* and *mouse,* respectively). Tricky plurals can be formed by modifying the root word, altering its pronunciation, adding an unusual ending, or a combination of the three. Sometimes, the pronunciation of the root word alters even when the spelling does not: for instance, the letter ‹i› makes a long /ie/ sound in *child,* but a short /i/ sound in *children.*

In the *Grammar 3 Pupil Book,* the children learnt that some plurals, such as *sheep, fish* and *deer,* are tricky because they have the same form for both singular and plural. In addition, they learnt that nouns ending in ‹o› usually take the ‹-es› suffix, except when the word is foreign, abbreviated, or has a vowel before the ‹o›, as in *pianos, kilos* and *studios.*

In the *Grammar 4 Pupil Book,* the children learnt that other plurals are tricky because their singular forms end in ‹f› or ‹fe›, whereas their plurals are made by removing the ending and adding ‹-ves›, as in *shelves* and *knives.* Not all singular nouns ending in ‹f› or ‹fe› make their plurals in this way, so the spellings have to be learnt. The children also learnt that, when using a plural in a sentence, the other words connected to it must agree. While most children will be making these adjustments automatically, the teaching was made more explicit in the *Grammar 4 Pupil Book* (see Grammatical Agreement, pages 20 and 21).

The *Grammar 5 Pupil Book* introduced the irregular plural ‹-i›, which is added to some words that have a Latin origin, such as *nucleus* and *alumnus.* It is irregular because not all words that derive from Latin and which end in ‹us› take this plural; in fact most are formed in the regular way by adding ‹-es›, as in *viruses* and *choruses.* However, a small number of scientific or academic words like *nuclei* and *alumni* do use this plural. Even more can take either plural, such as *hippopotamus, cactus, crocus* and *fungus*. In order to be sure, the children should look up words that end in ‹us› in the dictionary.

Pronouns

Pronouns are the little words used to replace nouns. Without them, language would become boring and repetitive. They can be divided into personal pronouns (such as *I* and *me*), possessive pronouns (such as *mine*), relative pronouns (such as *who*) and reflexive pronouns (such as *myself*). Only personal pronouns were taught in the early *Grammar Pupil Books*. Possessive pronouns were introduced in the *Grammar 3 Pupil Book*. The children learn about relative pronouns in *Grammar 6,* but reflexive pronouns can be taught when the children are older.

Personal Pronouns

Singular Pronoun Actions:

1st Person	**I / me**	point to oneself
2nd Person	**you / you**	point to someone else
3rd Person	**he / him**	point to a boy
3rd Person	**she / her**	point to a girl
3rd Person	**it / it**	point to the floor

Plural Pronoun Actions:

1st Person	**we / us**	point in a circle to oneself and others
2nd Person	**you / you**	point to two other people
3rd Person	**they / them**	point to the next-door class

Colour: The colour for pronouns is pink.

In the *Grammar 1 Pupil Book,* the children were taught the eight personal pronouns: *I, you, he, she, it, we, you* and *they*. In modern English, we use the same word, *you,* for both the singular and plural second person pronoun, but this is not the case in many foreign languages. In order to make learning such languages easier later on, the *Grammar Pupil Books* make the distinction between *you* used in the singular and *you* used in the plural.

In the *Grammar 3 Pupil Book,* the children learnt how to identify the subject and the object of a sentence. They also learnt that the personal pronouns can change, depending on whether they are the subject or the object of the sentence. The personal pronouns that were previously taught are subject pronouns; the corresponding object pronouns are *me, you, him, her, it, us, you* and *them*. The children practise using the subject pronouns whenever they conjugate verbs. They do the actions and say, for example, *I swim, you swim, he swims, she swims, it swims, we swim, you swim, they swim*. The same actions can also be used to revise the object pronouns.

In the *Grammar 4 Pupil Book,* the children learnt that personal pronouns are called 'personal' because they mostly relate to people: when talking about ourselves, we use *I* and *we*; when talking directly to one or more people, we say *you*; and when talking about someone or something else, we use *he, she* and *it* for the singular and *they* for the plural. These three groups are known as first, second and third person and they can be singular or plural (see above). Once the children were introduced to grammatical person, they were given regular practice parsing the verb in the spelling lessons. They also learnt that when the person in a sentence is changed, the verb and the rest of the sentence must agree.

Possessive Pronouns

In the *Grammar 3 Pupil Book,* the children learnt about the eight possessive pronouns: *mine, yours, his, hers, its, ours, yours* and *theirs*. These pronouns correspond to the personal pronouns (*I/me, you/you, he/him, she/her, it/it, we/us, you/you* and *they/them*) and the possessive adjectives (*my, your, his, her, its, our, your* and *their*). A possessive pronoun replaces a noun and its possessive adjective, so that *my hat* becomes *mine,* and *their house* becomes *theirs*. These pronouns are possessive because they indicate who the noun (which they are also replacing) belongs to. Possessive pronouns can be practised using the same colour and actions as for the personal pronouns.

Relative Pronouns

Relative pronouns are introduced in the *Grammar 6 Pupil Book,* alongside relative adverbs and relative clauses (see pages 14 and 17). The most common relative pronouns are *who, which, that, whom* and *whose*. They are often used at the beginning of relative clauses – which is a special kind of dependent clause that acts as an adjective – to relate the clause to the person or thing that it is describing. The relative pronouns *who* and *whom* are used for people: *who* is used for the subject of the clause and *whom* for the object, as in *the girl* **who** *won the race* and *the boys* **whom** *we met yesterday*. We use *which* to refer to things, as in *the book* **which** *you lent me,* while *that* can

9

be used for both people and things, as in *the scarf **that** I bought* or *the nurse **that** bandaged my knee*. The relative pronoun *whose* is used to indicate possession, as in *the chef **whose** recipes we like*.

Verbs

A verb denotes what a person or thing does or is. It can describe an action, an event, a state or a change. From the beginning, the children were encouraged to talk about verbs in the infinitive

Action: The action for **verbs** in general is to clench both fists and move arms backwards and forwards at one's sides, as if running.
Colour: The colour for all types of verb is red.

form rather than as gerunds. (Gerunds, such as *running, hopping, singing* and *playing*, are the noun form of verbs.) The infinitive form is made by putting the word *to* before the verb root, as in *to run, to hop, to sing* and *to play*. Early on the children learnt that an infinitive is the 'name' of the verb, but gradually the term *infinitive* should be introduced. In the *Grammar 4 Pupil Book* the children learnt that the infinitive can be used in a sentence (as in *I want **to stay***), although it is never the main verb and does not have a subject. The *Grammar 6 Pupil Book* also introduces the bare infinitive, which is the infinitive form of the verb without *to*. The children learn to use it with either modal verbs (as in *You **must go** home*) or the auxiliary *to do* (as in *I **do like** ice cream*), or when forming imperative sentences, like ***Sit** down over there*.

When the children are young, they find it easiest to think of verbs as 'doing' words. This was the working definition used throughout *Grammar Pupil Books 1* to *5*. However, during this time the children's understanding was gradually refined. For example, from the *Grammar 3 Pupil Book* onwards, they learnt about auxiliary verbs, which do not stand alone but are found 'helping' another verb in the sentence (such as the auxiliaries *will* and *shall*, which indicate the future). In the *Grammar 6 Pupil Book*, they also learn that some verbs are more accurately described as 'being' words, because they describe a state of being or change. Rather than taking a direct object, these verbs link the subject of the sentence to its complement. A complement is so called because it *completes* our understanding of the subject. It does this either by identifying the subject as a noun, noun phrase or pronoun (as in *Kate is an **engineer***) or by describing it using an adjective or adjective phrase (as in *Kate is very **clever***). The children learn that 'doing' words are more commonly called action verbs and that 'being' words are known as linking (or copular) verbs. The most common linking verb is *to be*, but other common examples include *to seem, to appear, to become, to remain, to look, to sound, to smell, to taste* and *to feel*. Most linking verbs can also act as action verbs, so the children need to think about what the verb is doing in the sentence before they decide what type it is.

Verb Tenses and Conjugation

The children were introduced to verbs in the *Grammar 1 Pupil Book*, where they learnt to conjugate regular verbs in the present, past and future. (Because verbs in English are very complicated, only the simple tenses were introduced initially.) Conjugating means choosing a particular verb and saying the pronouns in order with the correct form of the verb after each one. Conjugating verbs aloud with the pronoun actions is very good practice for children. It promotes a strong understanding of how verbs work, which helps them make sense of their own language, and it is invaluable when they come to learn foreign languages later on. Revise the conjugations regularly, using the pronoun actions.

Simple Past	*I jumped*	*you jumped*	*he jumped*	*she jumped*	*it jumped*
	we jumped	*you jumped*		*they jumped*	
Simple Present	*I jump*	*you jump*	*he jumps*	*she jumps*	*it jumps*
	we jump	*you jump*		*they jump*	
Simple Future	*I shall/will jump*	*you will jump*	*he will jump*	*she will jump*	*it will jump*
	we shall/will jump	*you will jump*		*they will jump*	

The children need to remember the following points:

- In the simple present tense, the verb changes after the third person singular pronouns: *he, she* and *it*. For regular verbs, ‹-s› is added to the root, unless the word ends in ‹sh›, ‹ch›, ‹s›, ‹z› or ‹x›, when ‹-es› is added. This is called the third person singular marker.
- The simple past tense of regular verbs is formed by adding the suffix ‹-ed› to the root. If the root ends in ‹e› (as in *bake*), the final ‹e› must be removed before ‹-ed› is added. The ‹-ed› can be pronounced in one of three ways: /t/ (as in *slipped*), /d/ (as in *smiled*) or /id/ (as in *waited*).
- In the simple tense, we add the auxiliary verbs *shall* or *will* to the root verb to denote the future. The auxiliary verb *will* can be used with all the pronouns, but *shall* should only be used with *I* or *we*.

Teaching Ideas for Grammar

In the *Grammar 2 Pupil Book,* the children learnt that every sentence must contain a verb, and so time was spent helping them to identify verbs with confidence. They revised regular conjugations and were introduced to some of the most common irregular verbs and their 'tricky' past forms: for example, the verbs *to sit* and *to run,* which have the tricky pasts *sat* and *ran.* In addition, they learnt to conjugate and identify the irregular verb *to be* in both the present and past tenses. This is especially useful for those children who are not in the habit of using standard forms in their speech: children who say, for example, *we was* instead of *we were.* Chanting the conjugations regularly will help these children avoid making mistakes in their written work. In fact, this is good practice for all children, as most of them will find it difficult to identify *to be* in a sentence until they become familiar with its irregularities.

The verb *to be* is used frequently in English, both as a main verb and as an auxiliary. In the *Grammar 3 Pupil Book,* the children learnt how to conjugate *to be* in the simple future and were introduced to the continuous tenses. The continuous tenses use *to be* as an auxiliary, followed by the present participle, as in *I am walking, I was walking, I shall be walking.* Later, in the *Grammar 5 Pupil Book,* the children learnt the perfect tenses, which use *to have* as an auxiliary, followed by the past participle, as in *I had walked, I have walked, I shall have walked.* Participles are discussed in more detail below.

Once the children have learnt a new tense, it is important that they practice identifying all the verb tenses taught so far. It is also important that they develop their ability to write sentences in those tenses. The *Grammar 4 and 5 Pupil Books* provided lots of practice in both these skills. As a result, the children should be able to distinguish between the simple, continuous and perfect forms more easily and this in turn will help them understand how the different tenses are used.

For now it is enough that the children understand that the simple past and future describe actions that start and finish within a specific time, while the simple present describes repeated or usual actions (as in *I swim in the pool every day);* the continuous tenses describe actions that have started and are still happening, either at that very moment or as a longer action in progress (as in *I am learning to swim);* and the perfect tenses are used to describe actions that have already been completed, especially general experiences, events that happen at unspecified times (as in *I have swum in that pool several times),* or actions that – although complete – still have some connection to the present (as in *I had just finished swimming in the pool).* For reference, the table below shows all three forms in past, present and future.

	Past	Present	Future
Simple	*looked*	*look*	*will look*
Continuous	*was looking*	*is looking*	*will be looking*
Perfect	*had looked*	*have looked*	*will have looked*

| Action: Point backwards over one's shoulder with a thumb. | Action: Point towards the floor with the palm of the hand. | Action: Point towards the front. |

Technically there is no future tense in English since, unlike the past tense, the future is not formed by modifying the root verb itself. However, at this stage it is helpful for the children to think of verbs as taking place in the past, present or future. The complexities can be taught when the children are older.

Participles

The ‹-ing› suffix, which is added to root verbs, was introduced in the *Grammar 2 Pupil Book.* In the *Grammar 3 Pupil Book* the children learnt that this form of the verb is called the present participle and it is used with the verb *to be* to form the continuous tenses. In the *Grammar 4 Pupil Book,* they learnt that present participles can also be used as adjectives, as in *There is no running water.* Present participles should not be confused with gerunds, the noun form of the verb, which are introduced in the *Grammar 6 Pupil Book* (see page 8).

Past participles were introduced in the *Grammar 5 Pupil Book* in preparation for the perfect tenses. Past participles of regular verbs have the same form as the simple past tense. However, past participles of irregular verbs are 'tricky' and they have to be learnt. The *Grammar 5 Pupil Book* introduced two of the more common forms. Verbs like *to swim* change their vowel sound to indicate tense: *swim* is used in the simple present, *swam* is used in the simple past and the past participle *swum* is used in the perfect tenses. Verbs like *to write* and *to fall* change their vowel sound in the simple past, but keep the original vowel letter and add either ‹-n› or ‹-en› to form the past participle (as in *write, wrote, written* and *fall, fell, fallen).* A good dictionary will always list the irregular parts of a verb, so if the children are not sure which form to use in their writing, encourage them to look it up.

In the *Grammar 6 Pupil Book,* the children learn that past participles – like present participles – can be used as adjectives. Present participles that are used in this way usually indicate an action carried out by the noun

11

Teaching Ideas for Grammar

it is describing. This action is either still happening or happens regularly, as in a *galloping* horse or a *talking* parrot. Past participles, on the other hand, usually indicate an action that has already happened and that is done to the thing it is describing, as in *buried* treasure or a *mixed* salad. Past and present participles also differ when they concern feelings. For example, an activity might be *interesting, frightening* or *boring,* and we, in turn, may be *interested, frightened* or *bored* by the activity. Present participles describe the thing that makes us feel a certain way and past participles describe the way it makes us feel.

Phrasal Verbs

The *Grammar 5 Pupil Book* introduced phrasal verbs. These consist of a verb plus one or more other words, which are usually prepositions or adverbs. Put together, these words make a new verb with a new meaning, such as *to break down* (meaning *to stop working*) and *to break out* (meaning *to escape*). Like other verbs, phrasal verbs often have more than one meaning. For example, you can *blow up* (destroy) something with dynamite, or *blow up* (inflate) a balloon, or *blow up* (enlarge) a photograph. The parts of a phrasal verb can often be separated by the object (including any modifiers). For example, we can say either **I brought** your book **back** or **I brought back** your book. In fact, when a pronoun is the object of a sentence it always separates a separable phrasal verb: *I brought it back* can never be written *I brought back it*, for example. However, some phrasal verbs are always inseparable. We cannot say, for example, that *I looked your book for* or *I looked it for*: the correct form is **I looked for** your book and **I looked for** it.

Modal Verbs

The *Grammar 6 Pupil Book* introduces the children to modal verbs, which are a special kind of auxiliary. Modal auxiliaries are used with the bare infinitive of the main verb (the infinitive form without *to*) to help express things like certainty *(You **will** see me tomorrow)*, obligation *(You **must** see me tomorrow)*, permission *(You **may** see me tomorrow)* or ability *(You **can** see me tomorrow)*. They are also used to give advice *(You **should** see me tomorrow)* or make suggestions (You **could** see me tomorrow). The most common modal verbs are *will, shall, can, could, may, might, should, would* and *must*. Unlike other auxiliaries, they do not change depending on the grammatical person (so the verb stays the same whichever pronoun is used).

Imperatives

In the *Grammar 6 Pupil Book,* the children also learn about imperatives, which get their name from the Latin verb *imperare,* meaning *to command*. The imperative is a special form of the verb that is used not only to give commands *(Sit down!),* but also to give warnings *(Beware of the bull!),* instructions *(Add a pinch of salt)* and advice *(Read the instructions first)*. They can also be used to make suggestions *(Taste this ice cream)*, invitations *(Come back anytime)* and requests *(Please close the door)*. When we talk directly to someone we usually use the second person, *you,* but this is not the case in imperative sentences. Instead we use the bare infinitive and leave the subject unstated (although it can be used to add emphasis, as in *You be quiet)*. Negative imperatives are formed by using *to do* as an auxiliary, as in *Do not disturb,* although *do not* is often contracted to *don't* in speech.

The Active and Passive Voice

Sentences can be written in either the active voice or the passive voice. From the start, the children were taught how to write in the active voice, although the term itself is only introduced in the *Grammar 6 Pupil Book*. It is at this point that the children learn how to write in the passive voice, which uses *to be* as an auxiliary, together with the past participle of the main verb (as in *The painting **was stolen** in the night)*. There is more information on both the active and passive voice in relation to sentence structure on page 16.

Adjectives

An adjective is a word that describes a noun or pronoun. It can be used either directly before the noun or pronoun, as in *the **big** dog,* or elsewhere in the sentence, as in *the dog was **big**.* The

> Action: The action for all types of **adjective** is to touch the side of the temple with one's fist.
> Colour: The colour for all types of **adjective** is blue.

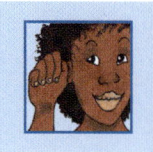

children are encouraged to use adjectives imaginatively in their writing.

Adjectives were introduced in the *Grammar 1 Pupil Book,* where the children learnt how to use them before a noun. In the *Grammar 2 Pupil Book,* adjectives were revised, and the children practised identifying them wherever they were placed in the sentence. In the *Grammar 3* and *4 Pupil Books,* the children learnt that adjectives can sometimes be formed by adding certain suffixes to other words: for example, by adding the suffixes ‹-y› or ‹-al› to a noun, as in *windy* and *logical,* or by adding suffixes like ‹-less›, ‹-ful› and ‹-able› to nouns and verbs, as in *worthless, helpful* and *enjoyable*. The children also learnt that other parts of speech can sometimes act as adjectives: for example, in the compound word **apple** *pie*, the first noun *apple* is describing the main noun *pie*; in the phrase *the* **running** *water,* the present participle *running*, which is a verb form, is describing the water; and possessive nouns always act as adjectives to describe another noun, as in *the* **peacock's** *tail*. Similarly, in the *Grammar 6 Pupil Book* the children learn that past participles and prepositional phrases can also act as adjectives (as in *the* **lost** *boy* and *the flowers* **in the vase**), while relative clauses (as in *the letter* **that I wrote**) always act as an adjective in a sentence (as discussed on pages 11, 15 and 17).

Before this, however, the *Grammar 5 Pupil Book* refined the children's understanding of adjectives by introducing them to adjective order. In English, we tend to write adjectives in a certain order, depending on which category they belong to. The children learnt that there are seven general categories, which are often written in the following sequence:

- Determiners (such as *a, an, one, two, some, many, any, this* and *that*)
- Opinion (such as *lazy, good, nasty, expensive* and *bad*)
- Size and shape (such as *fat, thin, small, broad, rectangular* and *oval*)
- Condition and age (such as *broken, battered, hungry, full, ancient* and *recent*)
- Colour and pattern (such as *black, brown, white, tartan* and *zigzag*)
- Origin (such as *Welsh, Polish, African, Japanese* and *Australian*)
- Material, including nouns acting as adjectives (such as *leather, iron* and *diamond*)

This is only a general rule and sometimes the order changes. For example, when shape and age are both included in a description, age tends to come before shape, as in *the old square box*. However, as a general guide it can be useful, especially for non-native English speakers.

Possessive Adjectives

The children's understanding of adjectives was extended in the *Grammar 2 Pupil Book* to include the eight possessive adjectives: *my, your, his, her, its, our, your* and *their*. These correspond to the personal pronouns (*I/me, you/you, he/him, she/her, it/it, we/us, you/you* and *they/them*) and the possessive pronouns (*mine, yours, his, hers, its, ours, yours,* and *theirs*). A possessive adjective replaces one noun and describes another, by saying whose it is. For example, in the sentence *Lucy fed her cat,* the possessive adjective *her* is used in place of *Lucy's* and describes *cat,* by saying whose cat it is. (As the possessive adjectives also function as pronouns, they are sometimes known as the weak set of possessive pronouns. However, to avoid any confusion with the strong set of possessive pronouns, which includes *mine* and *yours,* the *Grammar Pupil and Teacher's Books* do not use this terminology.)

Comparatives and Superlatives

The adjectives introduced in the *Grammar 1 Pupil Book* describe a noun or a pronoun without comparing it to anything else (as in *the girl is* **young**). These are known as *positive* adjectives, although this term is not used with the children. In the *Grammar 2 Pupil Book,* comparative and superlative adjectives were introduced. These adjectives describe a noun or a pronoun by comparing it to other items. A comparative is used when comparing a noun to one or more other items (as in *Sam is* **younger** *than Jim and Ted*). A superlative is used when comparing a noun to all the other items in its group (as in *Sam is the* **youngest** *boy in the team*). Short positive adjectives usually form their comparatives and superlatives with the suffixes ‹-er› and ‹-est› (as in *hard, harder, hardest*) and applying these suffixes correctly was the main focus in the earlier years. (There is more information on the rules for adding suffixes on page 30.) In the *Grammar 4 Pupil Book,* the children learnt that with longer adjectives, we often use the words *more* and *most*: for example, *difficult, more difficult, most difficult*. However, some two-syllable adjectives also make their comparative and superlative by adding *more* and *most,* especially those which have a suffix, as in *most careful, more helpless, most daring, more shaded* and *most famous*. The children need to listen and decide which sounds right in the sentence. The children also learn about other comparative and superlative forms, such as *less* and *least, better* and *best, worse* and *worst*.

Adverbs

In the *Grammar Pupil Books 1 to 4,* the children were taught that an adverb is similar to an adjective, in that they are both describing words, but that adverbs describe verbs rather than nouns. Usually, adverbs describe how, where, when, how much or how often something happens. In the *Grammar 5 Pupil*

> Action: The action for all types of **adverb** is to bang one fist on top of the other.
> Colour: The colour for all types of adverb is orange.

TEACHING IDEAS FOR GRAMMAR

Book, the children learnt that these types of adverb are called adverbs of manner, place, time, degree and frequency.

The children were introduced to adverbs in the *Grammar 1 Pupil Book*. Initially, they were taught to think of an adverb as a word often ending with the suffix ‹-ly›. In the *Grammar 2 Pupil Book,* adverbs were revised and the children were encouraged to identify less obvious adverbs by looking at the verb and deciding which word describes it. For example, in the sentence, *They arrived late last night,* the adverb *late* tells us something more about when they *arrived.* Point out examples of adverbs in texts whenever possible to help the children develop this understanding. In the *Grammar 3 Pupil Book,* the children learnt that adjectives can sometimes be turned into adverbs by adding the suffix ‹-ly›, as in *quickly, slowly* and *softly.* In the *Grammar 4 Pupil Book,* the children learnt that adjectives can be turned into adverbs by adding ‹-ly› or ‹-ally› when the adjective ends in ‹-ical› or ‹-ic›, as in *musically* and *basically.* In the *Grammar 5 Pupil Book,* the children looked at how adverbs do not always go next to the verb. They also learnt that adverbs do not always describe verbs: they can describe other adverbs (as in **really** *quickly*), as well as adjectives (as in **quite** *surprising*).

In the *Grammar 6 Pupil Book,* the children learn about modal adverbs and relative adverbs. Modal adverbs, like modal verbs, can be used to express degrees of certainty, as in *Ann will* **certainly** *go to town, Ann will* **probably** *go to town* and **Perhaps** *Ann will go to town.* They can be used with modal verbs like *will* (as in the previous examples) or with main verbs, as in *He* **clearly** *loves music.* Because modal verbs and adverbs express varying degrees of certainty, some do not work well together: for example, *perhaps,* which expresses a low level of certainty, is not usually used with *must,* which expresses a high degree of certainty.

Relative adverbs are adverbs that are commonly used to replace the more formal phrases *in which, on which, at which* and *for which* that are sometimes used in relative clauses. For example, we are more likely to use the adverb *when* than say *the day on which I was born* or the adverb *where* in *the house in which I was born.* Similarly, it is more common to use *why* to replace *for which* in a noun phrase like *the reason* **why** *he was late.* There is more information about relative clauses on page 17.

Adverbials

In the *Grammar 6 Pupil Book,* the children are introduced to the term *adverbial*. This is used to describe any word, phrase or clause that acts as an adverb in a sentence. The most common adverbials are adverbs, noun phrases, prepositional phrases and subordinate clauses. Adverbial noun phrases express time, telling us **when** something happens *(this Wednesday, next year, yesterday morning),* **how often** it happens *(every time, each winter),* or **how long** it takes *(all afternoon, the whole day).* Other adverbials can modify the verb in a range of ways, most commonly telling us more about **how** *(loudly, without complaint),* **where** *(in the house, wherever I go),* **when** *(during the week, after we had eaten)* or **why** *(for their wedding anniversary, because it was raining).*

Like adverbs, adverbials do not always appear next to the verb. When one is placed at the beginning of a sentence it is called a fronted adverbial, and it is usually separated from the rest of the sentence by a comma. When the children are parsing, encourage them to identify adverbials by putting orange brackets around all the words in the phrase or clause. Adverbs can be underlined in orange, as usual.

Prepositions

A preposition is a word that relates one noun or pronoun to another. For example, in the sentence *He climbed over the gate,* the preposition *over* relates the pronoun *he* to the noun *gate*. If the latter noun is part of a noun phrase, the preposition is always placed before all the words in it, as in **under** *the bridge,* **in** *my purse,* **after** *a long pause,* **on** *Sally's bicycle* and **from** *her dearest friend*.

Action: The action for **prepositions** is to point from one noun to another.
Colour: The colour for prepositions is green.

Prepositions, as introduced in the *Grammar 2 Pupil Book,* often describe where something is or the direction it is moving in. They can be practised by calling out examples and asking the children to suggest nouns to go with them. For example, the children might suggest *a box* or *the classroom* to follow *in,* and *the mat* or *the table* to follow *under.* Many prepositions are short words like *at, by, for, of, in, on, to* and *up.* Other common examples include *above, after, around, behind, beside, between, down, from, into, past, through, towards, under* and *with.* Care must be taken, however, as many of these words function as adverbs if they do not come before a noun or pronoun. In the sentence, *I fell down,* for example, the word *down* is an adverb describing *fell,* whereas in *I fell down the stairs,* it is a preposition relating *I* to *stairs.* It helps to remember that the word *preposition* has the prefix ‹pre-›, meaning *before,* and the root word *position,* meaning *to place,* so a preposition is always placed before a noun or pronoun.

In the *Grammar 5 Pupil Book,* the children learnt that not all prepositions are prepositions of place. Sometimes, a preposition relates something to a time or event, as in *Owls sleep* **during** *the day,* or *The seasons change* **throughout** *the year.* They also looked at phrases which start with a preposition, followed by a simple noun phrase or pronoun, and learnt that these are called prepositional phrases. They were taught that such phrases often act as an adverb in a sentence, describing how, where or when something happens, as in *I played* **with my friends***, They ran* **down the street***,* or *They arrived* **in the afternoon***.*

In the *Grammar 6 Pupil Book,* the children learn that prepositional phrases acting as adverbs are also known as *adverbials,* as is any word, phrase or clause that fulfils this function. (It is best to avoid the term *adverbial phrase* until the children are older, as it is so close to *prepositional phrase* that it can be confusing.) The children also learn that some prepositional phrases act as adjectives rather than adverbs, answering the question *which one?* or *what kind? (*as in *the girl **with red hair** or a bar **of milk chocolate**)*. They also look at longer prepositional phrases, which usually consist of two shorter phrases put together: for example, *at the front of the stage*; *in the heat of the moment;* and *by the house on the corner*.

Conjunctions

A conjunction is a word used to join parts of a sentence that usually, but not always, contain their own verbs. Conjunctions allow the children to write longer, less repetitive sentences. Instead of writing, for example, *I eat fish. I eat peas. I like the taste,* the children can use the conjunctions *and* and *because* to write *I eat fish and peas because I like the taste*. Where the shorter sentences are stilted and repetitive, the longer one flows because it joins together ideas that are closely related. The ability to vary the length of their sentences will greatly improve the quality of the children's writing. Display a list of common conjunctions in the classroom to encourage the children to use other words besides *and*: examples include *although, if, now, once, since, unless, until, when* and *whether*.

Action: The action for **conjunctions** is to hold one's hands apart with the palms facing up. Move both hands so one is on top of the other.
Colour: The colour for conjunctions is purple.

Conjunctions can often be categorised by meaning: *and* adds extra information, whereas *nor* excludes it; *or* provides an alternative and *so* reveals the consequences; *though, while, although, but* and *yet* provide a contrast; *for, because, since* and *as* provide an explanation; and *if* and *unless* imply a condition. Many indicate time, including *as, while, when, after, before, until, since* and *whenever,* and a few, such as *where, wherever* and *everywhere,* indicate place.

The *Grammar 2 Pupil Book* introduced conjunctions, focusing on six of the most useful ones: *and, but, because, or, so,* and *while*. Later, in the *Grammar 4 Pupil Book,* the children learnt that certain conjunctions can be used to join two simple sentences together in a compound sentence. In the *Grammar 6 Pupil Book,* they learn that there are two types of conjunction: those that coordinate parts of a sentence and those that subordinate one part to another.

Coordinating Conjunctions

The coordinating conjunctions are so called because they join together words, phrases or clauses of equal importance. There are only seven coordinating conjunctions: *for, and, nor, but, or, yet* and *so*, which can be remembered by the acronym FANBOYS. Some are used more often than others: *and, or, so, but* and *yet* are used quite widely; *nor* is used to join a negative clause to one in which the subject and verb are inverted (as in *She was not at home, **nor** was she at work*); and *for* – which introduces an explanation – is very formal and is rarely used in everyday speech.

In the *Grammar 4 Pupil Book,* the children learnt that the coordinating conjunctions are most notably used to join two simple sentences together in a compound sentence. The conjunctions *and, nor, but* and *or* are also used in pairs of correlative conjunctions, as in *He is neither tall nor handsome*, but the children can learn about this when they are older.

Subordinating Conjunctions

A subordinating conjunction joins the main clause in a sentence to a subordinate one. *Subordinate* means *ranked below*, so a subordinating conjunction indicates that the clause it belongs to is less important than the other. For example, in the sentence *They went home once it got dark,* the conjunction *once* tells us that the clause *once it got dark* is subordinate to (or dependent on) the main clause *They went home*. A clause with a subordinating conjunction is an adverbial (as explained on page 14), so it can be placed at the beginning of a sentence, as in *Once it got dark, they went home*.

Definite and Indefinite Articles: *the, a, an*

The words *a, an* and *the* are known as articles: *the* (the definite article) can be used before both singular and plural nouns, wheareas *a* and *an* (the indefinite articles) are only used before singular nouns. Articles, which belong to a group of words called determiners, are a special type of adjective because they always modify a noun. Determiners appear at the start of a noun phrase to show (or determine) the following: how known it is (articles); how many there are (quantifiers like *some, few, more* and *any*); who it belongs to (possessive adjectives like *my* and *ours*); and which particular one is referred to (the demonstratives *this, that, these* and *those*).

In the *Grammar 1 Pupil Book,* the children learnt when to use *an* instead of *a*. They were taught to choose the correct article by looking at the word that follows it. When the word begins with a vowel sound, the correct article is *an,* as in *an ant, an egg, an igloo, an octopus* and *an umbrella.* Otherwise, the correct article is *a.* This makes it easier to say the two words together fluently. Note that it is the first sound that is important, not necessarily the first letter. If, for example, a word starts with a silent consonant and the first sound is actually a vowel, the correct article is *an,* as in *an hour.* If, on the other hand, the word starts with the long vowel /ue/, pronounced /y-oo/, then the correct article is *a,* as in *a unicorn.*

In the *Grammar 6 Pupil Book,* the children look more closely at when the different articles are used. They learn that *definite* means *clearly known,* so *the* (the definite article) indicates that the noun it refers to is one we are likely to know already because, for example, it has been mentioned or is what we are expecting. *The* is also used before a superlative, because there can only be one thing or one group that is, for example, the tallest or the strongest. *Indefinite,* on the other hand, has the prefix ‹in-›, meaning *not,* and so *a* and *an* (the indefinite articles) are used to indicate that the nouns they refer to are unknown and are being introduced for the first time. The children are also introduced to the actions for the articles: they make a capital T with their hands for *the* and hold up their left hand, palm out, and point to their thumb for *a* and *an*. These actions, along with those for the other parts of speech, are used in the game *Grammar Action Sentences* (see pages 45 and 107).

Simple, Compound and Complex Sentences

The full definition of a sentence is complicated and so, in the *Grammar Pupil Books,* a simple working definition is gradually expanded and refined.

In the *Grammar 1 Pupil Book,* the children learnt that a sentence must start with a capital letter, end with a full stop and make sense. In the *Grammar 2 Pupil Book,* the children learnt that a sentence must always have a verb and end with a full stop, question mark or exclamation mark. In the *Grammar 3 Pupil Book,* this definition was further refined when the children learnt that a sentence always has a subject and may have an object; the subject is the noun or pronoun that **does** the verb action, as in **Sam** *hit the ball,* and the object is the noun or pronoun that **receives** the verb action, as in *The ball hit* **Sam**. In the *Grammar 4 Pupil Book,* the children learnt that when two or more sentences are joined together with one of the coordinating conjunctions (*for, and, nor, but, or, yet* and *so*), it is called a **compound** sentence, and the two original sentences are called **simple** sentences.

Later, in the *Grammar 5 Pupil Book,* the children were introduced to the idea that subjects and objects can also have simple and compound forms. The simple form consists of the head noun only rather than the whole noun phrase; the children are encouraged to identify it when parsing or writing on the sentence walls (see pages 21 and 22). A compound subject or object consists of two or more subjects or objects in the one simple sentence, as in ***Jack*** *and* ***Jill*** *went up the hill,* or *He bought two* ***shirts*** *and a* ***tie***. The children were also introduced to the idea that at its most basic level, a sentence has two parts: the **subject**, including any words that modify it, and everything else, including the verb, which is known as the **predicate**. They also learnt that verbs that have an object are called **transitive** and those that do not are called **intransitive**.

In the *Grammar 6 Pupil Book,* the children are taught that a compound sentence may be joined by a **semicolon** – rather than by a coordinating conjunction – as long as the two independent clauses are closely related. They learn that a sentence with a main (or independent) clause and a subordinate (or dependent) clause is called a **complex** sentence. They are also introduced to the idea that a sentence with a **direct object** may also have an **indirect object** for whom or to whom the verb action is done, as in *The twins made Dad a birthday card*.

The children also learn that a sentence can be written in either the **active voice** or the **passive voice**. In the active voice, the subject and object function in the usual way. In the passive voice, however, the subject of the sentence is the **receiver** of the verb action and the **agent**, who does the verb action, may not be mentioned at all. If the agent is mentioned, it is introduced in a prepositional phrase, as in *The ball was hit* ***by Sam***. The passive voice is used when the agent of the verb is not known or is considered unimportant. The verb is formed by using the auxiliary *to be* with the past participle.

Statements, Questions and Exclamations

In the *Grammar 1* and *2 Pupil Books,* the children learnt to recognise a question as a sentence that asks for further information and ends in a question mark. They were also taught the ‹wh› question words (*what, why, when, where, who, which* and *whose*). In the *Grammar 2 Pupil Book,* the children's knowledge was extended as they were introduced to exclamation marks, which are used at the end of exclamations to show that the writer or speaker feels strongly about something. Later, in the *Grammar 3 Pupil Book,* they learnt how to write questions and exclamations in direct speech.

In the *Grammar 4 Pupil Book,* the children learnt that sentences ending in a full stop are called statements, and they looked at some simple ways to turn statements into questions. For example, if a statement's main verb is *to be,* it can be made into a question by putting the verb at the beginning and replacing the full stop with a question mark. As a result, *This* ***is*** *the way to the park* becomes ***Is*** *this the way to the park?* Similarly, if there is a main verb and an auxiliary, it is the auxiliary verb that is moved to the front. In this way, *I **can** go to the park* becomes ***Can*** *I go to the park?*

Later, in the *Grammar 6 Pupil Book,* the children learn that statements written in the simple past and simple present cannot be turned into questions in the usual way because they have no auxiliary verb. Instead, the verb *to do* is used as an auxiliary, together with the bare infinitive of the main verb. This means that a sentence like *You* **went** *to the park* can be turned into the question **Did you go to the park?** The children also learn that *to do* can be used in a similar way to add emphasis to a positive statement *(I **do** like ice cream)* or to make a statement negative *(She **does** not **like** ice cream)*.

Phrases

A phrase is a group of words that makes sense but has no verb or subject. In the *Grammar 3 Pupil Book*, the children learnt to distinguish between a sentence and a phrase. In the *Grammar 4 Pupil Book*, the children learnt that a noun, together with the words that describe (or modify) it, is called a noun phrase. There can be more than one noun phrase in a sentence and each noun phrase can be replaced with a pronoun. For example, in the sentence *I took three juicy apples from the big wooden bowl*, there are two noun phrases: *three juicy apples* and *the big wooden bowl*. These can be replaced by the pronouns *them* and *it* and still make grammatical sense: *I took them from it*. Not all words in a noun phrase come before the noun, as in *a girl with blonde hair*. This kind of noun phrase generally has a main noun (in this example it is *girl*) and another noun helping to describe it (*hair*).

In the *Grammar 5 Pupil Book*, the children were introduced to prepositional phrases. These are phrases that start with a preposition followed by a simple noun phrase or pronoun, as in *down the steep hill,* or *between them*. They learnt that prepositional phrases often act as adverbs of manner *(He sat **in silence**)*, place *(She walked **to the door**)* or time *(They jog **in the morning**)*. In the *Grammar 6 Pupil Book*, the children learn that prepositional phrases can also act as adjectives, as in *the room **at the top*** or *a tube **of toothpaste***.

Clauses

The *Grammar 4 Pupil Book* introduced clauses. A clause is a group of words that contains a subject and verb and makes sense. This is much like the working definition of a sentence; indeed, some clauses can stand alone as sentences, such as those in the compound sentence <u>Gran baked a cake</u> and <u>the children decorated it</u>. Such clauses are known as independent clauses. However, not all clauses are independent. In the sentence *While he waited, he read his book,* the clause *he read his book* could stand alone as a simple sentence, but *While he waited* could not. This is because – despite having a verb and subject – the clause does not represent a complete thought: it leaves us to ask what else the subject did during that time. This type of clause is called a dependent or subordinate clause. It is dependent because it relies on further information to express its full meaning, and it is subordinate (meaning *ranked below*) because its function is to give us extra information about the main (or independent) clause.

In the *Grammar 6 Pupil Book,* the children learn that a sentence with a main clause and a subordinate clause is called a complex sentence. They also learn more about the type of information that a subordinate clause provides. Clauses starting with a subordinating conjunction act as adverbs by telling us more about the verb within the main clause. They can tell us when, where or why something happens, as in *We went inside <u>before it started to rain</u>; It rained <u>wherever we went</u>;* and *We went inside <u>because it was raining</u>*. However, clauses that start with a relative pronoun or relative adverb, as in *the key <u>that I found</u>* or *the street <u>where you live</u>*, always act as adjectives. Sometimes the information in the relative clause is interesting, but it could easily be left out. The children learn to punctuate this type of relative clause with bracketing commas. However, some information is essential because it tells us what we need to know in order to identify which person or thing is meant. Relative clauses are therefore described as either **defining** or **non-defining** clauses (or sometimes as restrictive and non-restrictive clauses). As they fulfil the adjective function, relative clauses are also known as adjectival clauses; however, this is not a term that is used with the children at this stage.

Paragraphs and Cohesion

Paragraphs are used to organise information in a piece of writing so that it is easy to read and understand. Instead of one large block of text, the writing is broken down into smaller groups of sentences called paragraphs. Each paragraph starts on a new line (which is usually indented) and is made up of sentences that describe one idea or topic. By putting paragraphs in a particular order, a piece of writing can move from one idea to another in a way that makes sense.

In the *Grammar 3 Pupil Book,* the children learnt how to plan their work and write in paragraphs. They were taught to think about what they wanted to say and note down their ideas, arranging them under topic headings. The children were then asked to expand their thoughts into proper sentences and put their paragraphs in a logical order. Once children can do this, they should be encouraged to use paragraphs in their writing, organising their ideas before they write anything down. It is also a good idea to point out paragraphs in the texts the children are studying. This will help them appreciate how a well-structured piece of writing flows and keeps the reader interested.

In the *Grammar 6 Pupil Book,* the children look more closely at the structure of a paragraph. They learn that it needs a beginning, a middle and an end. The first sentence, called the topic sentence, usually explains what the whole paragraph is about. The sentences that follow provide the evidence to support the main idea. The final sentence usually acts as a conclusion, summing up what the paragraph is about, although not all paragraphs do this. This pattern echoes the structure of a longer piece of writing, which would normally have an introductory and closing paragraph. Writing in this way helps the children to avoid repeating or contradicting themselves.

The children also learn about cohesion, which is the use of words and phrases to link ideas or paragraphs in a fluid way. Many adverbs and conjunctions provide cohesion, as do phrases that act as these parts of speech. They are often referred to as *connectives* and can be categorised by function. They include, for example, words that indicate time or sequence *(meanwhile, next, then, firstly, secondly, thirdly)*; an opening *(at first, to begin with, initially)*; a summing-up *(finally, after all, in conclusion)*; place *(nearby, around the corner, down the road)*; cause and effect *(because, since, therefore, as a result)*; additional information *(also, as well as, moreover)*; and contrast *(instead, although, however, unless)*.

Punctuation

The *Grammar Pupil Books* emphasise the importance of punctuation. The children are taught that their writing will be easier to read if it is accurately punctuated. In the *Grammar 2 Pupil Book,* the children revised full stops, question marks and speech marks, and were introduced to exclamation marks, commas and apostrophes. In the *Grammar 3* and *4 Pupil Books,* the focus was on using the correct punctuation when writing direct speech. In direct speech, the words are written exactly as they are said: for example, *'I'm tired,' said Tim.* (This is different from reported speech: for example, *Tim said he was tired.*) The children also revised speech marks, full stops, commas and contractions, and learnt how to use question marks and exclamation marks in direct speech. They were also introduced to some of the more straightforward uses of hyphens. In the *Grammar 5 Pupil Book,* the children were shown how to use parentheses correctly in their writing and learnt how to punctuate vertical lists using a colon and bullet points. The children's knowledge is further extended in the *Grammar 6 Pupil Book,* when they learn that colons can be used in a sentence to introduce things like an idea, a list of examples or an explanation. They are also introduced to semicolons, which can be used to replace commas in a complicated list or to join closely related clauses in a compound sentence. They also learn how to punctuate imperative sentences, non-defining relative clauses and fronted adverbials.

Question Marks ‹?›

The children need to understand what a question is and how to form a question mark correctly. If a sentence is worded in such a way that it expects an answer, then it is a question and needs a question mark instead of a full stop. If the question is being written as direct speech, the question mark is kept at the end and not replaced with a comma.

Exclamation Marks ‹!›

When someone cries out suddenly, especially in anger, surprise or pain, they are said to exclaim or to make an exclamation. An exclamation mark is used at the end of a sentence, instead of a full stop, to show that the speaker or writer feels strongly about something. It is also used after interjections (such as *Hi! Well!* and *Sorry!*) and in some imperative sentences, if these express a forceful order, command or warning. If the exclamation is being written as direct speech, the exclamation mark is kept at the end and not replaced with a comma.

Commas ‹,›

Sometimes it is necessary to indicate a short pause in the middle of a sentence, where it would be wrong to use a full stop. This helps the reader separate one idea from another. For this sort of pause we use a comma. The children will be used to being told to pause when they see a comma in their reading. However, learning when to use commas in writing is more difficult. The *Grammar 2 Pupil Book* introduced two of the most straightforward ways commas are used:

1. We use commas to separate items in a list of more than two items: *red, white and blue,* or *Grandma, Grandpa, Aunt or Uncle.* (In the *Grammar 6 Pupil Book,* the children learn that if an item already has a comma, they can punctuate the list using semicolons instead.) Note that a comma is not used before the last item in a list, but is replaced by the word *and* or *or.*
2. We also use commas in sentences that include direct speech. Here, the comma indicates a pause between the words spoken and the rest of the sentence. If the speech comes before the rest of the sentence, the comma belongs inside the speech marks, after the last word spoken: *'I am hungry,' complained Matt.* (If the words spoken are a question or an exclamation, then a question mark or exclamation mark is used instead of a comma in the same position.) If the speech comes after the rest of the sentence, the comma goes at the end of the word that comes before the speech marks: *Matt complained, 'I am hungry.'*

Later, in the *Grammar 6 Pupil Book,* the children learn that a fronted adverbial is usually separated from the rest of the sentence by a comma: *When I got home, I went to bed*. They are also taught that a non-defining relative clause should be bracketed with commas, unless the clause appears at the end of the sentence, when the second comma is unnecessary. The commas show that the information, while interesting, is not essential, as in *The house, which has four bedrooms, is currently for sale.*

Apostrophes ‹'›

Apostrophes are very often incorrectly used. The rules on how and when to use apostrophes are fairly straightforward and it is important to teach them early on before any children develop bad habits in their writing. The *Grammar 2 Pupil Book* introduced both of the main ways that an apostrophe is used:

1. An apostrophe followed by the letter ‹s› is used after a noun to indicate possession, as in *Ben's new toy* or *the girl's father*. The apostrophe is needed to show that the ‹s› is not being used to make a plural. Understanding this distinction will help the children use apostrophe ‹s› correctly. Encourage the children to think about the meaning of what they write and decide whether each ‹s› is being used to make a plural or the possessive case. In the *Grammar 4 Pupil Book,* the children learnt that this type of noun is called a possessive noun. They also learnt how to make possessive nouns plural (as in *the boys' room* or *the women's hats*), as described on page 7. Later, the children can learn how to use apostrophe ‹s› with names that end in ‹es› (as in *James' cat*).
    Although the possessive adjectives (such as *my, your, his, her* and *its)* indicate possession, there is no risk of confusion with the plural, so they do not need an apostrophe. Knowing this will help the children avoid the common mistake of writing the possessive adjective *its* as *it's*.
2. An apostrophe is also used to show that a letter (or more than one letter) is missing in a contraction. Sometimes, we contract words by joining them together and leaving out some of their letters, as in *I'm (I am), didn't (did not)* and *you'll (you will)*. The apostrophe indicates where the missing letter(s) used to be.
    There are many common contractions and when the children come across them, they should be encouraged to listen to the word and identify which sound(s) are missing. This will help them to leave out the appropriate letter(s) and put the apostrophe in the right place, thereby avoiding some common mistakes. In *haven't,* for example, the /o/ of *not* is missing, so the apostrophe goes between ‹n› and ‹t›, to show where ‹o› used to be. It does not go between ‹e› and ‹n›, as in 'have'nt'. Knowing that *it is* and *it has* can be contracted in this way will also help the children not to confuse *it's* and *its*. For example, if the word to be written is short for either *it is* or *it has,* as in *It's late* or *It's fallen in the water,* the children should remember to use an apostrophe.
    It is important that the children learn how to spell and punctuate contractions correctly. However, they should only use contractions when writing direct speech or informal notes. Contractions are not traditionally used in formal writing.

Hyphens ‹-›

Sometimes it is necessary to show that two or more words (or parts of words) are linked closely together, either in use or meaning. This helps the reader understand the text properly and avoids any ambiguity. To do this we use a hyphen. Hyphens are found mostly in compound words and some words with a prefix. Using hyphens makes a word like *brother-in-law* easier to read. It also allows us to distinguish, for example, between *re-cover* and *recover*.

However, not all compound words or words with a prefix need a hyphen, and hyphens are not used so commonly now as they once were; whether or not a hyphen is used often changes over time, and varies between dictionaries. Also, the rules for when to use hyphens are quite complex for children of this age, and so they should be encouraged to use a dictionary and make sure that their spelling is consistent.

Nevertheless, there are some instances in which a hyphen is nearly always used and these, along with the term *hyphen,* were introduced in the *Grammar 4 Pupil Book*. The children learnt to use a hyphen when the numbers between 21 and 99 are written as words, as in *twenty-one* or *thirty-three,* and when the first part of a compound word is a capital letter, as in *X-ray* and *T-shirt*. Later, children can learn about other common uses of the hyphen. These include joining fractions (as in *three-quarters* and *two-thirds)* and compound adjectives (but only when the adjective comes before the noun it is describing, as in *the well-known phrase)*. For now it is enough that the children understand what a hyphen is and how it can be used to make meaning clearer.

Colons and Bullet Points ‹:› ‹•›

In the *Grammar 5 Pupil Book,* the children learnt how to write lists vertically down a page. Vertical lists are often used in presentations and reports or for practical reasons, like making a shopping list, as the layout makes the list easier to read at a glance. However it is written, a list always needs an introduction. The children learnt that a vertical list's introduction has a colon at the end, which is a punctuation mark written as two small dots, one above the other (:). Like full stops and commas, a colon marks the place where we should pause in speaking: it is a longer

Teaching Ideas for Grammar

pause than a comma, but not as long as a full stop. In normal writing, an introduction that ends in a colon should be able to stand alone as a simple sentence, but in vertical lists this is not so important.

The items in a vertical list are not separated by commas. Instead, each item starts on a new, slightly indented, line with a special symbol at the front. This symbol, known as a bullet, can vary in design, but most commonly appears as a large dot or circle. Both the symbol itself and the items in the list are called bullet points, although not all vertical lists use them; instead, the items could be numbered *1, 2, 3,* or *A, B, C,* for example. Unlike a traditional list, the *and* or *or* before the final item does not usually appear.

A vertical list item can be a word, phrase or clause and it can either have an open punctuation style (no full stop at the end and a lower-case letter at the start, except when writing proper nouns) or be more formally punctuated; either way is acceptable as long as the style is consistent, although it is more common for clauses to be punctuated as sentences. The wording itself also has to be consistent, so that the list makes sense. For example, if a vertical list begins *At school I:* and the first two bullet points are *study hard* and *play sports,* the other items should follow the same format, starting with a verb in the simple present tense; it would not make sense to change style by changing the tense, using a participle, or writing a whole sentence, for example.

In the *Grammar 6 Pupil Book,* the children look at how a colon can be used in a sentence and learn that when we see one, we know that some important information will follow, such as a list of examples, an idea or an explanation. As in a vertical list, the colon is used as part of the introduction, but unlike a vertical list, the words in front of the colon must always form an independent clause. This means that we should never use a colon to separate a verb from its object or complement: instead of using an unnecessary colon in *My sister has: two dogs, three cats and a hamster,* for example, we could say, *My sister has six pets: two dogs, three cats and a hamster.*

Semicolons

Like the colon, a semicolons marks a longer pause than a comma, but a shorter one than a full stop. Both punctuation marks look quite similar, except the semicolon has a comma-like mark rather than a bottom dot ‹;›. The children are introduced to the semicolon in the *Grammar 6 Pupil Book,* and learn the two main ways that it can be used:

1. Semicolons can be used to join independent clauses in a compound sentence. Normally, this is done by using one of the coordinating conjunctions to create a flow in our writing (as explained on page 15). However, when the relationship between the two clauses is obvious, the conjunction can be replaced with a semicolon, as in *Take your umbrella; it is going to rain.* The semicolon implies there is a connection between the two clauses without interrupting the flow.
2. Semicolons can also be used instead of commas to separate items in a complicated list. For example, the children learn that if any of the items already has a comma, it is better to separate them with a semicolon, as in *In the box there was an old, chipped cup; some old Roman coins; and some torn, faded postcards.*

Parentheses ‹( )›

In a piece of writing, we sometimes choose to provide further information which is interesting, but not essential. In the *Grammar 5 Pupil Book,* the children learnt that the main way to do this is to put the information in parentheses. Parentheses are round brackets that come in pairs, rather like speech marks do; an opening bracket is placed at the beginning and a closing bracket is put at the end. When something is written in parentheses, the reader knows that the sentence would still be complete even if the extra information were removed. The extra information provided can be varied, but often includes such things as dates, prices, page numbers, explanations and alternative names. It can even be a sentence, and if it is written as such, with a capital letter at the beginning and a full stop at the end, the full stop should go inside the parentheses. Parentheses can also be used in a list of options: for example, *These shirts are available in (a) small, (b) medium or (c) large.* The children should be encouraged to read their writing through and check that it would still make sense if the words in parentheses were removed.

Grammatical Agreement

From the beginning, the children were encouraged to think about the relationship between words in a sentence and to use their grammar knowledge to make their writing as clear and as accurate as possible. They learnt that the indefinite articles *a* and *an* are only used with a singular noun, whereas the definite article *the* can be used for both singular and plural. They learnt how to form a plural correctly and how to conjugate a verb. They also learnt the possessive adjectives and possessive pronouns and were shown, for example, how *It is my book* could be written as *It is mine.*

This knowledge will help the children to understand grammatical agreement. In most languages, certain word relationships have to match or *agree.* In English this agreement centres on person, number and sometimes gender. The form of a verb can change, for example, depending on which person is used for the subject: we say *I am* for the verb *to be* in the first person singular but *he is* for the third person singular. Whether the subject is singular or plural (grammatical number) can also affect the verb: we say *The rabbit **eats*** in the singular, but *The rabbit**s** eat* in the plural. When it comes to pronouns and possessive adjectives, gender can affect which word is used: in the singular, we say *he, him* or *his* for the masculine, *she, her* or *hers* for the feminine and *it* and *its* for the neuter.

While most children use simple grammatical agreement quite naturally in their spoken and written language, it is important that they understand the principles. This will help them as they start to produce longer, more complicated writing. The idea was introduced gradually in the *Grammar 4 Pupil Book*. First, the children looked at what happened when certain words in a sentence were changed, starting first with object nouns and the words that describe them and then with subjects and their verbs. Then, when the children had learnt about grammatical person, they looked at how changing this can affect the verb and the rest of the sentence. Encourage the children to proofread their work and to make sure that all the relevant words in the sentence agree.

Parsing: Identifying Parts of Speech in Sentences

Parsing means identifying the function, or part of speech, of each word in a sentence. The children must look at each word in context to decide what part of speech it is. This skill is worth promoting, as it reinforces the grammar teaching and helps the children to develop an analytical understanding of how our language works. Many words can function as more than one part of speech. For example, the word *light* can be a noun (*the light*), a verb (*to light*), or an adjective (*a light colour*). It is only by analysing a word's use within a sentence that its function can be identified.

The best way to introduce parsing is by writing extremely simple sentences on the board. A good example is *I pat the dog*, which is parsed like this: pronoun, verb, (article), noun. The children can be encouraged to identify the parts of speech they know and then take turns to underline them in the appropriate colours. Gradually, when most of the children have mastered this, move on to more complicated sentences that use more parts of speech: for example, *She cheerfully wrote a long letter to her friend*. This can be parsed as pronoun, adverb, verb (the infinitive of which is *to write*), (article,) adjective, noun, preposition, possessive adjective, noun. Ask the children to identify the nouns and verbs first, reminding them that every sentence must contain at least one verb. Also encourage them to say each verb in its infinitive form. If there is time, the children should identify as many of the other parts of speech as possible, underlining them in the appropriate colours (as shown below).

<u>Nouns</u>	<u>Verbs</u>	<u>Pronouns</u>	<u>Adjectives</u>	<u>Adverbs</u>	<u>Prepositions</u>	<u>Conjunctions</u>
(Black)	(Red)	(Pink)	(Blue)	(Orange)	(Green)	(Purple)

In the *Pupil Books* for *Grammar 3* onwards there is regular parsing practice in the spelling lessons to help the children become quick and competent at this task. If any children are unfamiliar with parsing, or find it difficult, they need to work on simpler sentences and build up their confidence.

Sentence Walls

Parsing a sentence can reveal a lot about the role of the individual words. It can also help the children identify its subject and object. This in turn allows them to decide whether a verb is transitive or intransitive. However, it does not always reveal the relationship between certain words or phrases; nor does it tell us much about the structure of the sentence. The *Grammar 5 Pupil Book* introduced the idea of sentence walls: a form of sentence diagramming* that has been simplified for younger children. Sentence walls represent the building blocks of a sentence in an accessible and visual way. They allow the children to see at a glance different parts of a sentence: the subject and predicate; the verb and direct object; an indirect object or subject complement; prepositional phrases acting as adverbs or adjectives; and the words that are essential to the meaning of the sentence and those that provide extra information.

To give some visual interest, the sentence walls on the activity pages are portrayed as old stone walls, but they basically consist of six boxes that can be drawn on the board and discussed with the children.

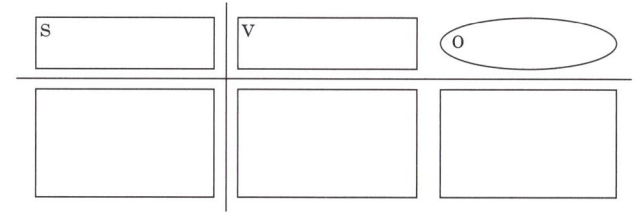

---

* Modern diagramming is based on Alonzo Reed and Brainerd Kellogg's work in *Higher Lessons in English: A Work on English Grammar and Composition,* first published in 1877. However, sentence walls were inspired by D. K. Thompson's work on box analysis, which is closer in format to Francis A. March's diagrams in *A Parser and Analyzer for Beginners* (1869), which were influenced by W. S. Clark and his 'balloon' system (*A Practical Grammar,* 1847).

Teaching Ideas for Grammar

A short vertical line separates the two basic parts of a sentence: the subject and predicate. A long horizontal line separates the essential information from the extra information. Everything above the line – the simple subject, verb and simple object (if there is one) is necessary to the sentence and reads rather like a short newspaper headline. Everything below the line (such as articles, determiners, adjectives, adverbs and prepositional phrases) is additional information that modifies the words above.

A simple sentence like *The young girl has decorated her picture beautifully* can be parsed as normal, and then it can be transferred to the boxes in the following way:

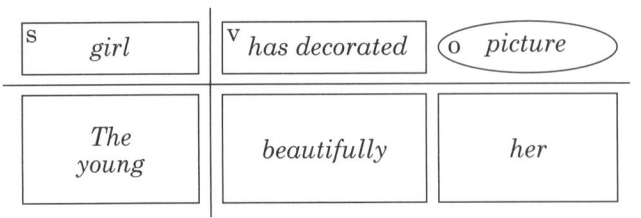

S girl	V has decorated	O picture
The young	beautifully	her

If the sentence contains a compound subject and object it will look like this:

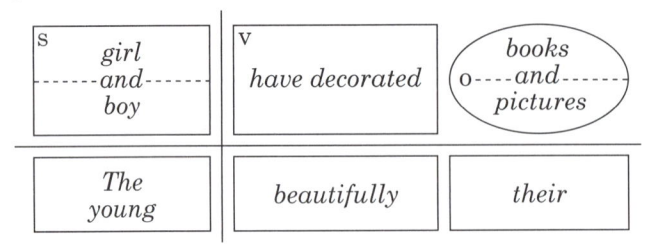

S girl -----and----- boy	V have decorated	O-----and----- books pictures
The young	beautifully	their

Similarly, if the main adverb is modified by another adverb or there is a prepositional phrase acting as an adverb, the boxes are completed like this:

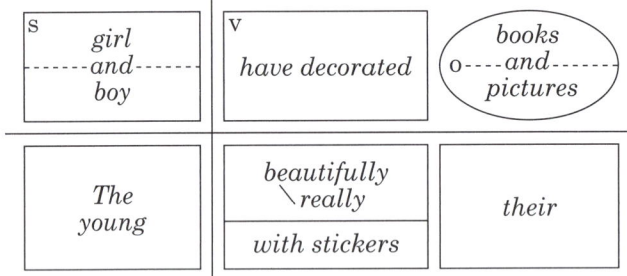

S girl -----and----- boy	V have decorated	O-----and----- books pictures
The young	beautifully \really with stickers	their

If an adverb modifies an adjective (as in ***really*** *beautiful*), or a prepositional phrase acts as an adjective rather than an adverb (as in *the book* *with stickers*)*,* they are written as above, but go in either the left- or right-hand bottom box, depending on whether they are describing the subject or object (see page 55).

Similarly, if *really beautiful* is a subject complement used with a linking verb like *to be* (as in *The stickers are really beautiful),* the top row is filled in like this:

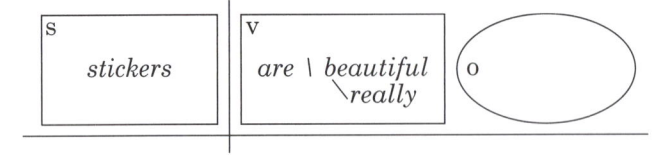

S stickers	V are \ beautiful \really	O

Finally, if a sentence has an indirect object, it is written like this:

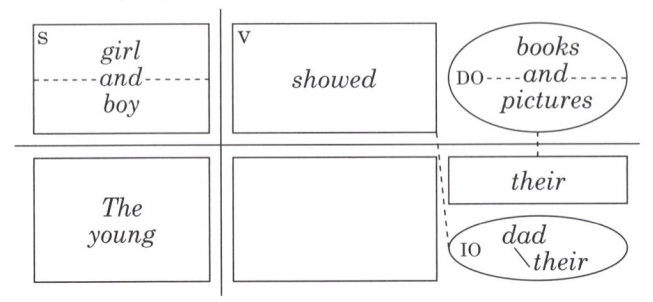

S girl -----and----- boy	V showed	DO-----and----- books pictures
The young		their IO dad \their

Alphabetical Order, Dictionary and Thesaurus Work

The more familiar children are with the order of the alphabet, the better they will be at using essential classroom resources like dictionaries, thesauruses and encyclopedias. In the *Grammar 1 Pupil Book,* the children learnt the alphabet thoroughly and were taught how to navigate a dictionary. They were encouraged to think of the dictionary as comprising four approximately equal parts, containing the following groups:

1. **A a B b C c D d E e**

2. **F f G g H h I i J j K k L l M m**

3. **N n O o P p Q q R r S s**

4. **T t U u V v W w X x Y y Z z**

It is a good idea to have a copy of the alphabet, divided into the four groups, available for the children to see. For easy reference it appears on the first page of the *Grammar 6 Pupil Book,* and the groups and colour-coding are incorporated into the *Jolly Phonics Alphabet Poster* and the *Jolly Dictionary.*

Knowing the alphabet groups saves the children time when using a dictionary. Before looking up a word, they decide which group its initial letter falls into and then narrow their search to that section of the dictionary. When looking up the word *pony,* for example, the children can turn directly to the third quarter of the dictionary because they know that the letter ‹p› is in the green group. The *Grammar 2 Pupil Book* improved the children's dictionary skills by teaching them to look beyond the initial letter of each word. The children practised putting into alphabetical order words that share the first two letters (such as *sheep* and *shoe*) and then words that share the first three letters (for example, *penny, pencil* and *penguin*). This skill was reinforced in the *Grammar 3* and *4 Pupil Books,* which include a common activity that asks the children to put the words from the weekly spelling list into alphabetical order. This activity is also found in the *Grammar 6 Pupil Book.*

In the *Grammar 3* and *4 Pupil Books,* looking up words in the dictionary for spelling and meaning was a regular activity in the spelling lessons. It helps the children understand how useful dictionaries are and aims to develop the skills they need to become regular and proficient dictionary users. Most children can become quite proficient at using a dictionary designed for schools. When they finish a piece of writing, the children should proofread their work, identify any words that look incorrectly spelt and look them up in the dictionary. The children should also be encouraged to use a dictionary to make sure they are using the right word, especially one that is a homophone, near homophone or homograph. Homophones are words that sound similar to one another but have different spellings and meanings (as in *hear* and *here*). Homographs are words that share the same spelling but have different meanings. There are two types of homographs: Those that look and sound the same are called homonyms (as in *There was a **fly** on my sandwich* and *I will **fly** to Australia*); those that look the same but sound different are called heteronyms (as in *The two rocky paths **wind** among the trees* and *The **wind** blew the leaves off the tree*). There is a strong focus on homophones throughout the *Grammar Pupil Books,* particularly in the *Grammar 4 Pupil Book,* while homographs were introduced in the *Grammar 5 Pupil Book.*

In the *Grammar 2 Pupil Book,* the children were introduced to thesauruses. Instead of giving a definition for a word, a thesaurus provides a group of words with a similar meaning and often suggests words with the opposite meaning. The children can make their work more interesting by using a thesaurus to find alternatives to words that are commonly overused, like *nice* or *said.* In the *Grammar 4 Pupil Book,* the children learnt the technical names for the two types of word found in a thesaurus: words with similar meanings are called synonyms and their opposites are known as antonyms. The children also developed their knowledge of antonyms, learning that many prefixes and some suffixes can be used to create them: for example, ‹un-›, ‹im-› and ‹non-› mean *not*; ‹de-› and ‹dis-› mean *undo* or *remove*; ‹mis-› means *wrongly* or *not*; and ‹ex-› means *out* or *away from.* The suffixes ‹-less› and ‹-ful›, which mean *without* something or *full* of it, can be added to the same root word to make a pair of adjectives with the opposite meaning, as in *thoughtful* and *thoughtless.*

Having their own Spelling Word Book can help the children improve their independent writing. In it the children can record the weekly spellings, other useful vocabulary (including homophones, antonyms and synonyms) and any interesting examples of literacy devices that they find (such as idioms and alliterative phrases).

The following extension activities can be used to improve alphabet and dictionary skills, or with those children who finish their work ahead of time:

- The children take the words from a page in their Spelling Word Book and rewrite them in alphabetical order.
- The children use a dictionary to check which spelling of a word is correct. For this activity, write out a word three or four times on the board. Spell it slightly differently each time, but ensure that one of the spellings is correct. It is a good idea to choose a word which contains a sound or spelling pattern that has alternative spellings: for example, *delicious,* which uses the ‹ci› spelling of /sh/ before the suffix ‹-ous›. The options for the children could then be *delitious, delixious, desicious* or *delicious.* The children write the correct spelling in their Spelling Word Book.
- In pairs, the children race one another to find a given word in the dictionary.

Teaching Ideas for Spelling

Most children need to be taught to spell correctly. In the *Grammar Pupil Books,* spelling is the main focus for one lesson each week. The spelling activities in the *Grammar 6 Pupil Book* are designed to consolidate the children's existing knowledge and introduce new spelling patterns. Its main focus is on the more unusual spellings of the vowel sounds, less common silent letter digraphs, number prefixes, and closely related suffixes like ‹-ity› and ‹-ety›, ‹-ious› and ‹-eous›, and ‹-ure› and ‹-our›.

The children first learnt to spell by listening for the sounds in a word and writing the letters that represent those sounds. They also systematically learnt the tricky words, which are frequently used words that either have an irregular spelling or use phonic knowledge that the children do not know yet. After completing the *Pupil Books* for *Phonics* and *Grammar 1,* most children have a reading age of at least seven years, and they are starting to spell with far greater accuracy. As research has shown, children with a reading age of seven years or more are able to use analogy in their reasoning. This is a useful strategy for spelling. For example, children who know the word *would* and who want to write *should,* might notice that the end of both words sound the same. They can then use this knowledge to write *should,* replacing the ‹w› with ‹sh›. If the children are unsure of a spelling, they may be able to find it by writing the word in several ways (such as *should, shood* and *shud*) and choosing the version that looks correct. If they have already encountered the word several times in their reading, they will probably be able to choose the right one. By introducing groups of spelling words that each feature a particular spelling pattern, the *Grammar Pupil Books* encourage the children to think analogically.

A focus on revising the alternative spellings of vowel sounds and learning new ones helps the children consolidate and extend their learning. The alternative vowel spellings are what makes English spelling difficult and, by this stage, the children need to be not only revising the main ways of spelling the vowel sounds, but also improving their ability to remember which words take which spelling.

The *Grammar 6 Pupil Book* builds on the teaching of the previous *Pupil Books* and assumes that the children have some knowledge of the following spelling features, which are outlined in greater detail below:

1. Vowel Digraphs
2. Alternative Spellings of the Vowel Sounds
3. New Spelling Patterns
4. Syllables
5. The Schwa
6. Silent Letters
7. Identifying the Short Vowels
8. Spelling Rules

1. Vowel Digraphs

The vowel digraphs were introduced and revised in the *Pupil Books* for *Phonics* and *Grammar 1.* The focus in the *Grammar 2* and *Grammar 3 Pupil Books* is on consolidating this learning. *Vowel digraph* is the term for two letters that make a single vowel sound. Often, the two letters are placed next to each other in a word, as in h**ay**, s**ea**, **ou**t, **oi**l and f**ew**. At least one of these letters is always a vowel, and two vowel letters are usually needed to make one of the long vowel sounds: /ai/, /ee/, /ie/, /oa/, /ue/. (The long vowel sounds are the same as the names of the vowel letters: ‹a›, ‹e›, ‹i›, ‹o›, ‹u›.) Generally, the sound made by a digraph is that of the first vowel's name, hence the well-known rule of thumb: *When two vowels go walking, the first does the talking.*

Sometimes, the long vowel sound is made by two vowels separated by one or more consonants. In monosyllabic words, the second vowel is usually an ‹e›, known as a *magic* ‹e› because it modifies the sound of the first vowel letter. Digraphs with a magic ‹e› can be thought of as *hop-over* ‹e› digraphs: ‹a_e›, ‹e_e›, ‹i_e›, ‹o_e› and ‹u_e›. Once again, the sound they make is that of the first vowel's name; the magic ‹e› is silent. Children like to show with their hand how the 'magic' from the ‹e› hops over the preceding consonant and changes the short vowel sound to a long one.

The hop-over ‹e› digraphs are an alternative way of writing the long vowel sounds, and are found in words such as *bake, these, fine, hope* and *cube.* The children need to be shown many examples of such words, which are available in the *Jolly Phonics Word Book.* To help the children understand how magic ‹e› works, ask them to read a word twice: first with the magic ‹e› showing and then with it hidden by a piece of paper. In this way *pipe* becomes *pip, hate* becomes *hat, hope* becomes *hop,* and *late* becomes *lat.* It does not matter if, as in the *late/lat* example, the children find themselves producing nonsense words; the exercise will still help them to understand the spelling rule. When looking at words on the board or in other texts, the children can be encouraged to look for and identify words with a magic ‹e›.

Although hop-over ‹e› words are generally quite common, there are only a few words with the ‹e_e› spelling pattern: examples include *these, scheme* and *complete*. Words with an ‹e_e› spelling are not only rather rare, but often quite advanced. For this reason, the ‹e_e› spelling is not given quite as much emphasis as the other long vowel spellings, and it is not made the focus of a whole lesson until the *Grammar 3 Pupil Book*.

2. Alternative Spellings of the Vowel Sounds

Children who have learnt to read with *Jolly Phonics* are used to spelling new words by listening for the sounds and writing the letters that represent those sounds. This skill enables the children to spell accurately the many regular words that do not contain vowel sounds with more than one spelling: words like *hot, plan, brush, drench* and *sting*.

However, trying to spell words like *train, play* and *make* presents a problem. All three words feature the same vowel sound, /ai/, but in each case it is spelt differently. The adjacent table shows the first spelling taught for each sound and the main alternatives introduced.

These vowel sounds and their alternative spellings were the main focus for spelling in the *Grammar 1 Pupil Book*. They were then revised in the *Grammar 2* and *3 Pupil Books* and should be familiar to the children. The alternative vowel spellings are what make English spelling difficult and it is very important to keep consolidating the teaching. This can be achieved by revising the spelling patterns regularly with flash cards, and by asking the children to list the alternative spellings for a particular sound. The children should be able to do this automatically and apply their knowledge when writing unfamiliar words. For example, with a word like *frame*, they should be able to write *fraim, fraym, frame* on a scrap of paper, before deciding which version looks correct.

First spelling taught	Alternative spellings for sound	Examples of all spellings in words
‹ai›	‹ay›, ‹a_e›	rain, day, came
‹ee›	‹ea›, ‹e_e›	street, dream, these
‹ie›	‹y›, ‹i_e›, ‹igh›	pie, by, time, light
‹oa›	‹ow›, ‹o_e›	boat, snow, home
‹ue›	‹ew›, ‹u_e›	cue, few, cube
‹er›	‹ir›, ‹ur›	her, first, turn
‹oi›	‹oy›	boil, toy
‹ou›	‹ow›	out, cow
‹or›	‹al›, ‹au›, ‹aw›	corn, talk, haunt, saw

3. New Spelling Patterns

Many of the less common spellings for familiar sounds were introduced in the *Pupil Books* for *Grammar 2* and *3*. A few were taught earlier in the *Grammar 1 Pupil Book*, and others have been introduced in subsequent levels. The adjacent table (and the tables on the following pages) show the spellings first taught and the new spelling patterns introduced. The children need to memorise which words use each of these new spelling patterns. It is helpful to make up silly sentences for each spelling, using as many of the words as possible. For example, for the ‹ie› spelling of the /ee/ sound, the children could chant the following: *I bel**ie**ve my n**ie**ce was the ch**ie**f th**ie**f who came to gr**ie**f over the p**ie**ce of sh**ie**ld she hid in the f**ie**ld.*

The *Pupil Books* for *Grammar 2* and *3* also featured a few sounds that had not been a focus for spelling before. The *Grammar 2 Pupil Book* introduced the new sounds /zh/ (written as ‹si›, as in *vision*) and /ear/ (written as ‹ear›, as in *hear* and *earring*). It also taught the ‹air›, ‹are› and ‹ear› spellings of /air/ (as in *hair, care* and *bear*). In the *Grammar 3 Pupil Book*, the children learnt that /ear/ can also be written as ‹eer› and ‹ere› (as in *deer* and *here*); that ‹ere› also makes the /air/ sound (as in *there* and *where*); and that ‹s› makes a /zh/ sound in words like *pleasure* and *treasure*. Later, in the *Grammar 6 Pupil Book*, ‹ere› is revised as an alternative spelling of both /air/ and /ear/, and the spelling pattern ‹eir› is introduced as another alternative for both sounds (as in *their* and *weird*).

Throughout the *Grammar* levels, the children's knowledge of the spelling pattern ‹ure› is revised and extended. In the *Grammar 2 Pupil Book*, the children learnt that ‹ture› says /cher/ in words like *picture* and

First spelling taught for sound(s)	New spelling(s) for sound(s)	Examples of new spellings in words
Spellings taught in the *Grammar 1 / 2 Pupil Books*		
‹ai›	‹ei›, ‹eigh›	veil, eighteen
‹cher›*	‹ture›	capture, nature
‹e›	‹ea›	breakfast, ready
‹ee›	‹ey›, ‹ie›, ‹y›**	key, field, fairy**
‹f›	‹ph›	graph, photo
‹j›	soft ‹g›	gem, giant
‹k›	‹ch›, ‹ck›	chord, cricket
‹ngk›	nk**	ink, bank, trunk
‹ool›*	‹le›	handle, little
‹or›	‹ore›	more, snore, wore
‹s›	soft ‹c›	cell, city, cycle
‹sh›	‹si›, ‹ti›	tension, station
‹u›	‹o›, ‹ou›	month, touch
‹w›	‹wh›**	whale, whistle
‹(w)o›	‹(w)a›	swan, watch, wasp

Teaching Ideas for Spelling

future. In the *Grammar 3 Pupil Book,* they looked at how ‹ure› can follow other letters to make words like *leisure, pressure, figure, failure* and *conjure.* In the *Grammar 5 Pupil Book,* the children learnt that in short words, ‹ure› usually keeps its pure sound, /ue-r/ (as in *pure* and *cure*), but that in words like *sure, unsure* and *ensure,* ‹sure› says /shor/. Finally, in the *Grammar 6 Pupil Book,* the children look at how the ‹ure› in longer, multisyllabic words is often swallowed in an unstressed syllable, becoming a schwa, or neutral vowel.

In the *Grammar 6 Pupil Book,* the children are also introduced to ‹ough›, which is one of the trickiest spellings in English because it can say a number of different sounds: /ou/ (as in *drought*), /uff/ (as in *enough*), /or/ (as in *bought*), a schwa (as in *thorough*), /oa/ (as in *doughnut*), /off/ (as in *cough*) and /oo/ (as in *breakthrough*). It even says /up/ in *hiccough,* which is an alternative spelling of *hiccup.* There are no rules to help the children work out when to use these spellings, so the words must be learnt; however, there are only a small number of common words that use ‹ough› for each of these sounds and this is why, when mastered, they can be remembered as **o**h y**o**u **g**et **h**appy words!

4. Syllables

An understanding of syllables will help to improve the children's spelling. A number of spelling rules depend on the children's ability to identify the number of syllables in a given word and to hear where the stress is placed. Although the rules of English sometimes let us down, they are worth acquiring. The more the children know, the more skilful they become and the better equipped they are to deal with any irregularities.

In the *Grammar 2 Pupil Book* the children were encouraged to count the syllables in a word by doing *chin bumps.* This is a fun, multisensory way of teaching syllables. The children place one hand under their chin (with the hand flattened as though they are about to pat something). Then they slowly say a word and count the number of times they feel their chin go down and bump their hand. When saying *cat,* for example, the children feel one bump, which means the word has one syllable; they will feel two bumps for *table,* which has two syllables; *any* also has two bumps and two syllables; *screeched* has one bump and one syllable; and *idea* has three bumps and three syllables.

In the *Grammar 3* and *4 Pupil Books,* the teaching of syllables was extended and refined. In the *Grammar 3 Pupil Book,* the children learnt that a syllable is a unit of sound which is organised around a vowel sound: If a word has three vowel sounds, for example, it will have three syllables. Words with two or more syllables are referred to as multisyllabic or polysyllabic. If a word only has one vowel sound, and therefore one syllable, it is referred to as monosyllabic. The *Grammar 4 Pupil Book* introduced the idea that, in English, stress is placed on at least one of the syllables in a multisyllabic word. This is achieved by saying the syllable a little louder and lengthening the vowel slightly, which keeps the vowel sound pure. However, the vowel in an unstressed syllable is often swallowed and

First spelling taught for sound(s)	New spelling(s) for sound(s)	Examples of new spellings in words
Spellings taught in the *Grammar 3 Pupil Book*		
‹ai›	‹a›	able, taste, haste
‹air›, ‹are›, ‹ear›*	‹ere›	where, there
‹ar›	‹a›	koala, vase, lava
‹ch›	‹tch›	match, itch, fetch
‹ear›*	‹eer›, ‹ere›	cheer, deer, here
‹ee›	‹e›, ‹e_e›	athlete, secret
‹f›	‹gh›	enough, cough
‹i›	‹y›	myth, pyramid
‹ie›	‹i›	child, microwave
‹j›	‹dge›	edge, bridge, judge
‹n›	‹gn›	gnome, resign
‹ng›	‹n›	trunk, finger
‹oa›	‹o›	only, ogre, ago
‹qu(o)›	‹qu(a)›	squad, quantity
‹ue›	‹u›	menu, emu
‹z›	‹s›, ‹se›, ‹ze›	easy, pause, bronze
Spellings taught in the *Grammar 4 Pupil Book*		
‹er›	‹ear›	earth, pearl
‹g›	‹gh›	ghost, aghast
‹oo›	‹u›	truth, flu
‹or›	‹ough›, ‹augh›	ought, caught
‹s›	‹se›, ‹st›	goose, listen
‹v›	‹ve›	solve, curve
‹(w)er›	‹(w)or›	worm, worker
Spellings taught in the *Grammar 5 Pupil Book*		
‹iez›	‹ize›, ‹ise›	capsize, surprise
‹ij›	‹age›, ‹ege›	advantage, privilege
‹sh›	‹ch›, ‹che›, ‹sch›	chef, moustache, schwa
‹shor›*	‹sure›	sure, assure
‹shul›*	‹cial›, ‹tial›, ‹sial›	special, initial, controversial
‹shun›*	‹ssion›, ‹cian›	mission, musician
‹shus›*	‹cious›, ‹xious›, ‹tious›	delicious, anxious, cautious
‹sk›	‹sch›	school, scheme
‹us›*	‹ous›	famous, dangerous

26

becomes – most commonly – a neutral schwa, sounding something like /uh/.

In the *Pupil Books* for *Grammar 3* onwards, the children are given regular practice identifying the syllables in words. They find doing this aurally (with chin bumps or by clapping the syllables) quite easy with practice, but the children are also required to identify the syllables on paper. In the *Grammar 3* and *4 Pupil Books,* they did this by underlining the letters that make the vowel sounds and drawing a vertical line between the syllables. In the *Grammar 5* and *6 Pupil Books,* the children go through the spelling list and write each word again, with a space between the syllables. There are some simple rules the children can learn that will help them split words with double consonants, or with ⟨ck⟩ and ⟨le⟩ spellings:

- **Double consonants**: when a consonant is doubled, the line goes between the two letters, as in *kit/ten*. However, the children should take care with words like *hopped, stopped* and *nipped,* where the ⟨e⟩ in ⟨-ed⟩ is silent. These may look like two-syllable words but they are, in fact, monosyllabic.

- **⟨ck⟩ words**: although ⟨c⟩ and ⟨k⟩ make the same sound and so act like double consonants, the line goes after the ⟨k⟩, as in *pock/et*.

- **⟨le⟩ words**: the sounds represented by the ⟨le⟩ spelling are the same as those for ⟨el⟩ and ⟨il⟩ and consist of a small schwa before the /l/. This swallowed vowel sound can clearly be seen in *label* and *pencil* but not in *candle*. In ⟨le⟩ words there is no written vowel to underline in the last syllable. Instead, when the children see a word like this, they must listen for the schwa and draw a line before the consonant preceding it, as in *can/dle* and *sad/dle*. Again, ⟨ck⟩ words are an exception; the line goes after the ⟨k⟩, as in *pick/le, cack/le* and *buck/le*.

Exactly how a word is split into syllables often depends on stress (as in the noun **pres**/ent and the verb pre/**sent**) or whether the syllable is open or closed. Open syllables are syllables ending in a long vowel sound, and closed syllables are syllables with a short vowel that end in a consonant. A word like *paper,* for example, tends to be split into *pa/per* rather than *pap/er*. The type of syllable is not always easy to determine, as many long vowels become swallowed and are pronounced as schwas in English. The guidance given in the lesson plans aims to follow these rules, but in practice there is no definitive way to split the syllables and different dictionaries will often do it in different ways. For now, the focus should be on improving the children's ability to identify the vowel sounds in a word and hear how many syllables there are.

First spelling taught for sound(s)	New spelling(s) for sound(s)	Examples of new spellings in words
Spellings taught in the *Grammar 6 Pupil Book*		
⟨ai⟩	⟨ea⟩, ⟨ey⟩, ⟨et⟩, ⟨e_e⟩, ⟨aigh⟩	*great, they, ballet, fete, straight*
⟨air⟩*	⟨eir⟩	*their, heirloom*
⟨e⟩	⟨ei⟩	*heifer, leisure*
⟨ear⟩*	⟨eir⟩	*weir, weird*
⟨ee⟩	⟨ei⟩	*ceiling, receive*
⟨g⟩	⟨gu⟩, ⟨gue⟩	*guess, league*
⟨gw⟩	⟨gu⟩	*penguin, language*
⟨i⟩	⟨ei⟩, ⟨ui⟩, ⟨u⟩	*counterfeit, building, busy*
⟨ie⟩	⟨ei⟩, ⟨eigh⟩	*eiderdown, height*
⟨ius⟩*/⟨us⟩*	⟨eous⟩	*hideous, gorgeous*
⟨k⟩	⟨cc⟩, ⟨que⟩	*hiccup, queue*
⟨m⟩	⟨mb⟩, ⟨mn⟩, ⟨me⟩	*numb, column, welcome*
⟨ne⟩	⟨n⟩	*examine, migraine*
⟨ng⟩	⟨gue⟩	*tongue, meringue*
⟨oa⟩	⟨oe⟩, ⟨oo⟩, ⟨ew⟩, ⟨ou⟩, ⟨au⟩, ⟨ough⟩	*toe, brooch, sewn, shoulder, mauve, dough*
⟨off⟩	⟨ough⟩	*cough*
⟨oo⟩	⟨ui⟩, ⟨ou⟩, ⟨o⟩, ⟨oe⟩, ⟨ough⟩	*fruit, soup, movie, shoe, through*
⟨or⟩	⟨ough⟩	*bought, thought*
⟨ou⟩	⟨ough⟩	*bough, drought*
⟨sh⟩	⟨ci⟩	*ancient, social*
⟨t⟩	⟨bt⟩, ⟨te⟩, ⟨tte⟩, ⟨th⟩, ⟨cht⟩	*doubt, paste, palette, thyme, yacht*
⟨uff⟩	⟨ough⟩	*tough, enough*

* As the relevant lesson plans explain, this is only an approximation of the sound made by the new spelling.
** ⟨y⟩ as /ee/, ⟨wh⟩ and ⟨nk⟩ are introduced in the *Grammar 1 Pupil Book*.

5. The Schwa

In the *Grammar 4 Pupil Book,* the children were introduced to the schwa, which is the most common vowel sound in English. It is used when the vowel in an unstressed syllable is swallowed and loses its purity, becoming more like an /uh/ sound. Although it is the most common vowel sound, the schwa is not taught earlier because it can be made by any unstressed vowel. This means that there is no helpful spelling rule for the children to use and so the spellings have to be learnt. To help them remember the spelling, encourage the children to 'say it as it sounds', stressing the pure form of the vowel sound and saying, for example, *doct-**or*** rather than *doct-**uh***. This is a useful strategy for any word that is difficult to spell.

TEACHING IDEAS FOR SPELLING

The schwa often appears in suffixes that have similar spellings, making it difficult for children to choose the correct one simply by listening for the sounds. The later *Grammar Pupil Books* focus on this type of suffix and include the following:

- ‹-ant›, ‹-ent›
- ‹-ance›, ‹-ence›
- ‹-ancy›, ‹-ency›
- ‹-ary›, ‹-ery›, ‹-ory›
- ‹-able›, ‹-ible›
- ‹-ious›, ‹-eous›
- ‹tial›, ‹cial›, ‹sial›
- ‹tious›, ‹cious›, ‹xious›
- ‹-tion›, ‹-sion›, ‹ssion›, ‹cian›, ‹-ation›

A swallowed vowel in an unstressed syllable does not always become neutral, but sometimes changes to an /i/ sound, as can be seen in words like *village, college* and *society*. It happens to ‹e› in particular, especially when it appears at the beginning of a word (as in *exam, enjoy, enough, extend, expand, efficient, enormous, emergency, encourage, equipment, embarrass* and *essential*) or is part of a prefix like ‹re-› (as in *rely, remove, refer, recruit, revise, receive, receipt, relation, retrieve, revere* and *reprieve*), ‹pre-› (as in *prefer, prepare, pretend, prevent, predict, precise, presume, precede, presenter, precaution, precarious* and *preliminary*) or ‹de-› (as in *deny, delay, decide, deliver, defeat, debate, deduct, deprive, despise, devise, deceive* and *determine*). In the *Grammar 5* and *6 Pupil Books*, the lesson plans point out when an unstressed vowel in a spelling word changes to /i/ in this way.

6. Silent Letters

A number of English words contain letters that are not pronounced at all. These are known as silent letters. Some silent letters, such as the ‹k› in *knee,* show us how the word was pronounced in the past. Other silent letters, like the ‹h› in *rhyme,* indicate the word's foreign origins. Encouraging the children to 'say it as it sounds' will help them to remember these spellings. If the word *lamb* is called out, for example, the children should respond with /lamb/, emphasising the /b/, which would normally be silent. The *Grammar Pupil Books* introduce the following silent letters:

- silent ‹b›, as in *lamb*
- silent ‹c›, as in *scissors*
- silent ‹h›, as in *rhubarb*
- silent ‹k›, as in *knife*
- silent ‹w›, as in *wrong*
- silent ‹g›, as in *gnome*
- silent ‹t›, as in *castle*
- silent ‹p›, as in *attempt*
- silent ‹n›, as in *hymn*
- silent ‹e›, as in *active*.

The first five silent letters (shown in the left-hand column) were introduced in the *Grammar 2 Pupil Book*. Later, the children learnt that silent letters often go with a particular letter to form a common spelling pattern. For example, in the *Grammar 3 Pupil Book*, the children looked at how silent ‹g› comes before ‹n› in words like **g**nome, **g**nat and si**g**n. Similarly, in the *Grammar 4 Pupil Book*, they learnt that silent ‹t› follows ‹s› in words such as cas**t**le, lis**t**en and nes**t**le. From the *Grammar 4 Pupil Book* onwards, the children were encouraged to think of these and other examples (including ‹mb›, ‹wr›, ‹kn›, ‹wh›, ‹rh›, ‹wh›, ‹sc› and ‹gh›) as silent letter digraphs. Further examples, introduced in the *Grammar 6 Pupil Book*, appear in more advanced words. Some of them, like the silent ‹p› digraphs in attem**p**t, **p**salm and **p**neumonia, share a common silent letter. Others use different silent letters, but make the same sound, such as the digraphs in nu**mb**, hy**mn** and so**me**, which make the /m/ sound.

Several spelling patterns, introduced over the course of the *Grammar Pupil Books,* include a silent ‹e› at the end, making words like *more, bronze, geese, twelve* and *examine*. A silent ‹e› should not be confused with magic ‹e›, which is explained on page 24.

7. Identifying the Short Vowels

One of the most reliable spelling rules in English is the consonant doubling rule. Consonant doubling is governed by the short vowels, so the children need to be able to identify short vowel sounds confidently. In the *Grammar 1* and *Grammar 2 Pupil Books,* a puppet was used to encourage the children to listen for the short vowels.

- For /a/, put the puppet **a**t the side of the box.
- For /e/, make the puppet wobble on the **e**dge of the box.
- For /i/, put the puppet **i**n the box.
- For /o/, put the puppet **o**n the box.
- For /u/, put the puppet **u**nder the box.

TEACHING IDEAS FOR SPELLING

The children pretended that their fist was the box and their open hand was the puppet. Initially, the children were encouraged to do the appropriate action when the short vowel sounds were called out. Then they learnt to do the actions when they heard short words with a short vowel sound (such as *hat, red, dig, pot* and *bun*). Once the children had learnt to distinguish between short vowels and long vowels (and the other vowel sounds) they were able to repeat the activity, listening to short words with a variety of vowel sounds. For those words that did not have a short vowel sound, the children kept their hands still.

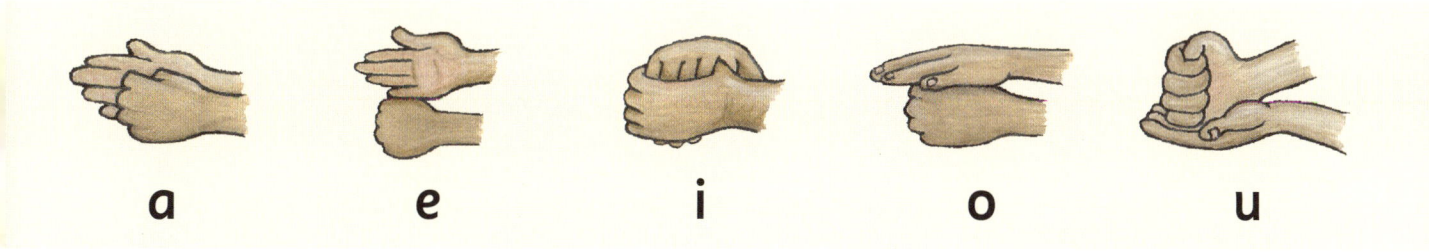

Once the children know the short vowel sounds, it is important that they revise them regularly. A simple way to do this is by using the vowel hand. The children hold up one hand so that their palm is facing them; then, using the index finger of their other hand, they point to the tip of each finger, saying the vowel sounds in turn. First they point to the tip of their thumb for /a/, then to the first finger for /e/, and so on. The vowel hand can also be used to revise the long vowel sounds: the children point to the base of each finger as they say /ai/, /ee/, /ie/, /oa/ and /ue/. Activities like these help to keep the children tuned in to identifying the sounds in words and, in turn, help to prepare them for the consonant doubling rules.

8. Spelling Rules

An ability to identify syllables and short vowels will help the children apply the following rules for consonant doubling and adding suffixes.

Spelling Rules for Consonant Doubling

a. In a monosyllabic word with a short vowel sound, ending in ‹f›, ‹l›, ‹s› or ‹z›, the final consonant letter is doubled, as in the words *cliff, bell, miss* and *buzz*. (Some common exceptions to this rule are the two-letter words *as, if, is, of* and *us*.)

b. In a monosyllabic word with a short vowel sound, if the last consonant sound is /k/, this is spelt ‹ck›, as in the words: *back, neck, lick, clock* and *duck*.

c. If there is only one consonant after a short, stressed vowel sound, this consonant is doubled before any suffix starting with a vowel is added. For example, when the suffixes ‹-ed›, ‹-er›, ‹-est›, ‹-ing›, ‹-y› and ‹-able› are added to the words *hop, wet, big, clap, fun* and *hug*, the final consonants are doubled so that we get *hopped, wetter, biggest, clapping, funny* and *huggable*. Note that when ‹y› is a suffix, it counts as a vowel because it has a vowel sound.

This rule does not apply to words that end in ‹x›, because ‹x› is really two consonant sounds, /k/ and /s/, blended together as /ks/. This means that consonant doubling is unnecessary in words like *faxed, boxing* and *mixer*.

The rule can be understood more easily if the children think of the consonant(s) as a wall between two vowels. With only one consonant, the wall

29

Teaching Ideas for Spelling

is not thick enough to prevent the 'magic' hopping over from the vowel in the suffix and changing the short vowel sound to a long one. With two consonants, the wall becomes so thick that the 'magic' cannot get over.

d. When a word ends in the letters ⟨le⟩ and the preceding syllable contains a short, stressed vowel sound, there must be two consonants between the short vowel and the ⟨le⟩. This means that the consonant before the ⟨le⟩ is doubled in words like *paddle, kettle, nibble, topple* and *snuggle*. No doubling is necessary in words like *handle, twinkle* and *jungle* because they already have two consonants between the short vowel and the ⟨le⟩.

e. The doubling rule also applies to words ending in ⟨fer⟩, but only if the syllable containing ⟨fer⟩ is stressed once the suffix is added. This is why the ⟨r⟩ is doubled in *preferred, referral* and *conferring,* but remains single in *offered* and *conference*. The main exception to this rule is the word *transferable*, in which ⟨fer⟩ is stressed but there is only one ⟨r⟩.

Spelling Rules for Adding Suffixes

a. If the root word ends in a consonant that is not immediately preceded by a short vowel sound, simply add the suffix. So, *walk* + ⟨-ed⟩ = *walked*, *quick* + ⟨-est⟩ = *quickest*, *look* + ⟨-ing⟩ = *looking* and *avoid* + ⟨-able⟩ = *avoidable*.

b. If the root word ends in the letter ⟨e⟩ and the suffix starts with a consonant, simply add the suffix, so *care* + ⟨-less⟩ = *careless*. If the suffix starts with a vowel, remove the ⟨e⟩ before adding the suffix. So, *love* + ⟨-ed⟩ = *loved*, *brave* + ⟨-er⟩ = *braver*, *like* + ⟨-ing⟩ = *liking* and *value* + ⟨-able⟩ = *valuable*.

When the suffix ⟨-ing⟩ is added to a root word ending in ⟨ie⟩, not only is the ⟨e⟩ removed, but *shy* ⟨i⟩ is replaced by *toughy* ⟨y⟩. This avoids the problem of having two ⟨i⟩s next to each other and makes the word easier to read. So, *tie, die* and *lie* + ⟨-ing⟩ = *tying, dying* and *lying*, but *tie, die* and *lie* + ⟨-ed⟩ = *tied, died* and *lied*.

Once exception to this rule is when the suffix ⟨-able⟩ is added to words ending in ⟨e⟩. Many of these words can be spelt either with or without the ⟨e⟩: both *lovable* and *loveable* are correct, for example. In these cases, it is better for the children to be consistent and drop the ⟨e⟩ in their writing.

c. If the root word ends in ⟨ce⟩ or ⟨ge⟩ and the suffix is ⟨-able⟩, do not remove the ⟨e⟩. This is because the ⟨e⟩ is part of the soft ⟨c⟩ and ⟨g⟩ spellings, making the ⟨c⟩ say /s/ and the ⟨g⟩ say /j/, as in *noticeable* and *changeable*.

d. If the root word ends in ⟨ce⟩ and the suffix is ⟨-al⟩, replace ⟨e⟩ with ⟨i⟩ before adding the suffix. So *commerce* + ⟨-al⟩ = *commercial*.

e. If the root word ends in a consonant that is immediately preceded by a short, stressed vowel sound and the suffix starts with a consonant, simply add the suffix, so *sad* + ⟨-ness⟩ = *sadness*. If the suffix starts with a vowel, however, double the final consonant before adding the suffix. So, *stop* + ⟨-ed⟩ = *stopped*, *sad* + ⟨-er⟩ = *sadder*, *run* + ⟨-ing⟩ = *running* and *control* + ⟨-able⟩ = *controllable*.

Remind the children that two consonants are needed to make a thicker 'wall' between the two vowels. This prevents 'magic' from the vowel in the suffix from jumping over to change the short vowel sound (see Spelling Rules for Consonant Doubling, rule c, on page 29.)

f. If the root word ends in a letter ⟨y⟩ that is immediately preceded by a consonant, replace *toughy* ⟨y⟩ with *shy* ⟨i⟩ before adding the suffix. So, *hurry* + ⟨-ed⟩ = *hurried*, *dirty* + ⟨-est⟩ = *dirtiest*, *beauty* + ⟨-ful⟩ = *beautiful*, *vary* + ⟨-able⟩ = *variable* and *pity* + ⟨-ful⟩ = *pitiful*. However, if the suffix starts with the letter ⟨i⟩, the rule does not apply, so *worry* + ⟨-ing⟩ = *worrying*.

The letter ⟨y⟩ is unique in being able to function as either a vowel or a consonant. As a vowel, ⟨y⟩ replaces ⟨i⟩. In the *Phonics Pupil Books*, the children learnt that *shy* ⟨i⟩ does not like to go at the end of a word, so *toughy* ⟨y⟩ takes its place. It is interesting to note that when ⟨y⟩ is the last syllable of a multisyllabic word, the sound it makes is somewhere between the short /i/ in *tin* and the long /ee/ in *bee*. (The same sound is made in the rare instances when the letter ⟨i⟩ is the final syllable in a multisyllabic word, as in *taxi* and *spaghetti*.) Despite this confusing pronunciation, it is important for the children to think of ⟨y⟩ as replacing *shy* ⟨i⟩. This will help them to remember that the ⟨i⟩ returns when such words are extended (except in words like *worrying*, where it would look odd to have two ⟨i⟩s next to each other).

Prefix and Suffix Fish

In the *Grammar Pupil Books*, suffixes and prefixes are taught using prefix and suffix fish. Prefixes are shown on the fish's head; the root (or *base*) word is shown on the fish's body and suffixes are shown on the fish's tail.

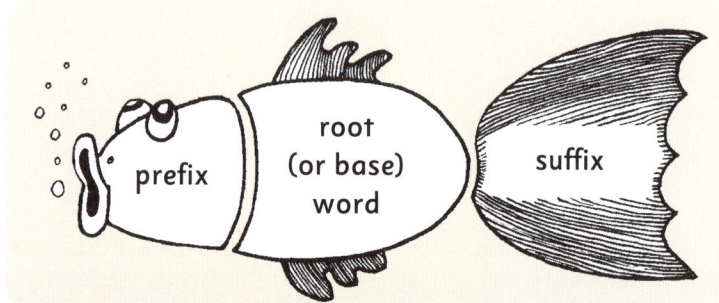

Spelling Rule: ‹i› before ‹e›?

In the *Grammar 6 Pupil Book,* the children are introduced to the well-known spelling rule that governs whether ‹i› goes before ‹e› in our writing. This rule is usually misunderstood and often rejected because it seems to have too many exceptions: for example, the words *weird, their, height, vein* and *weight* are all spelt ‹ei› even though the preceding letter is not ‹c›. This misunderstanding occurs when an important part of the rule is omitted: as long as the children are taught that *It's ‹i› before ‹e›, except after ‹c›,* **if you want to say /ee/***,* it is a very reliable rule and will help the children with their spelling of words like *niece, shriek, achieve, receive, deceive,* and *ceiling*. There are a few exceptions, however, and these can be remembered as *S**ei**ze n**ei**ther prot**ei**n nor caff**ei**ne*.

Spelling and Grammar Lessons

For each lesson, there is at least one activity page in the *Pupil Book* for the children to complete and an accompanying lesson plan in the *Teacher's Book*. The recommendations in the teacher's lesson plans are intended to be followed systematically. However, if a suggestion seems inappropriate for a particular class situation, it can of course be adapted to suit. Each lesson plan also features a reduced copy of the relevant activity page(s) in the *Pupil Book*. It can be helpful to refer to this prior to, or during, the lesson.

Grammar Lessons

Each grammar lesson has its own particular focus and the lesson plans vary accordingly. However, the grammar lessons all follow the same standard format, which helps to give them a recognisable shape. The format of the grammar lessons is as follows:

a. Aim
b. Introduction
c. Main Point
d. Activity Page
e. Extension Activity
f. Rounding Off

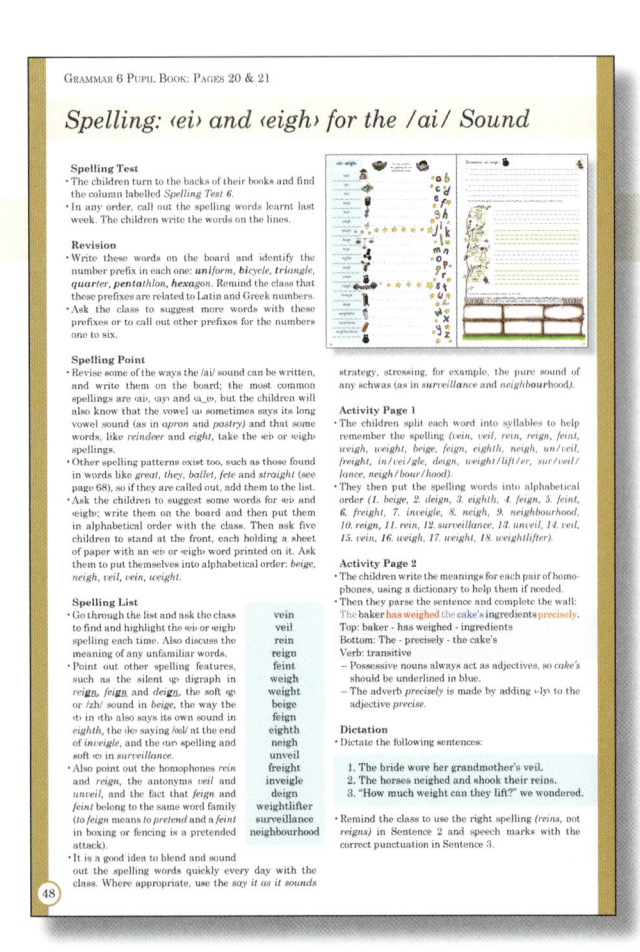

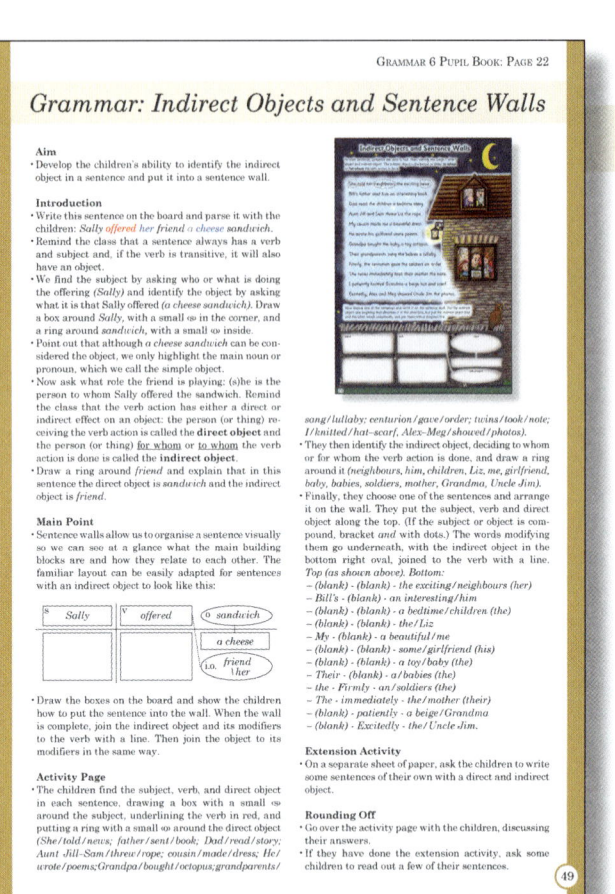

Spelling Lessons

The spelling lessons all follow the same basic format:

a. Spelling Test
b. Revision
c. Spelling Point
d. Spelling List
e. Activity Pages 1 and 2
f. Dictation

Many teaching points are common to all of the spelling lessons, so these are explained in further detail on the following pages.

SPELLING AND GRAMMAR LESSONS

a. Spelling Test

Six pages have been provided at the back of the *Grammar 6 Pupil Book* for the children's spelling tests (pages 110 to 115). Start by telling the children to turn to the back of their books and find the space for that particular week's spelling test. Call out the words one at a time for the children to write on the lines. Repeat each word twice, giving the children just enough time to write each word before moving on to the next one. The words can be called out in the same order as they appear in the list, but it is best if they are called out in a random order. Those children who are finding it difficult can be given fewer words to learn.

b. Revision

Each lesson should start with a short burst of revision. Early lessons concentrate on commonly confused homophones, such as *its* and *it's*; *to, two* and *too*; *our, hour* and *are*; *your* and *you're*; *there, their* and *they're*; and *where, wear* and *were*. After that, they focus on the prefixes, suffixes, spelling rules and spelling patterns introduced in recent lessons. The lesson plans provide suitable words to write on the board and discuss with the class.

c. Spelling Point

In the *Grammar 6 Pupil Book,* the focus of many spelling lessons is on the more unusual vowel spellings and silent letter digraphs, and on commonly used prefixes and suffixes. Analysing different parts of a word and understanding how they convey meaning, or recognising when they form a certain part of speech, can help the children enormously with their comprehension, particularly when reading unfamiliar words for the first time.

d. Spelling List

Each week, the children are given eighteen words with a particular spelling pattern to learn for a test. It is a good idea to give the spelling homework at the beginning of the week and to test at the end of the week, or on the following Monday. The spelling words have been carefully selected to enable every child to have some success. The eighteen words can be divided into three groups of six. The words in the first group are usually short, regular and fairly common; those in the second group are a bit longer and may have more alternative spellings in them; and the third group has longer, often less common words, with more varied spellings.

For those children who find spelling difficult, it may be appropriate to give them only the first six spelling words; the number can be increased when the children are ready. The number of spelling words given to the children is at the teacher's discretion, based on his or her knowledge of the children in the class.

It is important to go over the words during the spelling lesson. Look carefully at each spelling list with the class: discuss the meanings of any unfamiliar words, and look to see which parts of a word are regular and identify those parts that are not. The lesson plans in the *Teacher's Book* point out the words that need particular attention and suggest suitable learning strategies. The spelling activity pages will also help the children become more familiar with the words and their spellings. Go over the spelling words as often as possible during the week, ideally blending and sounding out the words with the children every day. The class can also work in pairs, testing each other on their spellings in spare moments.

Each child takes the list of spellings home to learn. If the children usually leave their *Pupil Books* at school, the words can be copied out into a small homework book for the children to take home. If the children do the writing, check that they have copied the words clearly and accurately before the books go home.

Test and mark the spellings each week. The results should be written in the children's *Pupil Books* for the parents to see. Write in the mark out of eighteen or use a coded system, if preferred, such as coloured stars: a gold star for 18/18, a silver star for 17/18 and a coloured star for 16/18, for example. Most parents like to be involved in their children's homework and are interested to see how many words were spelt correctly and which words were misspelt.

Children need to be aware that accurate spelling is important for their future. Unfortunately, there is no magic wand that can be waved to make them good at spelling. In addition to knowing the letter sounds and alternative spellings thoroughly, a certain amount of dedication and practice is needed.

e. Activity Pages 1 and 2

Now that the children are older, there are two spelling activity pages per lesson. As in previous *Pupil Books,* the focus of each spelling page reflects the main teaching point. Every week, there are two activities on Activity Page 1 that use the words from the spelling list. In the first activity, the children have to write out the spelling words, splitting them into syllables: the children should be familiar with doing this now, so they are given no clues and have to work out the number of syllables for themselves. (The lesson plans show how the words should be split, but as long as the children are able to hear the syllables, which are organised around the vowel sounds, and can indicate them approximately, their work should be marked as correct. For more information on syllables, see pages 26 and 27.) The second activity is more varied: it could be writing in the missing letters; putting words in alphabetical order; using them to solve crossword clues; finding them in word searches; identifying their meanings in quizzes and multiple-choice questions; solving anagrams; drawing pictures; making word families; adding prefixes and suffixes; matching words to their root words; writing the meanings of words; or using words in a noun phrase or sentence. These activities allow the children to engage actively with the spelling words, which makes learning the words more meaningful.

Activity Page 2 has three activities. The top and bottom activities are the same every week. At the top of the page, lines are provided for the weekly dictation. At the bottom of the page there is a parsing activity. Parsing involves identifying the part of speech for each word in a sentence and underlining it in the appropriate colour. The children then identify the subject and (if there is one) the object of the sentence, before transferring the words to the sentence wall. (Sentence walls are explained in more detail on pages 21 and 22.) The middle activity on Activity Page 2 sometimes focuses on the main spelling point but, more often than not, it provides some cross over with recent grammar lessons. This consolidates the grammar the children are learning and puts it into a spelling context.

f. Dictation

As a weekly exercise, dictation is useful in a number of ways. It gives the children regular practice listening for the sounds in the words they write, and it is a good way of monitoring their progress. Dictation helps the children to develop their independent writing and encourages the slower writers to increase their speed. It also provides a good opportunity for the children to practise their punctuation, such as commas, speech marks and question and exclamation marks. The dictation sections in each lesson plan suggest the important things to point out to the children.

There are three sentences each week for dictation. All of the sentences revise the spelling focus for that week, and may also feature spelling patterns and grammar points from previous lessons. For example, when the spelling focus is ‹que›, the dictation sentences feature words like *antique, technique, unique* and *boutique*, but they also use previous spelling words like *sculpture, valuable, bought* and *fashionable*. Furthermore, grammar points like the passive voice, questions formed by using the verb *to do*, and positive and negative imperatives all appear in the dictation sentences once they have been taught.

The children can write the dictation sentences on the lines provided at the top of Activity Page 2. Begin by calling out the first sentence for the children to write down. Give the children a reasonable amount of time to finish writing, but not too long, and then move on to the next sentence. The few children who have not yet finished should leave the sentence incomplete and move on. This encourages them to get up to speed. Afterwards, it is important to go over the sentences with the children and discuss the spellings, grammar and punctuation points.

Part 2

Teaching with the Grammar 6 Pupil Book

The following pages provide detailed lesson plans and teaching guidance for use alongside the activity pages in the *Grammar 6 Pupil Book*. It is a good idea to read through the relevant teaching guidance prior to each lesson, and to prepare any additional materials that might be required.

For a typical spelling lesson or grammar lesson, the teacher will need to prepare coloured pens or pencils, highlighters, dictionaries and thesauruses for the children's use. The teacher may also find it helpful to prepare a set of grammar action cards to use in the *Grammar Action Sentences* game (see the *Parts of Speech* grammar lesson on page 45). A number of the extension activities in the grammar lessons also require lined paper for extended writing.

GRAMMAR 6 PUPIL BOOK: PAGES 2 & 3

Spelling: Numerical Prefixes for 1

Spelling Test
- As the children have not been given any spelling words to learn yet, there is no spelling test in this lesson.

Revision
- Revise homophones, which are words that sound the same but have different spellings and meanings.
- Write *its* and *it's* on the board and ask the children to identify the different meanings: *its* is a possessive adjective that describes a noun by saying who it belongs to and *it's* is a contraction of either *it is* or *it has*.
- Write a sentence on the board and ask the class which spellings are needed to complete it: (*It's*) cold so the dog will need (*its*) coat.
- Ask the class to suggest some other sentences using either *its* or *it's* and to say which spelling is needed each time.

Spelling Point
- Write the words *unicycle* and *monocle* on the board and ask the children whether they know what ‹uni› and ‹mono› mean: the word *unicycle* describes a type of bicycle that only has one wheel and a *monocle* is like a pair of spectacles (glasses) with just one lens.
- Explain that both prefixes mean **one**: ‹uni-› is from the Latin *unus*, meaning *one* and ‹mono-› comes from the Greek *monos*, meaning *alone*. Ask the class to suggest other words starting with ‹uni› and ‹mono› and discuss how each prefix relates to the meaning.
- Write the words on the board and put them in alphabetical order with the class. Remind them to look at the letters after each prefix to help determine the correct order.

Spelling List
- Go through the list, asking the class to find and highlight the ‹uni-› or ‹mono-› prefix each time. Look at how it changes or adds meaning to each word. Also discuss the meaning of any unfamiliar words.
- Point out other spelling features, such as the ‹y› saying /ie/ in *unify* and *unicycle*, the soft ‹c› in *unicycle*, the /oo/ spellings at the end of *unicycle, monocle, monosyllable* and *universal*, the ‹io› saying /yoon/ when it follows ‹n› in *union*, the ‹se› saying /s/ in *universe*, the ‹gue› saying /g/ in *monologue*, the ‹y› saying /i/ in *monosyllable*, the ‹ch› saying /k/ in *monochrome* and the ‹tion› saying /shun/ in *unification*.
- It is a good idea to blend and sound out the spelling words quickly every day with the class. Where appropriate, use the *say it as it sounds* strategy, stressing the pure sound of any schwas, for

unit
unicorn
uniform
monogram
monorail
monotone
unify
unicycle
union
universe
monocle
monologue
monosyllable
universal
monochrome
monolith
unification
monopoly

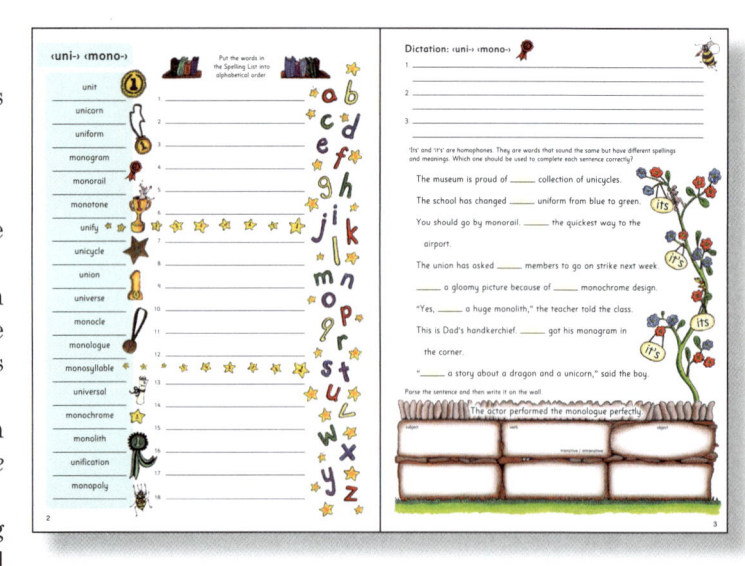

example. Alternatively, you could break down the words into prefix and root word.

Activity Page 1
- The children split each word into syllables to help remember the spelling (u/nit, u/ni/corn, u/ni/form, mon/o/gram, mon/o/rail, mon/o/tone, u/ni/fy, u/ni/cy/cle, u/nion, u/ni/verse, mon/o/cle, mon/o/logue, mon/o/syl/la/ble, u/ni/ver/sal, mon/o/chrome, mon/o/lith, u/ni/fi/ca/tion, mo/nop/o/ly).
- They then put the spelling words into alphabetical order (**mono** 1. -chrome, 2. -cle, 3. -gram, 4. -lith, 5. -logue, 6. -poly, 7. -rail, 8. -syllable, 9. -tone; **uni** 10. -corn, 11. -cycle, 12. -fication, 13. -form, 14. -fy, 15. -on, 16. -t, 17. -versal, 18. -verse).

Activity Page 2
- The children complete the sentences by writing in the correct homophone(s) (*its* collection; *its* uniform; *It's* the quickest; *its* members; *It's* a gloomy/*its* monochrome; *it's* a huge; *It's* got; *It's* a story).
- Then they parse the sentence and complete the wall:
The **actor** performed the **monologue** perfectly.
Top: actor - performed - monologue
Bottom: The - perfectly - the
Verb: transitive (see page 16)
  – The adverb *perfectly* is made by adding ‹-ly› to the adjective *perfect*.

Dictation
- Dictate the following sentences:

  1. The man in the painting was wearing a monocle.
  2. How many stars are in the universe?
  3. "Turn to the first unit in your textbook," said the teacher.

- Sentence 2 needs a question mark. Remind the class to use speech marks with the correct punctuation in Sentence 3.

36

Grammar: Homophone Mix-Ups

Aim
- Reinforce the children's understanding of homophones and develop their ability to choose between similar-sounding words in their writing.

Introduction
- Ask the children what we call words like *its* and *it's,* which sound the same but have different spellings and meanings *(homophones).*
- Remind them that some of the most commonly used homophones are possessive adjectives and contractions, such as *your* and *you're, its* and *it's,* and *their* and *they're,* while others are parts of the verb *to be* (*are* is often confused with *our* and *were* with *where*).
- These commonly used homophones are revised in upcoming lessons (see pages 40, 42, 44 and 46), so now is a good time to quickly remind the class about possessive adjectives (*my, your, his, her, its, our, your, their*), about how an apostrophe replaces the missing letters in a contraction, and about the irregular parts of the verb *to be*. For more information, see pages 13 and 19.
- As well as using homophones correctly, the children also need to take care using different types of homograph:
  – Homonyms are words that look and sound the same but have different meanings, as in *the **second** time* and *in a **second**).*
  – Heteronyms are words that look the same but sound different and have different meanings, as in *to **lead** the way* and *a **lead** pencil.*
- Ask the children if they can think of any other examples of homophones and homographs.

Main Point
- Remind the children that it is important to use the correct spelling when writing homophones, otherwise their writing will not make sense.
- Write the homophones from the activity page on the board, look at the spellings and check that the class know what they mean: *led/lead, aloud/allowed, aisle/isle, precede/proceed, steal/steel, mourning/morning, bridal/bridle, compliment/complement.*
- If the children are unsure of any meanings, ask them to look up the words in the dictionary and see who can find them first.
- Remind the children that they need to stop and think before writing a homophone, decide which meaning is needed, and think how the word with that meaning is spelt. Using the information they already know can sometimes help them remember the different spellings and meanings. For example:
  – *Allowed* is the simple past tense of the verb *allow,* made by adding the suffix ‹-ed›, whereas *aloud* is an adverb meaning *out loud*.
  – To *complement* something means to create a good combination (and comes from the verb *to complete,* which explains the ‹e› spelling); so, for example, a scarf complements a dress and makes the outfit more complete.
- Ask the children to think of sentences for some of the homophones and discuss which spelling they would use.

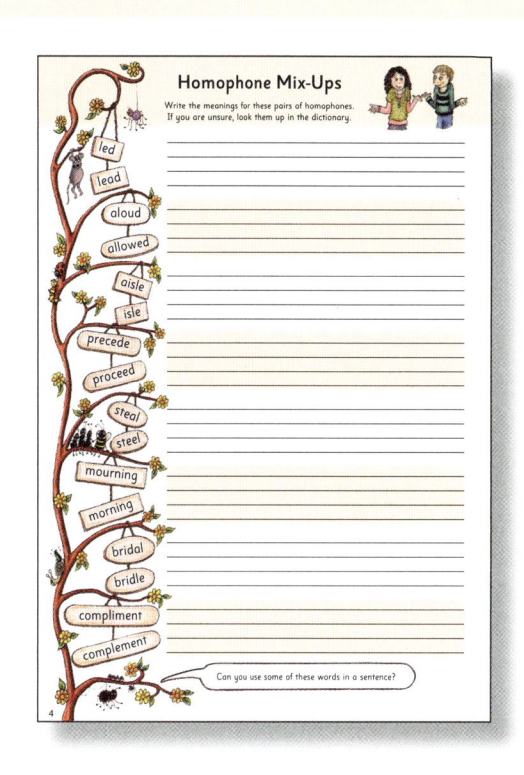

Activity Page
- The children write the meaning for each homophone. Encourage them to use a dictionary, if needed, to remind them of the meaning or to check the spelling.
- Writing on a separate sheet of paper, they then use each homophone in a sentence. (Alternatively, this could be done as part of the extension activity.)

Extension Activity
- Write some more homophones on the board and ask the children to write meanings or sentences for them.
- These could be words that the children have particular problems with or other common homophones, such as one/won, be/bee, son/sun, knot/not, main/mane, fair/fare, plain/plane, ball/bawl, grate/great, heal/heel/he'll, missed/mist, scene/seen, berry/bury, accept/except, affect/effect.

Rounding Off
- Go over the activity page with the children, discussing their answers.
- If they have done the extension activity, ask some of the children to read out their sentences and meanings before checking which spelling they have used.

37

GRAMMAR 6 PUPIL BOOK: PAGES 5 & 6

Spelling: Numerical Prefixes for 2

Spelling Test
- The children turn to the backs of their books and find the column labelled *Spelling Test 1*.
- In any order, call out the spelling words learnt last week. The children write the words on the lines.

Revision
- Revise the homophones, *to*, *two* and *too*, discussing their spellings and meanings: *to* is used with a verb to make the infinitive or is a preposition relating two objects; *two* is a number; and the adverb *too* means *also* or *excessively*.
- Write a sentence on the board and ask the class which spellings are needed to complete it: *It was (too) late for the (two) girls (to) go out*. Repeat with some other examples suggested by the class.

Spelling Point
- Write the words *bicycle*, *digraph* and *duet* on the board and ask the children whether they know what ‹bi-›, ‹di-› and ‹du-› mean: a *bicycle* is a vehicle with two wheels; a *digraph* is a pair of letters that make one sound; and a *duet* is a piece of music for two performers.
- Explain that these prefixes mean **two**, **twice** or **double** and come from the Latin *duos*, meaning *two*, and the Greek *dis*, meaning *twice*. Ask the class to suggest other words starting with each prefix and discuss how it relates to the meaning.

Spelling List
- Go through the list, asking the class to find and highlight the ‹bi-›, ‹di-› or ‹du-› prefix each time. Look at how it changes or adds meaning to each word. Also discuss the meaning of any unfamiliar words.
- Point out other spelling features, such as the vowel saying its long sound in *duo* and *bicentenary*, the soft ‹c› in *biceps*, *bicycle*, *bicentenary* and *bicentennial*, the ‹y› saying /i/ in *bicycle*, the /oo/ spellings at the end of *bicycle*, *duel*, *biennial*, *bilingual* and *bicentennial*, the soft ‹g› in *diverge*, the ‹ph› saying /f/ in *digraph*, the ‹io› saying /yoon/ when it follows ‹ll› in *billion* and the ‹gu› saying /gw/ in *bilingual*.
- Also explain that *bicentennial* is another word for *bicentenary*.
- It is a good idea to blend and sound out the spelling words quickly every day with the class. Where appropriate, use the *say it as it sounds* strategy, stressing the pure sound of any schwas, for example. Alternatively, you could break down the words into prefix and root word.

duo
duet
biceps
biplane
bicycle
duel
dilemma
biathlon
binary
diverge
duplicate
digraph
billion
biennial
binoculars
bicentenary
bilingual
bicentennial

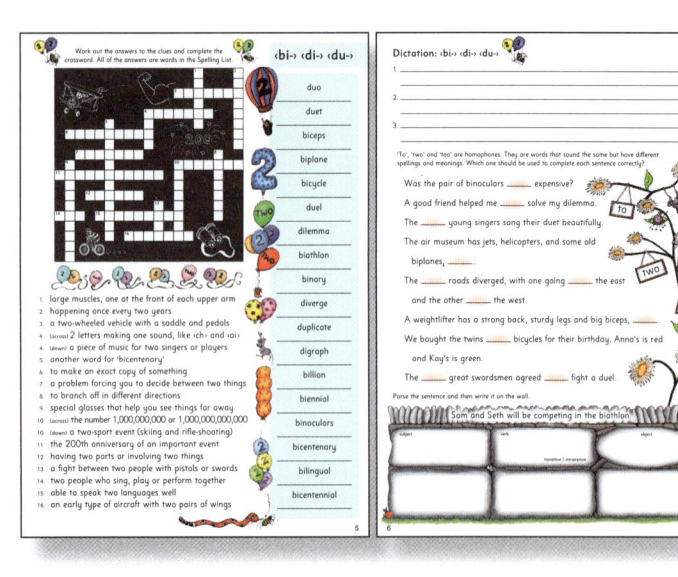

Activity Page 1
- The children split each word into syllables to help remember the spelling *(du/o, du/et, bi/ceps, bi/plane, bi/cy/cle, du/el, di/lem/ma, bi/ath/lon, bi/na/ry, di/verge, du/pli/cate, di/graph, bil/lion, bi/en/ni/al, bi/noc/u/lars, bi/cen/te/na/ry, bi/lin/gual, bi/cen/ten/ni/al)*.
- They then work out the answers to the crossword clues and write them in *(1. biceps, 2. biennial, 3. bicycle, 4. digraph (across) duet (down), 5. bicentennial, 6. duplicate, 7. dilemma, 8. diverge, 9. binoculars, 10. billion (across) biathlon (down), 11. bicentenary, 12. binary, 13. duel, 14. duo, 15. bilingual, 16. biplane)*.

Activity Page 2
- The children complete the sentences by writing in the correct homophone(s) *(too expensive; to solve; two young singers; biplanes, too; two roads/to the east/to the west; biceps, too; two bicyles; two great/to fight)*.
- Then they parse the sentence and complete the wall: Sam and Seth will be competing (in the biathlon).
Top: Sam–and–Seth - will be competing - [blank]
Bottom: [blank] - in the biathlon - [blank]
Verb: intransitive
  – The word *and* can be bracketed with dotted lines to show it is not one of the subjects (see page 22).
  – The prepositional phrase *in the biathlon* is acting as an adverb, so orange brackets can be put around it.

Dictation
- Dictate the following sentences:

  1. There are over seven billion people on the planet.
  2. "Can you make me a duplicate set of keys?" he asked.
  3. My parents gave me a new bilingual dictionary.

- Remind the class to use speech marks with the correct punctuation in Sentence 2.

Grammar: Simple, Continuous and Perfect Tenses

Aim
- Reinforce the children's understanding of the simple, continuous and perfect tenses, and develop their ability to identify tenses in sentences.

Introduction
- Write *to push* on the board and ask what form of the verb this is *(the infinitive)*. Discuss with the class how the infinitive is the name of the verb and without more information we cannot say who did the pushing or when it was done.
- Draw a simple grid of nine boxes on the board (or make it look like the Tense Tent on the activity page), reminding the children that verbs describe what is happening in the past, present or future. Then ask the children what tenses they know *(simple, continuous and perfect)* and label the grid as shown below.
- Fill in the grid with the class, discussing how each tense is formed (see *Verbs:* pages 10 and 11), and remind the children that the third person singular in the present tense takes the suffix ‹-s›, unless the verb ends in ‹sh›, ‹ch›, ‹s›, ‹z› or ‹x›, when ‹-es› is added.
- The verbs *to be* and *to have,* which act as auxiliary verbs in the continuous and perfect tenses respectively, are irregular, so now is a good time for the class to conjugate them in the simple past and present tense, using the pronoun actions.

	Past	*Present*	*Future*
Simple	pushed	push/pushes	shall/will push
Continuous	was/were pushing	am/are/is pushing	shall/will be pushing
Perfect	had pushed	have/has pushed	shall/will have pushed

Main Point
- Write these sentences on the board: *We rode our bicycles yesterday; We were riding our bicycles to school;* and *We have ridden our bicycles recently.*
- Discuss these sentences and remind the class that:
  – The **simple tenses** describe actions that start and finish within a specific time.
  – The **continuous tenses** describe actions that have started and are still happening.
  – The **perfect tenses** describe general experiences that have already been completed, usually at an unspecified point in the past.
- Also remind the class that while present participles (used in the continuous tenses) are completely regular, past participles (used in the perfect tenses) are often irregular and can be formed in a variety of ways, with no clear rules for which verbs take which spellings.
- Revise the two most common patterns for past participles, as in:

  – *swim, swam, swum,* where a change in vowel letter indicates a change in tense, and
  – *ride, rode, ridden,* where ‹-n› or ‹-en› is added to the root verb to form the past participle.
- Point out that the ‹d› is doubled in *ridden* to keep the short vowel sound /i/, and remind the children of the spelling rules for adding a suffix that starts with a vowel (see pages 29 and 30).

Activity Page
- The children write inside the outlined word *Verbs,* using a red pencil.
- They then choose one of the verbs listed, writing it in each tense to complete the Tense Tent. Remind the class that *to run away* is a phrasal verb meaning *to flee* or *to escape.*
- A good dictionary will always list the verb name and irregular past tense and past participle of a verb, so encourage the children to look these up where necessary. (Six of the verbs are irregular: *wear/wore/worn; sing/sang/sung; drink/drank/drunk; eat/ate/eaten; read/read/read* – pronounced /reed, red, red/; *run/ran/run.*)

Extension Activity
- The children think of a sentence, using one of the verbs, and write it out nine times on a separate sheet of paper, changing the tense each time.

Rounding Off
- Go over the activity page with the children, discussing their answers.
- If they have done the extension activity, ask some of the children to read out a sentence and say which tense is being used.

GRAMMAR 6 PUPIL BOOK: PAGES 8 & 9

Spelling: Numerical Prefixes for 3

Spelling Test
- The children turn to the backs of their books and find the column labelled *Spelling Test 2*.
- In any order, call out the spelling words learnt last week. The children write the words on the lines.

Revision
- Revise the possessive adjectives: *my, your, his, her, its, our, your, their*. Ask the class how to spell *its* and discuss how it differs in spelling and meaning to the contraction *it's*.
- Briefly revise the other homophones covered in recent lessons: *to, two* and *too*. Then look at the spelling of *our* and compare it to the spellings and meanings of the noun *hour*, with its silent ‹h›, and the word *are*, which is part of the verb *to be*. Remind the class that *our* is more properly pronounced /ou-r/ but in practice it is often pronounced /ar/ and can be confused with *are*.
- Write a sentence on the board and ask the class which spellings are needed to complete it: *We (are) riding (our) bicycles for an (hour)*. Repeat with some other examples suggested by the class.

Spelling Point
- Write the words *triangle, triplet* and *tricycle* on the board and ask the children whether they know what the letters ‹tri› mean: a *triangle* is a flat shape with three straight sides and three angles; a *triplet* is one of three brothers or sisters born at the same time; and a *tricycle* is a young child's bicycle with three wheels.
- Explain that ‹tri› comes from the Latin *tres* and Greek *treis*, meaning **three**.
- Ask the class to suggest other words starting with the prefix ‹tri› and discuss how it relates to the meaning of each one.

Spelling List
- Go through the list, asking the class to find and highlight the ‹tri› prefix each time. Look at how it changes or adds meaning to each word. Also discuss the meaning of any unfamiliar words.
- Point out other spelling features, such as the ‹o› saying its long sound in *trio*, the /oo/ spellings at the end of *triple, tricycle, triangle* and *triennial*, the soft ‹c› in *tricycle, triceps* and *triceratops*, the ‹y› saying /i/ in *tricycle*, the soft ‹g› in *trilogy*, the ‹our› in *tricolour*, and the ‹ion› saying /yoon/ when it follows ‹ll› in *trillion*.
- It is a good idea to blend and sound out the spelling words quickly every day with the class. Where appropriate, use the *say it as it sounds* strategy.

trio
triple
trident
triplane
tricycle
tripod
trilogy
triathlon
triangle
triplet
triceps
tricolour
triceratops
triangular
triplicate
triennial
tricorn
trillion

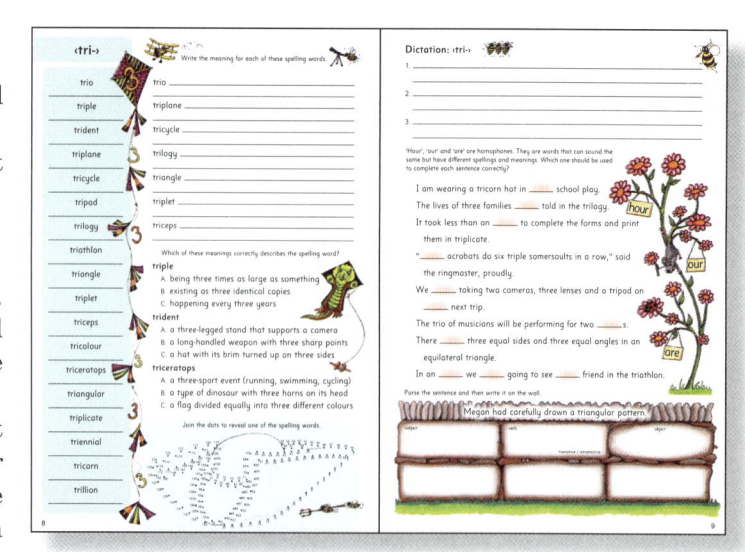

- Stressing the pure sound of any schwas will help the children to remember the spelling (such as in *trident* and *triplicate*). Alternatively, you could break down the words into prefix and root word.

Activity Page 1
- The children split each word into syllables to help remember the spelling *(tri/o, tri/ple, tri/dent, tri/plane, tri/cy/cle, tri/pod, tril/o/gy, tri/ath/lon, tri/an/gle, trip/let, tri/ceps, tri/col/our, tri/cer/a/tops, tri/an/gu/lar, trip/li/cate, tri/en/ni/al, tri/corn, tril/lion)*.
- They then write the meanings for the spelling words shown, using a dictionary if needed, and identify the correct meaning of *triple* (A), *trident* (B) and *triceratops* (B).

Activity Page 2
- The children complete the sentences by writing in the correct homophone(s) *(our school play; are told; an hour; Our acrobats; We are/our next trip; two hours; There are; an hour/we are/our friend)*.
- Then they parse the sentence and complete the wall: Megan had carefully drawn a triangular pattern.
  Top: Megan - had drawn - pattern
  Bottom: [blank] - carefully - a triangular
  Verb: transitive
  – The adverb *carefully* is made by adding ‹-ly› to the adjective *careful*.

Dictation
- Dictate the following sentences:

  1. "Have you read the trilogy?" asked the triplets.
  2. The mayor put on his red robe and tricorn hat.
  3. A triennial meeting takes place every three years.

- Remind the class to use speech marks with the correct punctuation in Sentence 1.

Grammar: Definite and Indefinite Articles

Aim
- Reinforce the children's understanding of the definite article (*the*) and the indefinite articles (*a* and *an*), and develop their knowledge of when to use *an* instead of *a*.

Introduction
- Revise the vowel sounds:
  – The short vowel sounds: /a, e, i, o, u/
  – The long vowel sounds: /ai, ee, ie, oa, ue/
  – Other vowel digraphs: /or, oo, oo, ou, oi, er, ar/
  Remind the children that many vowels have alternative spellings.
- Ask them what we call alphabet letters that are not vowels (*consonants*). Compared to vowels, the consonant sounds are more constant in their spelling, although there are some obvious exceptions, such as the soft ‹c› (for /s/), soft ‹g› (for /j/), ‹f›, ‹ph› and ‹gh› (for /f/), and ‹ch› (for /ch/, /k/ and /sh/).

Main Point
- Ask the children what they think is the most frequently used word in English (*the*). *The* is used before singular and plural nouns and is called the *definite article*, while *a* and *an* are used before singular nouns and are called the *indefinite articles*.
- *Definite* means *clearly known* and *the* is used to determine that the noun it refers to is one we are likely to know because, for example, it has already been mentioned or is what we are expecting.
- *Indefinite* has the prefix ‹in-›, meaning *not*, and so *a* and *an* are used to determine that the nouns they refer to are unknown and are being introduced for the first time.
- Write the following sentence on the board and discuss the use of *a* and *the*: I saw a dog in the park. The dog was barking.
  – The word *a* is used to introduce the dog for the first time and after that it can be referred to as *the* dog.
  – The word *the* is used with *park* to show that it is the familiar, local park, rather than an unspecified one.
  – Also point out that *the* is always used before a superlative, because there can only be one thing or one group that is the tallest or the strongest, for instance.
- The articles belong to a group of words called *determiners*, which always modify a noun and so are a special type of adjective. Determiners appear at the start of a noun phrase to show (or determine) the following:
  – How known it is (the articles: *a, an, the*)
  – How many there are (quantifiers like *some, few, more, any*)
  – Who it belongs to (possessive adjectives like *my* and *ours*)
  – Which particular one is referred to (the demonstratives *this, that, these* and *those*)
- Ask the children when and why they would use *an* instead of *a* (when the word following it starts with a vowel sound, as in **an** ant, **an** arm, **an** empty nest, **an** eel, **an** inch, **an** order, **an** umbrella; because it makes it easier to say the words together fluently).
- Call out some words and discuss whether *a* or *an* should be used. End with *unicorn* and ask the class to listen carefully to its first sound. As it starts with a long vowel, /ue/, we would expect to say *an unicorn*, but /ue/ is really two sounds – /y-oo/ – and so we say *a unicorn*, because /y/ is a consonant sound.
- Now try the word *hour* and remind the class that it is the first sound that is important, not the first letter, and so we say *an hour* because the ‹h› in *hour* is silent.
- Introduce the actions for *the* (making a capital T with your hands) and for *a* and *an* (showing the palm of your hand and pointing to your thumb).

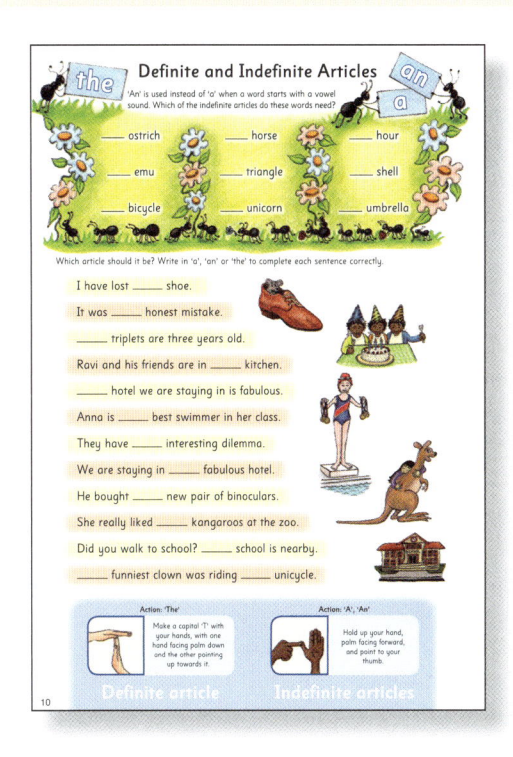

Activity Page
- The children write inside the outlined words *the, a* and *an* (in pencil or blue, as preferred).
- They then fill in the correct article to complete the noun phrases (*an ostrich, a horse, an hour, an emu, a triangle, a shell, a bicycle, a unicorn, an umbrella*) and sentences (*a shoe, an honest, The triplets, the kitchen, The hotel, the best, an interesting, a fabulous, a new, the kangaroos, The school, The funniest; a unicycle*).

Extension Activity
- The children write down their own sentences on a separate sheet of paper, leaving blank spaces for the articles. They then swap them with a partner and fill in the missing words.

Rounding Off
- Go over the activity page with the children, discussing their answers. If they have done the extension activity, ask some of them to read out a few sentences.

GRAMMAR 6 PUPIL BOOK: PAGES 11 & 12

Spelling: Numerical Prefixes for 4, 5 and 6

Spelling Test
- The children turn to the backs of their books and find the column labelled *Spelling Test 3*.
- In any order, call out the spelling words learnt last week. The children write the words on the lines.

Revision
- Revise the possessive adjectives: *my, your, his, her, its, our, your, their*. Ask the class how to spell *its* and *our* and compare them to *it's*, *hour* and *are*. Also revise *to*, *two* and *too*.
- Now look at the spelling of *your* and compare it to *you're*, which is a contraction of *you are*. Write a sentence on the board and ask the class which spellings are needed to complete it: (*You're*) visiting (*your*) granny today. Repeat with other examples suggested by the class.
- Ask the children if they can remember any of the prefixes for words relating to the numbers one, two and three.

Spelling Point
- English words relating to the numbers four, five and six also have prefixes influenced by Latin and Greek:
  – Words beginning with ‹quad(r)-› or ‹quar-› come from the Latin words *quattuor* and *quartus*, meaning **four** and **fourth**.
  – ‹Quin-› comes from the Latin word *quinque* and ‹penta› from the Greek word *pente*, both meaning **five**.
  – ‹Sex-› and ‹hexa-› come from the Latin and Greek words for **six** (*sex* and *hex*).
- Ask the children if they can think of any words beginning with these prefixes.

Spelling List
- Go through the list, asking the class to find and highlight the prefix each time. Look at how it changes or adds meaning to each word. Also discuss the meaning of any unfamiliar words.
- Point out other spelling features, such as the ‹a› saying /o/ and ‹ar› saying /or/ after ‹qu› in words starting with ‹quad› and ‹quar›, and the /ool/ spellings at the end of *quadru**ple***, *hexagon**al***, *quadrang**le*** and *quadrilateral*.
- It is a good idea to blend and sound out the spelling words quickly every day with the class. Where appropriate, use the *say it as it sounds* strategy, stressing, for example, the pure sound of any schwas (as in *hexagon*). Alternatively, you could break down the words into prefix and root word.

quad
quintet
quadrant
quartet
sextet
hexagon
pentagon
quarter
quadruple
hexagonal
pentathlon
sextant
quadrangle
pentagram
quadruped
pentameter
sextuplet
quadrilateral

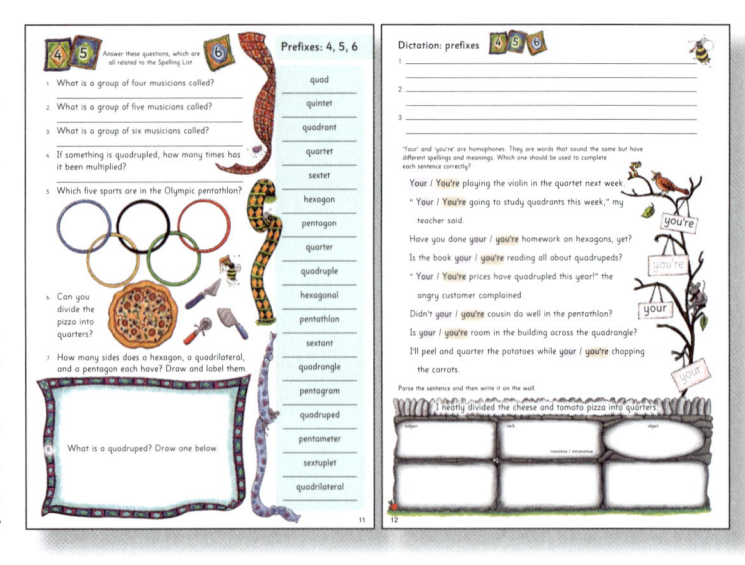

Activity Page 1
- The children split each word into syllables to help remember the spelling (*quad, quin/tet, quad/rant, quar/tet, sex/tet, hex/a/gon, pen/ta/gon, quar/ter, quad/ru/ple, hex/ag/o/nal, pen/tath/lon, sex/tant, quad/ran/gle, pen/ta/gram, quad/ru/ped, pen/tam/e/ter, sex/tu/plet, quad/ri/lat/er/al*).
- They then answer each question in the quiz (1. quartet, 2. quintet, 3. sextet, 4. four, 5. running; swimming; horse riding; fencing; shooting, 6. the pizza should be divided into four equal parts, 7. six (hexagon); four (quadrilateral); five (pentagon), 8. a picture of an animal with four legs, such as a sheep, cow, horse, etc).

Activity Page 2
- The children complete each sentence by crossing out the wrong homophone. (The correct spellings are *You're* playing; *You're* going; *your* homework; *you're* reading; *your* prices; *your* cousin; *your* room; *you're* chopping.)
- Then they parse the sentence and complete the wall:
  I neatly divided the cheese and tomato pizza (into quarters).
  Top: I - divided - pizza
  Bottom: [blank] - neatly / into quarters - the cheese and tomato
  Verb: transitive
  – *Cheese* and *tomato* are nouns acting as adjectives.
  – The prepositional phrase *into quarters* is acting as an adverb, so orange brackets can be put around it.

Dictation
- Dictate the following sentences:

  1. "Please draw a quadrilateral," said Miss Beech.
  2. The quintet will be singing in the concert.
  3. Does a pentagon have more sides than a square?

- Remind the class to use speech marks with the correct punctuation in Sentence 1. *Miss Beech* is a proper noun and needs initial capital letters, while Sentence 3 requires a question mark.

Grammar: Countable and Uncountable Nouns

Aim
- Refine the children's knowledge of nouns, and introduce the concept of countable and uncountable nouns.
- These are also known as *count* nouns and *non-count* (or *mass*) nouns.

Introduction
- Revise proper nouns and common nouns:
  – Proper nouns start with a capital letter and are the names given to particular people, places and dates.
  – Common nouns are the names of everyday things and often have the articles *a, an* or *the* in front of them.
- Ask the children what kinds of common nouns they know. They should be familiar with **collective** nouns (the names for groups of people, animals or things), **concrete** nouns (things we can see, hear, smell, taste or touch) and **abstract** nouns (the names for things like ideas, feelings, actions, qualities and events). See pages 6 to 8 for more information.
- The class should also know about **possessive** nouns (proper and common nouns ending in ‹'s›, which show possession and act as adjectives).
- Revise the actions for proper, common, concrete and abstract nouns and remind the class that the colour for nouns is black.
- Ask the children to call out different nouns and say what type they are.

Main Point
- Most nouns have a singular and plural form. Call out some regular plurals and ask the children how they would spell them: *girls, dogs, foxes, dishes, potatoes, pianos, boys, berries.* (See page 8 for when and how to add the suffixes ‹-s›, ‹-es› and ‹-ies›.)
- Now call out some irregular plurals *(men, women, children, mice, sheep, wolves, wives, cacti)* and compare them to their singular forms *(man, woman, child, mouse, sheep, wolf, wife, cactus).*
- Explain that nouns like these, which can be counted, that can have *a* or *an* in front of them and have a plural form, are called *countable* nouns.
- Now ask the children to imagine they are going on a picnic: what would they take? They might like some bread and butter, some honey and jam, or some cheese. Ask the children what is different about these nouns and explain that:
  – We do not usually count them or talk about them in the plural; we do not ask someone if they would like *a bread* or buy *two jams* at the supermarket. Instead, we use general descriptions like *some, a lot of* or *more*, and if we want to express a specific quantity, we use noun phrases like *a loaf of bread* or *a jar of jam*.
  – Nor do we ask *how many?* as we would with countable nouns, but *how much?* instead. This is because, in English, these things are thought of as a single idea or as something that is too hard to divide.
- Point out that some words can be countable or uncountable: for example, you might bring two cakes and a big roast chicken to the picnic *(countable)*, then sit down and eat some chicken and cake *(uncountable)*.
- Ask for suggestions of uncountable nouns and discuss them with the class. Possible words include *rice, sugar, pasta, flour, milk, food, rain, snow, thunder, lightning, weather, gold, silver, money, luggage, traffic, furniture, music.*

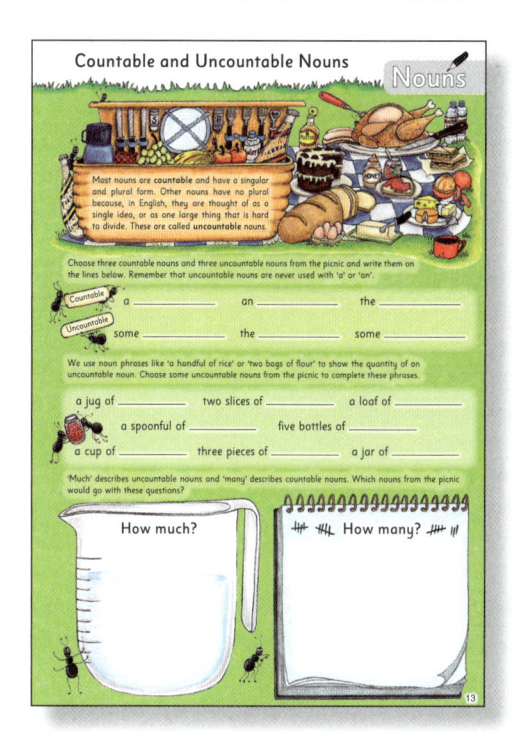

Activity Page
- The children write inside the outlined word *Nouns*, using a black pencil.
- They then choose suitable nouns from the picture to write on the lines or in the jug and notepad (Countable: *ant, apple, banana, basket, blanket, bottle, cake, chicken, cup, dish, egg, flask, fork, grape, jar, knife, napkin, orange, plate, spoon, sandwich*; Uncountable: *bread, butter, cake, cheese, chicken, coffee/soup/tea, fruit, grass, honey, jam, lemonade, mustard, pepper, salt, water.* Quantities: *a jug of lemonade/water; two slices of bread/cake/cheese/chicken; a loaf of bread; a spoonful of honey/jam/mustard/pepper/salt; five bottles of lemonade/mustard/water; a cup of coffee/soup/tea/lemonade/water; three pieces of bread/cake/cheese/chicken/fruit; a jar of coffee/honey/jam/mustard*).

Extension Activity
- The children write some sentences on a separate sheet of paper, using *much* with some suitable uncountable nouns and *many* with some countable nouns.

Rounding Off
- Go over the activity page and extension activity with the children, checking their answers.

GRAMMAR 6 PUPIL BOOK: PAGES 14 & 15

Spelling: Numerical Prefixes for 7, 8 and 9

Spelling Test
- The children turn to the backs of their books and find the column labelled *Spelling Test 4*.
- In any order, call out the spelling words learnt last week. The children write the words on the lines.

Revision
- Revise the possessive adjectives: *my, your, his, her, its, our, your, their*. Ask the class how to spell *its, our* and *your* and compare them to the homophones *it's, hour, are* and *you're*. Also revise *to, two* and *too*.
- Now look at the spelling of *their* and compare it to *they're* (a contraction of *they are*) and *there*, which is often used as an adverb to show position or as a pronoun to introduce the subject of a sentence (*There is..., There are...*).
- Write a sentence on the board and ask the class which spellings are needed to complete it: (*They're*) buying (*their*) school uniforms (*there*). Repeat with some other examples suggested by the class.
- Ask the children if they can remember any of the prefixes for words relating to the numbers one to six.

Spelling Point
- Like the numbers one to six, words relating to seven, eight and nine also have prefixes influenced by Latin and Greek:
  – ‹Sept-› comes from the Latin *septem* and ‹hepta-› from the Greek *hepta*, both meaning **seven**.
  – ‹Oct-› comes from *octo* in Latin and *okto* in Greek, which both mean **eight**.
  – ‹Novem-› and ‹nona-› come from *novem* and *nonus*, Latin words for **nine** and **ninth**.
- Ask the children if they can think of any words beginning with these prefixes.

Spelling List
- Go through the list, asking the class to find and highlight the prefix each time. Look at how it changes or adds meaning to each word. Also discuss the meaning of any unfamiliar words.
- Point out other spelling features, such as the ‹a› saying /oo/ in *octagonal*, the vowel saying its long sound in *October, November* and *octahedron*, and the soft ‹g› and ‹a› saying /air/ in *septagenarian, octogenarian* and *nonagenarian*.
- It is a good idea to blend and sound out the spelling words quickly every day with the class. Where appropriate, use the *say it as it sounds* strategy, stressing, for example, the pure sound of any schwas (as in *octagon* and *octave*). Alternatively, you could break down the words into prefix and root word.

septet
octet
heptagon
octagon
nonagon
octopus
octave
octagonal
September
October
November
heptathlon
septuplet
octuplet
octahedron
septuagenarian
octogenarian
nonagenarian

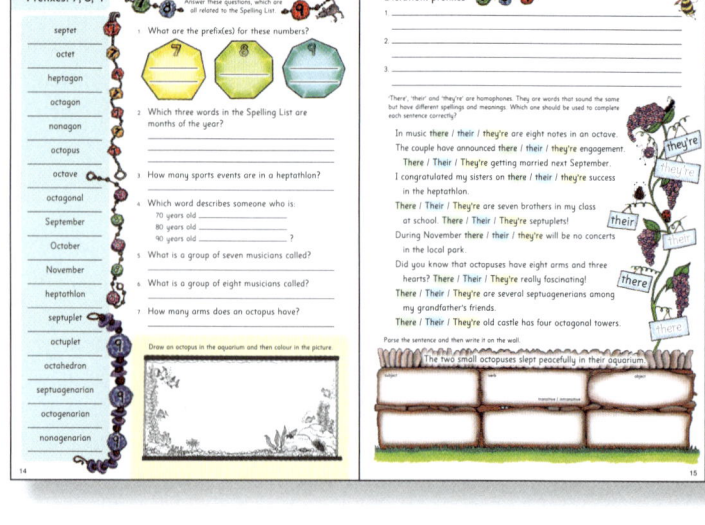

Activity Page 1
- The children split each word into syllables to help remember the spelling (*sep/tet, oc/tet, hep/ta/gon, oc/ta/gon, non/a/gon, oc/to/pus, oc/tave, oc/tag/o/nal, Sep/tem/ber, Oc/to/ber, No/vem/ber, hep/tath/lon, sep/tu/plet, oc/tu/plet, oc/ta/he/dron, sep/tu/a/ge/nar/i/an, oc/to/ge/nar/i/an, non/a/ge/nar/i/an*).
- They then answer each question in the quiz (1. sept-/hepta- (7); oct- (8); novem-/nona- (9), 2. September/October/November, 3. seven, 4. septuagenarian/octogenarian/nonagenarian, 5. septet, 6. octet, 7. eight), draw an octopus in the aquarium and colour it in.

Activity Page 2
- The children complete each sentence by crossing out the wrong homophone. (The correct spellings are *there are; their* engagement/*They're* getting; *their* success; *There are*/*They're* septuplets; *there* will; *They're* really; *There are; Their* old castle.)
- Then they parse the sentence and complete the wall: The two small octopuses slept peacefully (in their aquarium).
Top: octopuses - slept - [blank]
Bottom: The two small - peacefully / in their aquarium - [blank]
Verb: intransitive
  – The adverb *peacefully* is made by adding ‹-ly› to the adjective *peaceful*.
  – The prepositional phrase *in their aquarium* acts as an adverb, so orange brackets can be put around it.

Dictation
- Dictate the following sentences:

  1. How many people sing in a septet?
  2. The triplets became octogenarians last month.
  3. "We will see your cousins in October," said Dad

- Sentence 1 needs a question mark. Remind the class to use speech marks with the correct punctuation in Sentence 3. *October* and *Dad* are proper nouns and need a capital letter.

Grammar: Parts of Speech

Aim
- Revise all the parts of speech learnt so far (nouns, pronouns, adjectives, verbs, adverbs, prepositions and conjunctions; see pages 6 to 15) and introduce a new game to reinforce the learning.

Introduction
- Briefly look at **nouns**, which were revised in the previous grammar lesson, and ask the children what other parts of speech they know:
  - **Pronouns:** The small words that replace nouns, such as the personal pronouns (like *I/me* and *we/us*) and possessive pronouns (for example, *mine* and *ours*).
  - **Adjectives:** Words that describe nouns and pronouns (including possessive adjectives like *my* and comparatives and superlatives like *bigger* and *biggest*).
  - **Verbs:** Revised in the lesson on page 39, these are *doing* words that always appear in a sentence and describe past, present and future actions.
  - **Adverbs:** Words, commonly ending in ‹-ly›, that tell us more about how, where, when, how much or how often something happens. They mostly describe verbs, but can also modify other adverbs (as in *really* slowly) and adjectives (as in *really* happy).
  - **Prepositions:** Words that relate one noun or pronoun to another, such as *under* and *in*. (Such words can also be adverbs if they do not come before a noun or pronoun: for example, *We went in*.) Prepositional phrases can also act as adverbs.
  - **Conjunctions:** Words such as *and, but, or, so* and *because* that are used to join sentences, or parts of a sentence, to create longer, less repetitive sentences.
- Revise the action and colour for each part of speech, and remind the class that many words can act as different parts of speech, depending on how they are used.
- Write a sentence on the board and parse it with the class: *We saw clowns and acrobats (in the circus tent)*.

Main Point
- Knowing the parts of speech and being able to identify them in a sentence is fundamental to understanding grammar. This is why the children have regular parsing practice in their spelling lessons, underlining words in a particular colour to show how they are being used.
- Without this knowledge, children would struggle to understand the complexities of sentence structure and could not, for example, identify the subject and object of a sentence, another regular activity in the spelling lessons (see Sentence Walls: pages 21 and 22).
- Such multisensory activities are accessible and visual ways to help children understand how language works, and another example is the game *Grammar Action Sentences*.
- This game can be played either by doing the grammar actions themselves or by creating some action cards:
  - The actions should be ordered in a sequence, following the pattern of a simple sentence: for example, this could be indefinite article / adjective / common noun / verb / adverb.
  - The children call out possible words for each action and create a sentence, such as *A small kitten purred happily*.

Activity Page
- The children write five sentences, thinking of appropriate words for each action. The action sequences reflect five different sentence patterns:
  - indefinite article / adjective / common noun / verb (present) / adverb
  - indefinite article / adjective / adjective / common noun / verb (past)
  - pronoun / verb (future) / preposition / definite article / common noun
  - proper noun / verb (past) / preposition / definite article / adjective / common noun
  - proper noun / conjunction / proper noun / verb (present) / adverb.

Extension Activity
- Give the children some new sentence sequences, doing the grammar actions.
- Alternatively, the class can use the original sequences to write new sentences on a separate sheet of paper.

Rounding Off
- Go over the activity page with the children, discussing their answers.
- If they have done the extension activity, ask some of the children to read out a sentences and check that they have used the correct parts of speech.

GRAMMAR 6 PUPIL BOOK: PAGES 17 & 18

Spelling: Numerical Prefix for 10: ‹dec-›

Spelling Test
- The children turn to the backs of their books and find the column labelled *Spelling Test 5*.
- In any order, call out the spelling words learnt last week. The children write the words on the lines.

Revision
- Ask the class to spell the number *two* and the possessive adjectives *its, our, your* and *their*, and to give the spellings and meanings of their respective homophones (as revised in the previous lesson).
- Now discuss *where* (a question word relating to place), *wear* (a verb describing putting on things like clothes and shoes) and *were* (part of the irregular verb *to be*). Although *were* is not strictly a homophone of *where*, their spellings are often confused.
- Write a sentence on the board and ask the class which spellings are needed to complete it: (*Where*) (*were*) you hoping to (*wear*) the dress? Repeat with some other examples suggested by the class.
- Ask the children if they can remember any of the prefixes for words relating to the numbers four to nine.

Spelling Point
- English words relating to **ten** often have the prefix ‹dec-›, as the Latin and Greek words for that number are *decem* and *deka*. (The reason why September, October, November and December have their number prefixes is because they were the seventh, eighth, ninth and tenth months in the old Roman calendar.)
- Words starting with ‹cent-› and ‹milli-›, meaning *a hundred* and *a thousand*, also come from Latin, but other number-related words like *twice, twelfth, twentieth, forty* and *hundred* have their roots in Old English.

Spelling List
- Go through the list, discuss the meaning of each word, and ask the class to find and highlight the prefixes ‹dec-›, ‹cent-› and ‹milli-› when they appear.
- Point out other spelling features, such as the soft ‹c› in ‹cent›, *twice, December, decibel* and *decimal*, the /oo/ spelling in *decimal*, the ‹age› saying /ij/ at the end of *percentage*, and the ‹ion› saying /yoon/ after ‹ll› and silent ‹e› in both *millionaire* and *billionaire*.
- It is a good idea to blend and sound out the spelling words quickly every day with the class. Where appropriate, use the *say it as it sounds* strategy, stressing, for example, the pure sound of any schwas (as in

decagon
decade
twice
forty
hundred
December
twelfth
twentieth
percent
centurion
decibel
decimal
percentage
millennium
decathlon
millionaire
billionaire
decathlete

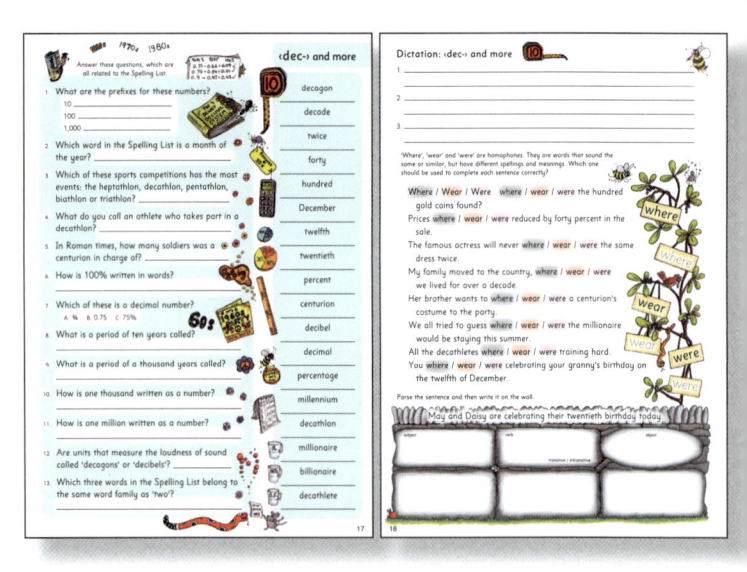

*dec**a**gon* and *twentie**th***). Alternatively, you could break down relevant words into prefix and root word.

Activity Page 1
- The children split each word into syllables to help remember the spelling (*dec/a/gon, dec/ade, twice, for/ty, hun/dred, De/cem/ber, twelfth, twen/ti/eth, per/cent, cen/tu/ri/on, dec/i/bel, dec/i/mal, per/cent/age, mil/len/ni/um, de/cath/lon, mil/lion/aire, bil/lion/aire, de/cath/lete*).
- They then answer each question in the quiz (*1. dec- (10); cent- (100); milli- (1,000), 2. December, 3. decathlon, 4. decathlete, 5. a hundred, 6. one hundred percent, 7. 0.75 (B), 8. a decade, 9. a millennium, 10. 1,000, 11. 1,000,000, 12. decibels, 13. twice; twelfth; twentieth*).

Activity Page 2
- The children complete each sentence by crossing out the wrong homophone. (The correct spellings are *Where/were ; were reduced; never wear; where we lived; wants to wear; guess where; were training; were celebrating.*)
- Then they parse the sentence and complete the wall:
May and Daisy are celebrating their twentieth birthday today.
Top: May–and–Daisy - are celebrating - birthday
Bottom: [blank] - today - their twentieth
Verb: transitive

Dictation
- Dictate the following sentences:

  1. A high percentage of tourists visit in December.
  2. "Remember where to put the decimal point," said Miss Beech.
  3. They celebrated the new millennium with hundreds of fireworks.

- *December* and *Miss Beech* are proper nouns and need initial capital letters. Remind the class to use speech marks with the correct punctuation in Sentence 2.

46

Spelling: ‹ei› and ‹eigh› for the /ai/ Sound

Spelling Test
- The children turn to the backs of their books and find the column labelled *Spelling Test 6*.
- In any order, call out the spelling words learnt last week. The children write the words on the lines.

Revision
- Write these words on the board and identify the number prefix in each one: **uni**form, **bi**cycle, **tri**angle, **quar**ter, **penta**thlon, **hexa**gon. Remind the class that these prefixes are related to Latin and Greek numbers.
- Ask the class to suggest more words with these prefixes or to call out other prefixes for the numbers one to six.

Spelling Point
- Revise some of the ways the /ai/ sound can be written, and write them on the board; the most common spellings are ‹ai›, ‹ay› and ‹a_e›, but the children will also know that the vowel ‹a› sometimes says its long vowel sound (as in *apron* and *pastry*) and that some words, like *reindeer* and *eight*, take the ‹ei› or ‹eigh› spellings.
- Other spelling patterns exist too, such as those found in words like *great, they, ballet, fete* and *straight* (see page 68), so if they are called out, add them to the list.
- Ask the children to suggest some words for ‹ei› and ‹eigh›; write them on the board and then put them in alphabetical order with the class. Then ask five children to stand at the front, each holding a sheet of paper with an ‹ei› or ‹eigh› word printed on it. Ask them to put themselves into alphabetical order: *beige, neigh, veil, vein, weight*.

Spelling List
- Go through the list and ask the class to find and highlight the ‹ei› or ‹eigh› spelling each time. Also discuss the meaning of any unfamiliar words.
- Point out other spelling features, such as the silent ‹g› digraph in *reign, feign* and *deign*, the soft ‹g› or /zh/ sound in *beige*, the way the ‹t› in ‹th› also says its own sound in *eighth*, the ‹le› saying /ool/ at the end of *inveigle*, and the ‹ur› spelling and soft ‹c› in *surveillance*.
- Also point out the homophones *rein* and *reign*, the antonyms *veil* and *unveil*, and the fact that *feign* and *feint* belong to the same word family (*to feign* means *to pretend* and a *feint* in boxing or fencing is a pretended attack).
- It is a good idea to blend and sound out the spelling words quickly every day with the class. Where appropriate, use the *say it as it sounds*

vein
veil
rein
reign
feint
weigh
weight
beige
feign
eighth
neigh
unveil
freight
inveigle
deign
weightlifter
surveillance
neighbourhood

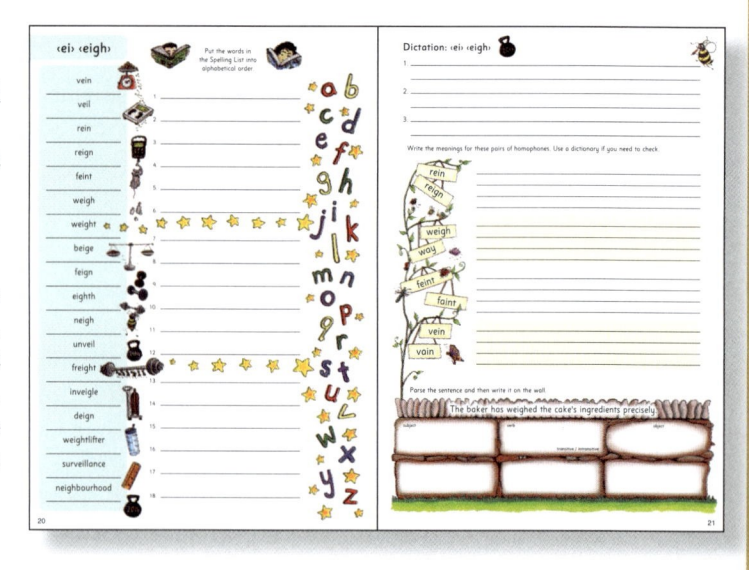

strategy, stressing, for example, the pure sound of any schwas (as in s**ur**veill**a**nce and neighb**our**hood).

Activity Page 1
- The children split each word into syllables to help remember the spelling (*vein, veil, rein, reign, feint, weigh, weight, beige, feign, eighth, neigh, un/veil, freight, in/vei/gle, deign, weight/lift/er, sur/veil/lance, neigh/bour/hood*).
- They then put the spelling words into alphabetical order (1. beige, 2. deign, 3. eighth, 4. feign, 5. feint, 6. freight, 7. inveigle, 8. neigh, 9. neighbourhood, 10. reign, 11. rein, 12. surveillance, 13. unveil, 14. veil, 15. vein, 16. weigh, 17. weight, 18. weightlifter).

Activity Page 2
- The children write the meanings for each pair of homophones, using a dictionary to help them if needed.
- Then they parse the sentence and complete the wall: The baker has weighed the cake's ingredients precisely.
Top: baker - has weighed - ingredients
Bottom: The - precisely - the cake's
Verb: transitive
  – Possessive nouns always act as adjectives, so *cake's* should be underlined in blue.
  – The adverb *precisely* is made by adding ‹-ly› to the adjective *precise*.

Dictation
- Dictate the following sentences:

  1. The bride wore her grandmother's veil.
  2. The horses neighed and shook their reins.
  3. "How much weight can they lift?" we wondered.

- Remind the class to use the right spelling (*reins*, not *reigns*) in Sentence 2 and speech marks with the correct punctuation in Sentence 3.

Grammar: Indirect Objects and Sentence Walls

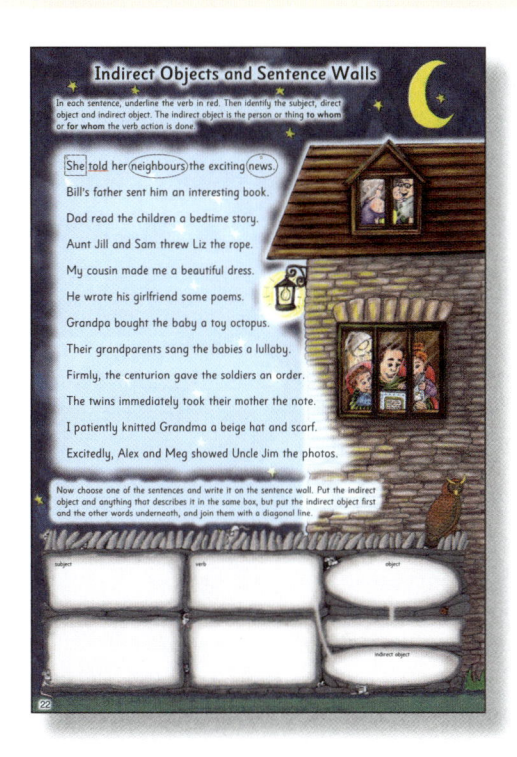

Aim
- Develop the children's ability to identify the indirect object in a sentence and put it into a sentence wall.

Introduction
- Write this sentence on the board and parse it with the children: *Sally offered her friend a cheese sandwich*.
- Remind the class that a sentence always has a verb and subject and, if the verb is transitive, it will also have an object.
- We find the subject by asking who or what is doing the offering *(Sally)* and identify the object by asking what it is that Sally offered *(a cheese sandwich)*. Draw a box around *Sally,* with a small ‹s› in the corner, and a ring around *sandwich,* with a small ‹o› inside.
- Point out that although *a cheese sandwich* can be considered the object, we only highlight the main noun or pronoun, which we call the simple object.
- Now ask what role the friend is playing: (s)he is the person to whom Sally offered the sandwich. Remind the class that the verb action has either a direct or indirect effect on an object: the person (or thing) receiving the verb action is called the **direct object** and the person (or thing) for whom or to whom the verb action is done is called the **indirect object**.
- Draw a ring around *friend* and explain that in this sentence the direct object is *sandwich* and the indirect object is *friend*.

Main Point
- Sentence walls allow us to organise a sentence visually so we can see at a glance what the main building blocks are and how they relate to each other. The familiar layout can be easily adapted for sentences with an indirect object to look like this:

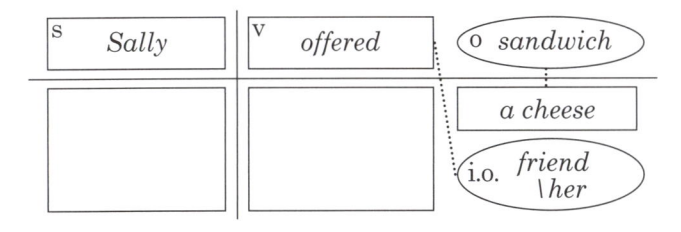

s Sally	v offered	o sandwich
		a cheese
		i.o. friend \ her

- Draw the boxes on the board and show the children how to put the sentence into the wall. When the wall is complete, join the indirect object and its modifiers to the verb with a line. Then join the object to its modifiers in the same way.

Activity Page
- The children find the subject, verb, and direct object in each sentence, drawing a box with a small ‹s› around the subject, underlining the verb in red, and putting a ring with a small ‹o› around the direct object *(She / told / news; father / sent / book; Dad / read / story; Aunt Jill–Sam / threw / rope; cousin / made / dress; He / wrote / poems; Grandpa / bought / octopus; grandparents / sang / lullaby; centurion / gave / order; twins / took / note; I / knitted / hat-scarf, Alex–Meg / showed / photos)*.
- They then identify the indirect object, deciding to whom or for whom the verb action is done, and draw a ring around it *(neighbours, him, children, Liz, me, girlfriend, baby, babies, soldiers, mother, Grandma, Uncle Jim)*.
- Finally, they choose one of the sentences and arrange it on the wall. They put the subject, verb and direct object along the top. (If the subject or object is compound, bracket *and* with dots.) The words modifying them go underneath, with the indirect object in the bottom right oval, joined to the verb with a line. *Top (as shown above). Bottom:*
  – (blank) - (blank) - the exciting / neighbours (her)
  – Bill's - (blank) - an interesting / him
  – (blank) - (blank) - a bedtime / children (the)
  – (blank) - (blank) - the / Liz
  – My - (blank) - a beautiful / me
  – (blank) - (blank) - some / girlfriend (his)
  – (blank) - (blank) - a toy / baby (the)
  – Their - (blank) - a / babies (the)
  – the - Firmly - an / soldiers (the)
  – The - immediately - the / mother (their)
  – (blank) - patiently - a beige / Grandma
  – (blank) - Excitedly - the / Uncle Jim.

Extension Activity
- On a separate sheet of paper, ask the children to write some sentences of their own with a direct and indirect object.

Rounding Off
- Go over the activity page with the children, discussing their answers.
- If they have done the extension activity, ask some children to read out a few of their sentences.

Spelling: ‹ei› and ‹ie› for the /ee/ Sound

Spelling Test
- The children turn to the backs of their books and find the column labelled *Spelling Test 7*.
- In any order, call out the spelling words learnt last week. The children write the words on the lines.

Revision
- Write these words on the board and identify the number prefix in each one: *September, October, November, December* (the seventh, eighth, ninth and tenth months in the old Roman calendar).
- Ask the class to suggest more words with these prefixes or to call out other prefixes for the numbers.

Spelling Point
- Probably the most well known, but most misunderstood, spelling rule in English is this: ‹i› before ‹e›, except after ‹c›.
- Many people find they cannot use the rule successfully, because it seems to have too many exceptions, like in *weird*, *their* and *height*, or in words like *vein* and *weight*, which the children learnt in the previous lesson.
- Write the words above on the board, add *niece* and *ceiling*, and discuss the different vowel sounds being made: /ear, air, ie, ai, ee/.
- Look at some more words from the spelling list and point out that the rule does work when you remember it like this: **If you want to say /ee/, it's ‹i› before ‹e›, except after ‹c›.** There are a few exceptions, however, and these can be remembered as *Seize neither protein nor caffeine*.

Spelling List
- Go through the list and ask the class to find and highlight the ‹ie› or ‹cei› spelling each time. Also discuss the meaning of any unfamiliar words.
- Point out other spelling features, such as the ‹k› in *shriek* and *handkerchief*, the soft ‹g› in *siege* and *hygiene*, the soft ‹c› in *niece* and ‹cei› words, the ‹e› saying /i/ (or becoming neutral) in *deceit*, *receive*, *deceive*, *retrieve* and *reprieve*, the ‹ve› saying /v/ in words ending in ‹ieve› or ‹eive›, the ‹y› saying /ie/ in *hygiene*, the ‹n› saying /ng/ and silent ‹d› in *handkerchief*, and the prefix ‹in-›, suffix ‹-able› and ‹le› saying /ool/ in *inconceivable*.
- It is a good idea to blend and sound out the spelling words quickly every day with the class. Where appropriate, use the *say it as it sounds* strategy, stressing, for example, the pure sound of any schwas (as in *achieve*, *perceive*, *handkerchief* and *inconceivable*).

shriek
wield
siege
yield
ceiling
fiendish
niece
deceit
receive
deceive
achieve
conceited
hygiene
retrieve
perceive
reprieve
handkerchief
inconceivable

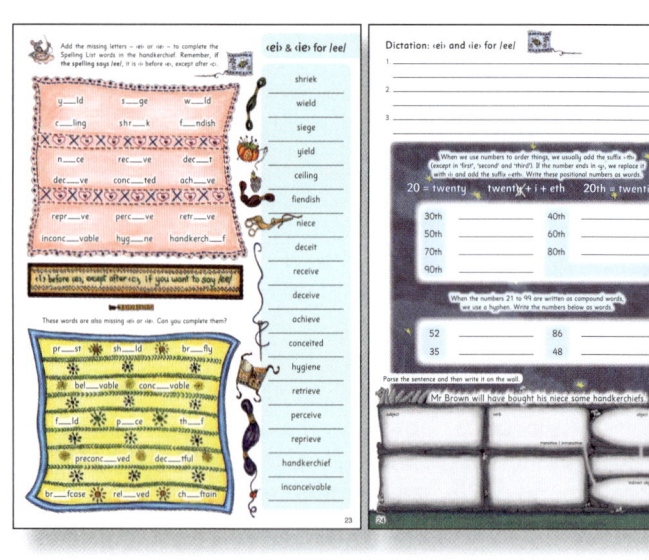

Activity Page 1
- The children split each word into syllables to help remember the spelling (*shriek, wield, siege, yield, cei/ling, fien/dish, niece, de/ceit, re/ceive, de/ceive, a/chieve, con/ceit/ed, hy/giene, re/trieve, per/ceive, re/prieve, hand/ker/chief, in/con/ceiv/a/ble*).
- They then add the missing letters (Top: *yield, siege, wield; ceiling, shriek, fiendish; niece, receive, deceit; deceive, conceited, achieve; reprieve, perceive, retrieve; inconceivable, hygiene, handkerchief* /Bottom: *priest, shield, briefly; believable, conceivable; field, piece, thief; preconceived, deceitful; briefcase, relieved, chieftain*).

Activity Page 2
- The children write the numbers as words, replacing *toughy* ‹y› with *shy* ‹i› before adding the suffix (*thirtieth, fortieth, fiftieth, sixtieth, seventieth, eightieth, ninetieth*), or by using a hyphen (*fifty-two, eighty-six, thirty-five, forty-eight*).
- Then they parse the sentence and complete the wall: Mr Brown will have bought his niece some handkerchiefs.
Top: Mr Brown - will have bought - handkerchiefs
Bottom: [blank] - [blank] - some
Indirect object: niece (his)   Verb: transitive
  – *Mr Brown* is a proper noun and should be underlined in black.
  – The possessive adjective *his* describes who the niece 'belongs' to.

Dictation
- Dictate the following sentences:

1. My niece is never vain or conceited.
2. "What a fiendish plan!" the reader exclaimed.
3. The knight wielded his sword many times in battle.

- Remind the class to use the right homophone (*vain*, not *vein*) in Sentence 1 and speech marks with the correct punctuation in Sentence 2.

Grammar: Linking Verbs

Aim
- Refine the children's understanding of verbs by introducing the idea that they are not all *doing* words; some are better thought of as *being* words, because they describe a state of being or change.
- These two types of verb are known as action verbs and linking verbs.

Introduction
- *To be* is one of the most common verbs in English, frequently used as a main verb and also as an auxiliary (helping to form the past, present and continuous tenses).
- It is also very irregular, at least in the simple past and present tenses, and has the 'tricky' past participle *been*.
- This can make it difficult to identify as a verb in a sentence, so conjugating the simple tenses with the class and doing the pronoun actions is particularly helpful:

Past	Present	Future
• I was, • you were, • he/she/it was, etc.	• I am, • you are, • he/she/it is, etc.	• I shall be, • you will be, • he/she/it will be, etc.

Main Point
- When the children are young, they are encouraged to think of verbs as *doing* words: the verbs *to run, to cook* and *to sing* all name a particular action.
- However, some verbs, including *to be,* are better described as *being* words, because they name a state of being or change.
- *Being* verbs act differently in a sentence: they do not take a direct object, but instead often link the subject to a word or phrase (called the *subject complement*) that completes our understanding of it. For example:
  - *The dog was really fierce:* Here, the verb *(was)* links the subject *dog* to the adjective *fierce,* which describes it.
  - *Jane is a farmer:* Here, the verb *(is)* links the subject *Jane* to the noun *farmer,* which identifies her. (Sentences like this are sometimes likened to an equation, with the verb as an equals sign: ⇔).
- Write the sentences on the board and discuss them with the class, identifying the verb and subject each time and underlining *fierce* in blue and *farmer* in black. Then link the complement back to the subject with an arrow.
- Explain that verbs like this are known as linking (or *copular*) verbs, while *doing* verbs are more commonly called action verbs. Other common linking verbs are *to seem, to appear, to become, to remain, to look, to sound, to smell, to taste* and *to feel.* However, most linking verbs can also act as action verbs, so care is needed when giving examples.
- Draw six boxes on the board and show the children how to put the two sentences into a wall. Put the verb and subject complement on the same line in the verb box and separate them with a diagonal line. If the subject complement has a modifier, put that underneath in the usual way:

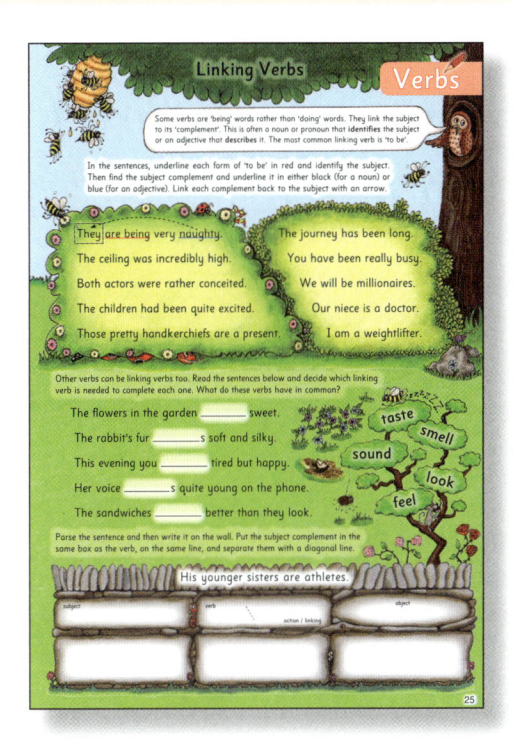

1. | v | was \ fierce
 \ really |
2. | v | is \ farmer
 \ a |

Activity Page
- The children write inside the outlined word *Verbs* in red.
- They then find the verb *to be* in each sentence, underline it in red, and identify the subject, drawing a box with a small ⟨s⟩ around it. Then they identify the subject complement, underlining it in the appropriate colour, and link it to the subject with an arrow. (In subject-verb-complement order: They/*are being*/naughty; ceiling/*was*/high; actors/*were*/conceited; children/*had been*/excited; handkerchiefs/*are*/present; journey/*has been*/long; You/*have been*/busy; We/*will be*/millionaires; niece/*is*/doctor; I/*am*/weightlifter).
- They then choose from the five verbs, all of which describe the senses, to complete the sentences *(smell, feel, look, sound, taste).*
- Then they parse the sentence and complete the wall: His younger sisters are athletes.
Top: sisters - are\athletes - [blank]
Bottom: His younger - [blank] - [blank]
Verb: linking

Extension Activity
- The children put some of the first ten sentences into sentence wall boxes on a separate sheet of paper.

Rounding Off
- Go over the activity page and extension activity with the children, discussing their answers.

GRAMMAR 6 PUPIL BOOK: PAGES 26 & 27

Spelling: ‹ei›, ‹eigh›, ‹eir›

Spelling Test
- The children turn to the backs of their books and find the column labelled *Spelling Test 8*.
- In any order, call out the spelling words learnt last week. The children write the words on the lines.

Revision
- Revise the spelling rule: ***If you want to say /ee/, it's ‹i› before ‹e›, except after ‹c›.***
- Write these words on the board and ask the class whether ‹ei› or ‹ie› is needed to complete them: ch(ie)f, f(ie)ld, c(ei)ling, th(ie)ves, p(ie)ce, dec(ei)ve, rec(ei)pt, br(ie)fcase.

Spelling Point
- Write the words *veil* and *eight* on the board in one column and *receive* in another. Remind the children that the spellings ‹ei› and ‹eigh› usually make the /ai/ sound, but ‹ei› can also make the /ee/ sound when it follows the letter ‹c›.
- Now write *height* and *feisty* in a third column and explain that ‹ei› and ‹eigh› can also make the sound /ie/.
- Then add *their* and *weird* in two new columns and explain that the ‹ei› in these words is actually part of the spelling pattern ‹eir›, which is one of the alternative spellings of both /air/ and /ear/.
- Finally, add the words *counterfeit* and *heifer* in two more columns and point out that ‹ei› occasionally makes an /i/ sound and can, on rare occasions, even make an /e/ sound.

Spelling List
- Go through the list, ask the class to find and highlight the ‹ei›, ‹eigh› or ‹eir› spelling each time, and discuss the sound it is making. Also discuss the meaning of any unfamiliar words.
- Point out other spelling features, such as the silent ‹h› in ***heir***, ***heirloom*** and ***Fahrenheit***, the ‹ur› spelling of /er/ in ***surfeit*** and the ‹ow› spelling of /ou/ in ***eiderdown***, the silent ‹g› digraph in ***foreign*** and ***sovereign***, the ‹s› saying /s/ and /z/ in ***seismic***, the ‹c› and ‹k› spellings in ***seismic*** and ***kaleidoscope***, and the capital F in ***Fahrenheit***.
- Also point out that the ‹ei› in *either* can say /ee/ or /ie/ and that *sovereign* has only two syllables as the /er/ is not usually pronounced.
- It is a good idea to blend and sound out the spelling words quickly every day with the class. Where appropriate, use the *say it as it sounds* strategy, stressing, for example, the pure sound of any schwas (as in *kaleidoscope*).

weir
their
heir
weird
forfeit
either
height
surfeit
foreign
heifer
feisty
sovereign
seismic
heirloom
eiderdown
counterfeit
kaleidoscope
Fahrenheit

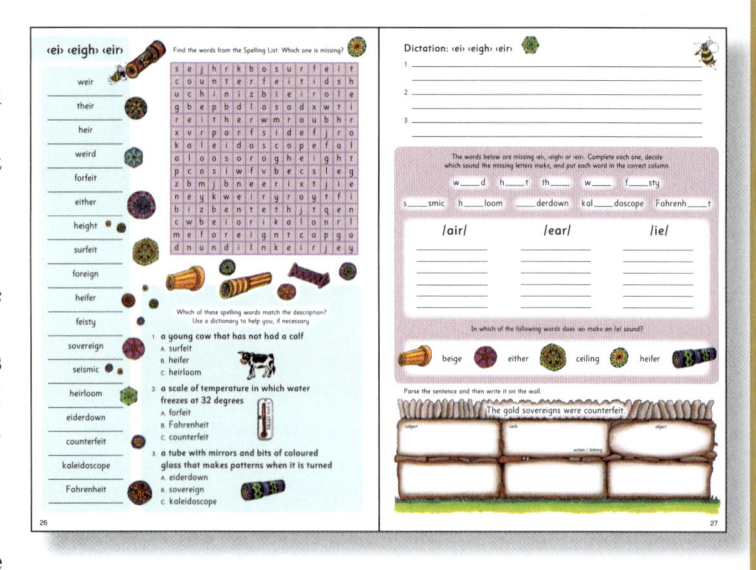

Activity Page 1
- The children split each word into syllables to help remember the spelling *(weir, their, heir, weird, for/feit, ei/ther, height, sur/feit, for/eign, heif/er, feist/y, sove/reign, seis/mic, heir/loom, ei/der/down, coun/ter/feit, ka/lei/do/scope, Fahr/en/heit)*.
- They then find the spelling words in the word search and work out which one is missing *(Fahrenheit)*.
- Then they read each phrase and identify which of the three spelling words it is describing *(1. B, 2. B, 3. C)*.

Activity Page 2
- The children add the missing letters in each word *(Top: weird, height, their, weir, feisty; Bottom: seismic, heirloom, eiderdown, kaleidoscope, Fahrenheit)*, and identify which sound they are making. *(They all say /ie/, except for* their *and* heirloom*, which say /air/, and* weird *and* weir*, which say /ear/.)*
- They then decide which of the four words below has an ‹ei› that is making an /e/ sound *(heifer)*.
- Then they parse the sentence and complete the wall:
The gold sovereigns were counterfeit.
Top: sovereigns - were \ counterfeit - [blank]
Bottom: The gold - [blank] - [blank]
Verb: linking
  – The verb *were* links the adjective complement *counterfeit* to the subject *sovereigns* it is describing.

Dictation
- Dictate the following sentences:

1. Their sovereign reigned for fifty-two years.
2. The farmer keeps eighty-two heifers in the field.
3. "What is your height and weight?" asked the nurse.

- Remind the class to write the compound numbers correctly in Sentences 1 and 2 and to use speech marks with the correct punctuation in Sentence 3.

Grammar: Prepositional Phrases as Adverbs

Aim
- Refine the children's understanding of how prepositional phrases can act as adverbs within a sentence and develop their ability to identify one when it comes at the beginning of a sentence.

Introduction
- Remind the class that a phrase is a group of words that makes sense but has no verb and subject.
- Briefly revise prepositional phrases, which begin with a preposition and are often followed by a noun phrase or pronoun.
- Call out some prepositions and ask the class to turn them into prepositional phrases: for example, *at the moment*, *in an hour*, *above the treetops*, *on the table*, *after the storm*, *without warning*.
- Remind the class that prepositional phrases are often used as adverbs in sentences. Write a few examples on the board and discuss how each prepositional phrase gives us more information about where, when or how the verb is happening:
  - When: *I will go in an hour*.
  - Where: *The birds soared above the treetops*.
  - How: *They left without warning*.
- Ask some children to come up and parse the prepositional phrases, underlining the prepositions in green and putting orange brackets around each phrase.

Main Point
- Write *Zack recently broke his arm* on the board and ask the children to identify the adverb in the sentence (*recently*).
- Discuss with the class how we know that *recently* is the adverb: it tells us more about when Zack broke his arm and, like a lot of adverbs, it is made by adding ‹-ly› to an adjective.
- Remind the class that even though adverbs often describe a verb, they do not always go next to it. Ask the children where else *recently* could go in the sentence: it could be moved to the end (*Zack broke his arm recently*) or to the beginning, where the adverb is separated from the rest of the sentence with a comma (*Recently, Zack broke his arm*).
- Explain that when prepositional phrases act as adverbs, they too can be found in different parts of a sentence; they usually go immediately after an intransitive verb or towards the end, following an object or adverb, but they can also be found at the beginning of a sentence.
- Write *I heard a strange noise in the middle of the night* on the board, and then write it again, with the prepositional phrase at the beginning: *In the middle of the night, I heard a strange noise*. Point out that here, too, the phrase at the beginning is often followed by a comma, particularly if it is a long one.
- Discuss how the emphasis has subtly shifted to when the action takes place, creating a sense of expectation and drama. Try this with some other sentences, discussing the effect each time.
- Look again at the prepositional phrase (*in the middle*) (*of the night*) and point out that many longer phrases are created by putting two shorter prepositional phrases together.

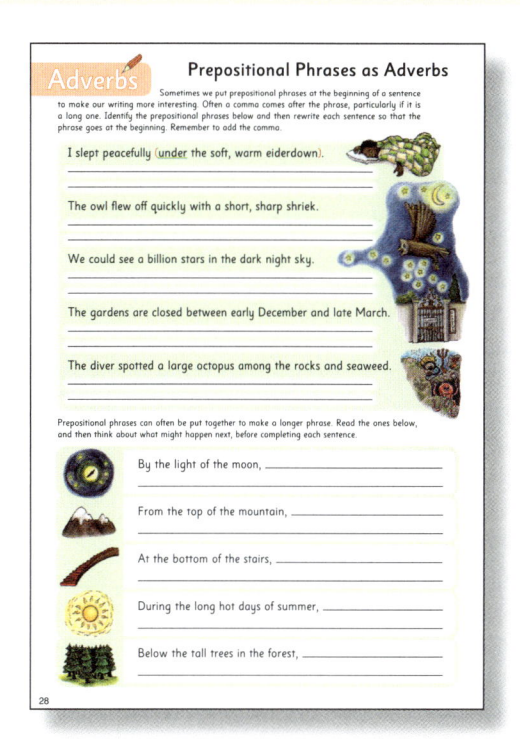

Activity Page
- The children write inside the outlined word *Adverbs*, using an orange pencil.
- They then identify the prepositional phrase that is acting as an adverb in each sentence, underlining the preposition in green and putting orange brackets around the phrase (*under the soft, warm eiderdown; with a short, sharp shriek; in the dark night sky; between early December and late March; among the rocks and seaweed*).
- Then the children rewrite each sentence, putting the prepositional phrase at the beginning of the sentence, followed by a comma.
- Lastly, they read the prepositional phrases at the bottom of the page, think about what might happen next, and complete the sentences.

Extension Activity
- The children write some more sentences on a separate sheet of paper, using other prepositional phrases as adverbs. They can then swap their sentences with a partner and rewrite them so that the phrase appears at the beginning, followed by a comma.

Rounding Off
- Go over the activity page with the children, discussing their answers.
- If they have done the extension activity, ask some of the children to read out their sentences.

GRAMMAR 6 PUPIL BOOK: PAGES 29 & 30

Spelling: ‹ci› for the /sh/ Sound

Spelling Test
- The children turn to the backs of their books and find the column labelled *Spelling Test 9*.
- Call out the spelling words learnt last week.

Revision
- Write these words on the board and ask the class to identify the letters saying /sh/ in each one: *man*s*ion, pre*ss*ure, ini*ti*al, mi*ss*ion, spe*ci*al, ma*ch*ine, *s*ure, an*xi*ous*. Apart from ‹ch›, which has French origins, words with these spellings usually come from Latin.
- Ask the children if they can think of other words with these spellings for /sh/.

Spelling Point
- Although it can be written in several different ways, /sh/ is most often spelt ‹ti› or ‹ci› in the middle of a longer word. These spellings can be combined with familiar suffixes to form words like *sta*ti*on*/*suspi*ci*on*, *nego*ti*able*/*so*ci*able*, *ter*ti*ary*/*benefi*ci*ary*, *pa*ti*ent*/ *an*ci*ent*, *pa*ti*ence*/*cons*ci*ence*, *Egyp*ti*an*/*musi*ci*an*, *nego*ti*ation*/*appre*ci*ation*, *nego*ti*ate*/*appre*ci*ate*, *cau*ti*ous*/*deli*ci*ous* and *ini*ti*al*/*so*ci*al*; the spelling depends on the word's original Latin root. All the words in the spelling list take the ‹ci› spelling.

Spelling List
- Go through the list and ask the class to find and highlight each ‹ci› saying /sh/. Also discuss the meaning of any unfamiliar words.
- Point out other spelling features, such as the long vowel sound(s) in words like *ancient* and *species*, the prefixes meaning *not* in *unsocial*, *insufficient* and *inefficient*, the /ᴏᴏ/ spellings in *unsocial*, *sociable*, *(e)specially* and *multiracial*, the ‹s› saying /z/ in *species*, the suffix ‹-ly› in *(e)specially*, the prefix in *multiracial*, the ‹e› saying /i/ in *(in)efficient*, *especially*, *beneficiary* and *excruciating*, the soft ‹c› in *conscience*, and the ‹u› saying /oo/ in *excruciating*.
- Also point out that *(in)efficient* and *(in)sufficient* have a double ‹f›, while *proficient* does not (as a result of the way certain prefixes behave when added to a root word in Latin). Also explain that the /sh/ in *conscience* is actually made by ‹sci› (you could also compare it to *science*, where the silent letter digraph ‹sc› says /s/).
- It is a good idea to blend and sound out the spelling words quickly every day with the class. Where appropriate, use the *say it as it sounds* strategy, stressing, for example, the pure sound of any schwas (as in *ancient*).

ancient
unsocial
species
sociable
specially
multiracial
efficient
sufficient
suspicion
conscience
proficient
especially
appreciation
insufficient
coercion
inefficient
beneficiary
excruciating

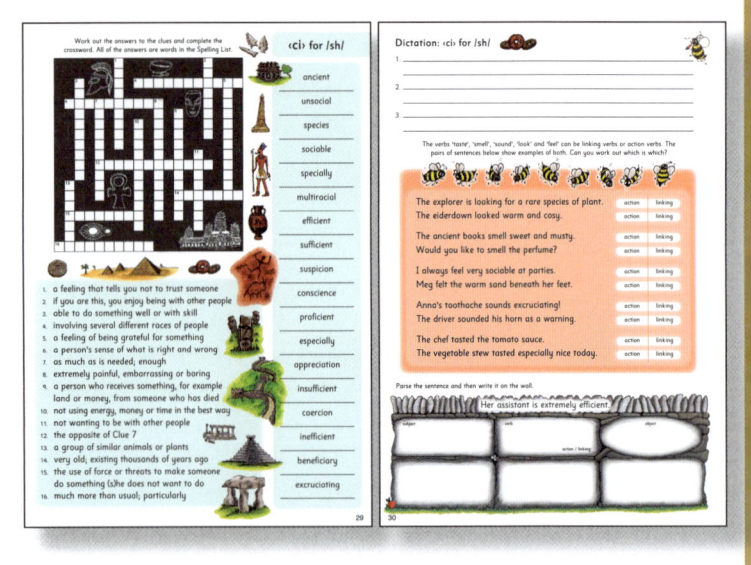

Activity Page 1
- The children split each word into syllables to help remember the spelling *(an/cient, un/so/cial, spe/cies, so/cia/ble, spe/cial/ly, mul/ti/ra/cial, ef/fi/cient, suf/fi/cient, sus/pi/cion, con/science, pro/fi/cient, es/pe/cial/ly, ap/pre/ci/a/tion, in/suf/fi/cient, co/er/cion, in/ef/fi/cient, ben/e/fi/cia/ry, ex/cru/ci/at/ing)*.
- They then work out the answers to the crossword clues and write them in *(1. suspicion, 2. sociable, 3. proficient, 4. multiracial, 5. appreciation, 6. conscience, 7. sufficient, 8. excruciating, 9. beneficiary, 10. inefficient, 11. unsocial, 12. insufficient, 13. species, 14. ancient, 15. coercion, 16. especially)*.

Activity Page 2
- The children read the sentences and identify the action verb and linking verb in each pair *(is looking for [action] / looked [linking]; smell sweet [linking] / to smell [action]; always feel [linking] / felt [action]; sounds [linking] / sounded [action]; chef tasted [action] / stew tasted [linking])*.
- Then they parse the sentence and complete the wall:
Her assistant is extremely efficient.
Top: assistant - is \ efficient (extremely) - [blank]
Bottom: Her - [blank] - [blank]
Verb: linking
  – The verb *is* links the adjective complement *efficient* to the subject *assistant* it is describing.

Dictation
- Dictate the following sentences:

1. The detective regarded everyone with suspicion.
2. "Is Jane a beneficiary of her mother's will?" we asked.
3. He had shown his appreciation for all their kindness.

- Remind the class to use speech marks with the correct punctuation in Sentence 2. The proper noun *Jane* needs a capital letter.

Grammar: Prepositional Phrases as Adjectives

Aim
- Extend the children's understanding of prepositional phrases by introducing the idea that they can act as adjectives as well as adverbs.

Introduction
- Write *The birds were singing in the old oak tree* on the board and ask the children to identify the prepositional phrase *(in the old oak tree)*.
- Ask them what the phrase is doing *(it describes where the birds were singing, so it is acting as an adverb)*, and ask a child to come and parse it, underlining the preposition *in* in green and putting orange brackets around all the words in the phrase.
- Ask another child to come and rewrite the sentence so the prepositional phrase is at the beginning; remind the class that when we do this, we usually add a comma, especially after a long phrase *(In the old oak tree, the birds were singing)*.
- If action cards were used in the *Parts of Speech* lesson on page 45, give them to some children and ask them:
  – to arrange themselves in the order of the first sentence: definite article / common noun / verb (past) / preposition / definite article / adjective / adjective / common noun,
  – then rearrange themselves so that the prepositional phrase goes at the beginning and ask another child to stand where the comma should go, holding a large *comma* card.

Main Point
- Now write on the board *The birds in the old oak tree were singing*. Ask the class what the phrase is describing now and explain that it is no longer describing the verb; instead, it is doing the job of an adjective, describing the birds by telling us **which ones** were singing. Similarly, in a sentence like *The birds of prey were singing*, the prepositional phrase tells us **what kind** of birds were singing.
- Write some noun phrases on the board and ask the children to identify the prepositional phrase in each one that is answering the question **which one?** or **what kind?** Possible examples include: *the boy (in the red coat); the handkerchief (with blue spots); a tube (of toothpaste); the plates (on the table)*.
- Parse each one, underlining the preposition in green and putting blue brackets around all the words in the phrase.
- Look again at the first sentence and discuss how it would be put into a word wall, along with other examples:

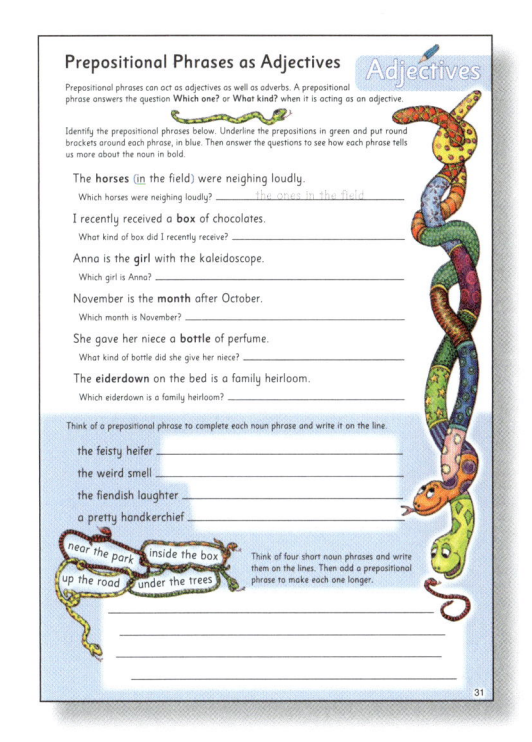

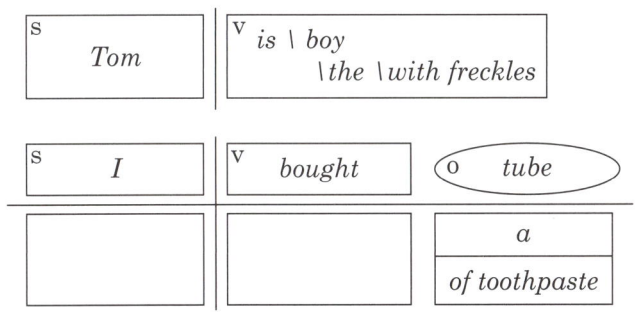

s birds	v were singing	o
The		
in the old oak tree		

Activity Page
- The children write inside the outlined word *Adjectives*, using a blue pencil.
- They then:
  – Identify the prepositional phrases acting as adjectives, underlining the preposition in green and putting blue brackets around each phrase *(in the field; of chocolates; with the kaleidoscope; after October; of perfume; on the bed)*.
  – Answer each question in the way shown *(except for answers 2 and 5: a box of chocolates / a bottle of perfume)*.
- Finally, the children create eight longer noun phrases by adding prepositional phrases of their own to four noun phrases and, similarly, their own noun phrases to four prepositional phrases.

Extension Activity
- The children put some of the sentences into sentence wall boxes on a separate sheet of paper.

Rounding Off
- Go over the activity page and extension activity with the children, discussing their answers.

GRAMMAR 6 PUPIL BOOK: PAGES 32 & 33

Spelling: ‹cious›

Spelling Test
- The children turn to the backs of their books and find the column labelled *Spelling Test 10*.
- Call out the spelling words learnt last week.

Revision
- Write these words on the board and ask the class to identify the letters saying /sh/ in each one: pen**si**on, rea**ss**ure, e**ss**ential, expre**ss**ion, offi**ci**al, **ch**ef, en**s**ure, obno**xi**ous. Apart from ‹ch›, which has French origins, words with these spellings usually come from Latin.
- Ask the children if they can think of other words with these spellings for /sh/.

Spelling Point
- Write the words *suspicious*, *ambitious* and *anxious* on the board and remind the class that ‹-ous› is often preceded by /sh/, which can be spelt ‹ti›, ‹ci› and, very occasionally, ‹xi›.
- In this suffix, the ‹ou› has a neutral schwa sound, and so ‹tious›, ‹cious› and ‹xious› all say /shus/. This makes knowing which spelling to use difficult, so words like this have to be learnt.
- It helps to remember that the suffix ‹-ous› is found in adjectives that describe something as having the quality of the root (word): so *suspicious* means *full of suspicion*, *ambitious* means *full of ambition* and *anxious* means *full of anxiety*.
- If the children already know the spelling of the root word, they can add the correct spelling of the suffix. All the words in the spelling list take the ‹ci› spelling.

Spelling List
- Go through the list and ask the class to find and highlight the ‹cious› spelling each time. Also discuss the meaning of any unfamiliar words.
- Point out other spelling features, such as the long vowel sound(s) in words like *graciously* and *atrocious*, the ‹-ly› suffix in the adverbs *graciously*, *viciously*, *suspiciously* and *ferociously*, the prefix in **un**conscious, **semi**-precious, **pre**cocious and **sub**conscious, the ‹e› saying /i/ in *tenacious* and *precocious*, and the ‹au› spelling in *audacious* and *auspicious*.
- Also point out that — like *conscience* in the previous lesson — *conscious*, *unconscious*, *luscious* and *subconscious* belong to the small group of words where /sh/ is spelt ‹sci›.
- It is a good idea to blend and sound out the spelling words quickly every day with the class. Where appropriate, use the *say it as it sounds* strategy, stressing, for example, the pure sound of any schwas (as in *malicious*).

graciously
conscious
viciously
unconscious
semi-precious
suspiciously
malicious
atrocious
luscious
vivacious
tenacious
ferociously
audacious
auspicious
officious
voracious
precocious
subconscious

Activity Page 1
- The children split each word into syllables to help remember the spelling (*gra/cious/ly, con/scious, vi/cious/ly, un/con/scious, sem/i/pre/cious, sus/pi/cious/ly, ma/li/cious, a/tro/cious, lus/cious, vi/va/cious, te/na/cious, fe/ro/cious/ly, au/da/cious, aus/pi/cious, of/fi/cious, vo/ra/cious, pre/co/cious, sub/con/scious*).
- They then unscramble the letters in the gemstones and add them to ‹cious› to make some of the spelling words (*semi-precious, viciously, graciously, unconscious, luscious, suspiciously, ferociously, tenacious, malicious, atrocious, precocious, voracious, subconscious, auspicious*).

Activity Page 2
- The children look up *semi-precious* in the dictionary, check its meaning, and make as many words as they can with its letters.
- Then they parse the sentence and complete the wall: The spiced pumpkin soup tasted delicious.
Top: soup - tasted \ delicious - [blank]
Bottom: The spiced pumpkin - [blank] - [blank]
Verb: linking
  — The verb *tasted* links the adjective complement *delicious* to the subject *soup* it is describing.

Dictation
- Dictate the following sentences:

  1. "What an atrocious song!" exclaimed Fred.
  2. The fierce pack of wolves howled ferociously.
  3. Her silver locket was decorated with semi-precious stones.

- Remind the class to use speech marks with the correct punctuation in Sentence 1. The proper noun *Fred* needs a capital letter.

Grammar: Relative Clauses

Aim
- Introduce relative clauses, which are a special kind of dependent (or subordinate) clause that starts with either a relative pronoun *(who, which, that, whom, whose)* or relative adverb *(why, where, when)*.

Introduction
- Write three simple sentences on the board and ask the children to identify the pronouns, underlining them in pink: *I have a dog. The dog belongs to me. It is mine*.
- Briefly revise personal and possessive pronouns (see page 9) and point out that the personal pronoun *I* (the subject) changes to *me* when it becomes the object, and that the possessive pronoun *mine* stands in for *my dog*.
- Now write *I have a dog because I love animals* on the board and remind the class that a long sentence often has more than one clause in it.
- Ask the children if they can remember what a clause is *(a group of words which makes sense and contains a subject and verb)* and discuss how the clause *I have a dog* can stand alone as a simple sentence, whereas *because I love animals* cannot, because it depends on the rest of the sentence for its meaning.
- Remind the children that the first kind of clause is called an independent clause and the second one is called a dependent or subordinate clause.

Main Point
- Write these two noun phrases on the board and compare them: *the girl in the green dress* and *the girl who has a green dress*.
- The children should recognise that the first contains a prepositional phrase *(in the green dress)* which acts as an adjective to describe the girl; in the second, however, this job is done by *who has a green dress*, which is a special kind of dependent clause, known as a relative clause. It is:
  – dependent because it has a verb *(has)* and subject *(who)* but does not represent a complete thought,
  – and it is relative because it starts with a pronoun that **relates** the clause to what it is describing.
- Underline the word *who* in pink and explain that there are five main relative pronouns that can be used in this way: **who, which, that, whom** and **whose**.
- To describe people, we use *who* for the subject of the clause and *whom* for the object, but we only use *which* to describe things; we can also use *that* to describe either people or things and *whose* to show possession.
- On the board, write some more examples of relative clauses describing nouns, and ask some children to underline the relative pronouns in pink and put blue brackets around each clause. Possible examples include *the letter (which arrived this morning); the music (that we like); the friend (whom I often visit); the writer (whose books you enjoy)*.
- Write three more noun phrases on the board and ask what is different about the relative clauses:
  – *the time (when I eat lunch)*,
  – *the town (where you live)*,
  – *the reason (why we were late)*.
- Point out that **when**, **where** and **why** are not pronouns but adverbs, and explain that they are usually used in everyday language to replace the more formal phrases *in which, on which, at which* and *for which*.
- Discuss which phrases are being replaced in the three examples *(at which, in which, for which)* and parse the clauses with the children, putting blue brackets around them and underlining the adverbs *when, where* and *why* in orange.

Activity Page
- The children write inside the outlined pronouns in pink and the outlined adverbs in orange.
- They then identify the relative clause acting as an adjective in each noun phrase, underlining the pronoun in pink and putting blue brackets around the clause *(whom I saw twice last year; that he bought for his camera; whose birthday is in September; which they built in the twelfth century; who won first prize in the competition)*.
- Finally, they rewrite the noun phrases, replacing each *which* phrase in the relative clause with the correct adverb *(when, where, why, where, when, why)*.

Extension Activity
- The children try parsing the relative clauses in the rewritten phrases, underlining the adverbs in orange and putting blue brackets around the clauses.

Rounding Off
- Go over the activity page and extension activity with the children, discussing their answers.

GRAMMAR 6 PUPIL BOOK: PAGES 35 & 36

Spelling: ‹-eous›

Spelling Test
- The children turn to the backs of their books and find the column labelled *Spelling Test 11*.
- Call out the spelling words learnt last week.

Revision
- Write these adjectives on the board, identify the ‹-ious› suffix in each one, and discuss whether the ‹i› is spoken (either as /i/ or /ee/) or is part of the spelling for /sh/ or /j/: gra**cious**, infec**tious**, nox**ious**, reli**gious**, ser**ious**, obv**ious**, dub**ious**.
- Ask the children if they can think of other words with the ‹-ious› suffix.

Spelling Point
- Write the words *hideous* and *gorgeous* on the board and ask the class what they have in common:
  – The children may recognise them as antonyms (words with opposite meanings).
  – They should also notice that these words are both adjectives in which the suffix ‹-ous› follows the letter ‹e›.
- The suffix ‹-eous› is a less common variant of ‹-ious›, and words with this spelling usually have Old French or Latin origins.
- Unlike the ‹i› in ‹-ious›, which is sometimes pronounced and sometimes not, the ‹e› in ‹-eous› is nearly always spoken, although the sound it makes is either /i/ or /ee/, not /e/.
- The main exception is when ‹e› is part of the soft ‹g› spelling, as in *gorgeous, outrageous, courageous* and *advantageous*.

Spelling List
- Go through the list and ask the class to find and highlight the ‹eous› spelling each time. Also discuss the meaning of any unfamiliar words.
- Point out other spelling features, such as the schwa (neutral vowel sound) in ‹-ous›, the ‹igh› spelling of /ie/ and ‹te› saying /ch/ in *righteous*, the long vowel sound in words like *outrageous* and *erroneous*, the ‹our› spelling of /er/ in *courteous* and *discourteous* (which are a pair of antonyms), the ‹e› saying /i/ in *erroneous* and *extraneous*, the ‹au› spelling in *nauseous* and the silent ‹c› digraph in *miscellaneous*.
- It is a good idea to blend and sound out the spelling words quickly every day with the class. Where appropriate, use the *say it as it sounds* strategy, stressing, for example, the pure sound of any schwas (as in *advantageous, miscellaneous* and *instantaneous*).

hideous
gorgeous
piteous
gaseous
righteous
outrageous
courageous
courteous
bounteous
erroneous
nauseous
advantageous
extraneous
simultaneous
spontaneous
miscellaneous
instantaneous
discourteous

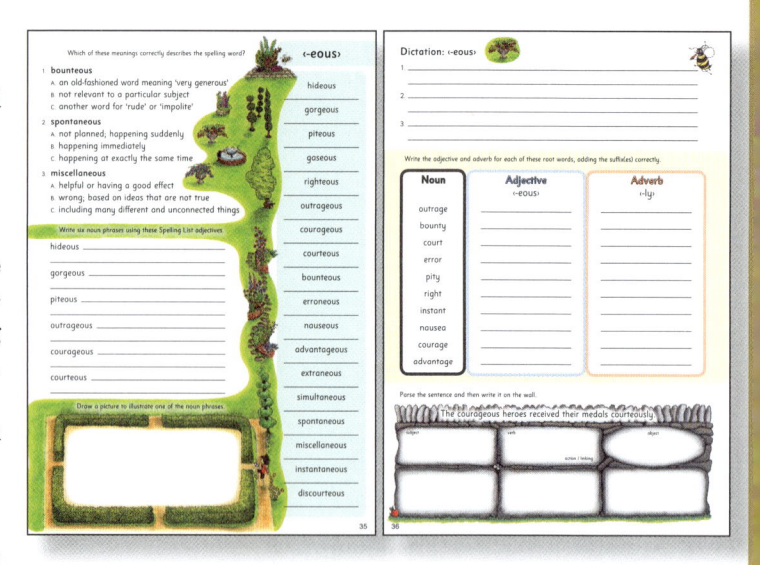

Activity Page 1
- The children split each word into syllables to help remember the spelling (*hid/e/ous, gor/geous, pit/e/ous, gas/e/ous, right/eous, out/ra/geous, cou/ra/geous, cour/te/ous, boun/te/ous, er/ro/ne/ous, nau/se/ous, ad/van/ta/geous, ex/tra/ne/ous, sim/ul/ta/ne/ous, spon/ta/ne/ous, mis/cel/la/ne/ous, in/stan/ta/ne/ous, dis/cour/te/ous*).
- Then they identify the correct meaning of *bounteous* (A), *spontaneous* (A) and *miscellaneous* (C).
- Lastly, they write a noun phrase for each of the six spelling words shown and draw a picture to illustrate one of them.

Activity Page 2
- The children write the adjective and adverb for each root word (*outrageous[ly], bounteous[ly], courteous[ly], erroneous[ly], piteous[ly], righteous[ly], instantaneous[ly], nauseous[ly], courageous[ly], advantageous[ly]*).
- Then they parse the sentence and complete the wall:
  The courageous heroes received their medals courteously.
  Top: heroes - received - medals
  Bottom: The courageous - courteously - their
  Verb: action
  – *Their* is a possessive adjective and should be underlined in blue.
  – *Courteously* is an adverb made by adding ‹-ly› to the adjective *courteous*.

Dictation
- Dictate the following sentences:

  1. "What gorgeous flowers!" I exclaimed.
  2. The smell of rotten eggs is nauseous.
  3. Do you think it is an outrageous idea?

- Remind the class to use speech marks with the correct punctuation in Sentence 1. Sentence 3 needs a question mark.

Grammar: Relative Clauses in Sentences

Aim
- Develop the children's understanding of how relative clauses act as adjectives, either to give important information that helps us identify who or what is being described *(defining clauses)*, or to add extra information that is interesting, but not essential *(non-defining clauses)*.

Introduction
- Briefly revise what the children have learnt about relative clauses so far:
  – Relative clauses are a special kind of dependent clause, so they have a verb and subject, but do not represent a complete thought.
  – They start with a relative pronoun *(who, which, that, whom, whose)* or adverb *(where, when, why)* that **relates** the clause to what it is describing.
- Call out the beginnings of some noun phrases and ask the class to complete the relative clauses: possible examples include *the day (when ...); my friend (who ...); some trees (which ...); the house (that ...); a place (where ...); the actor (whom ...); an artist (whose ...).*
- Write the completed phrases on the board and ask some children to come and identify the relative clauses, underlining the pronouns in pink and adverbs in orange, and putting each clause in blue brackets.

Main Point
- Relative clauses cannot stand on their own as simple sentences. They act as adjectives, giving us more information about a noun or pronoun.
- When a relative clause is used in a sentence, the information it provides does one of two things:
  – It either defines the noun, giving us the information we need to identify which person or thing is meant,
  – or it provides some extra detail which, while interesting, could easily be left out.
- We call these two kinds of clauses **defining** and **non-defining** clauses. Write two sentences on the board and identify the relative clause in each one, underlining the pronoun in pink and putting blue brackets around the clause:
  – *She is the girl (who won the race).*
  – *Paris, (which is the capital of France), is a beautiful city.*
- Discuss them with the class and explain that in the first sentence, the relative clause defines which girl we are talking about: without it we would be left asking *which girl?*; whereas in the second sentence, the clause tells us more about Paris, but it does not aim to help us understand *which* Paris is being referred to.
- Point out that the non-defining clause is separated from the main clause by a pair of bracketing commas. These work in a similar way to parentheses, telling us that the information inside is extra information that could easily be removed without changing the sense.
- In our writing, it is important to know when to put commas in, because it will affect the meaning: for example, the sentence *John is in the park where his friends are playing*, tells us which park John is in (the one where his friends are playing); whereas *John is in the park, where his friends are playing*, tells us that John is in the park and his friends are also playing there.
- Point out that in this last example, the closing comma is not needed because the clause comes at the end of the sentence.
- Clauses starting with *that* are always defining clauses and never have a comma.

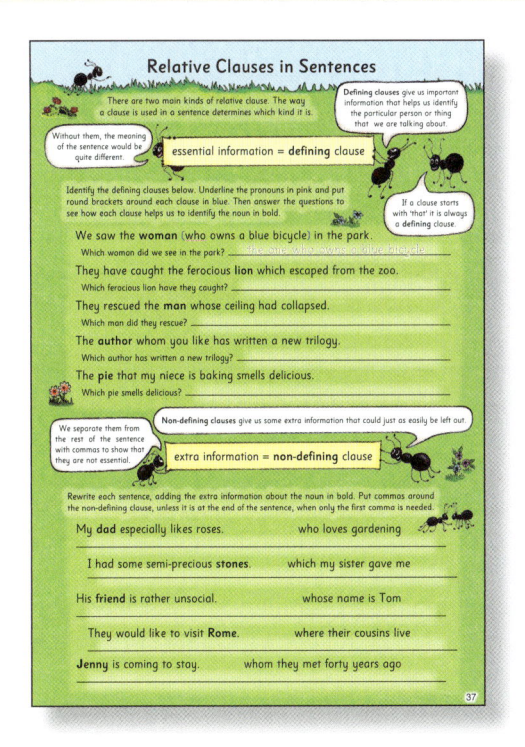

Activity Page
- The children identify the defining clauses, underlining the pronoun in pink and putting blue brackets around the clause *(who owns a blue bicycle; which escaped from the zoo; whose ceiling had collapsed; whom you like; that my niece is baking).*
- They then answer each question in the way shown.
- Then they rewrite the next set of sentences, adding the extra information given and putting commas around each non-defining clause *(My dad, who loves gardening, especially likes roses; I had some semi-precious stones, which my sister gave me; His friend, whose name is Tom, is rather unsocial; They would like to visit Rome, where their cousins live; Jenny, whom they met forty years ago, is coming to stay).*

Extension Activity
- The children write some sentences of their own with defining or non-defining relative clauses.

Rounding Off
- Go over the activity page and extension activity with the children, discussing their answers.

GRAMMAR 6 PUPIL BOOK: PAGES 38 & 39

Spelling: Double Letters

Spelling Test
- The children turn to the backs of their books and find the column labelled *Spelling Test 12*.
- Call out the spelling words learnt last week.

Revision
- Write the words *fell, back, hopped* and *nibble* on the board, underline the double letters, and then compare them to *feel, bark, hoped* and *nimble*.
- Revise the rules for consonant doubling, when two letters form a 'wall', either to end a short word with a short vowel sound (if the final letter is ‹f›, ‹l›, ‹s› or ‹z›) or to stop the 'magic' of one vowel changing the short, stressed sound of another (see pages 29 and 30).

Spelling Point
- The rule for consonant doubling is very reliable when adding a suffix that starts with a vowel (as in *equipped* and *programmed*) but elsewhere in a word, it can be dependent on other factors like word meaning or origin.
- For example, some words with a Latin root have a prefix like ‹sub-› or ‹ad-›, which adapts its final consonant to the first letter of the stem, as in *suppose* (from *sup + ponere*), *address* (from *ad + directus*), *aggressive* (from *aggression: ag + gredi*) and *apparent* (from *appear: ap + parere*).
- This makes spelling difficult and so time must be spent looking at words and noting when double letters appear.

Spelling List
- Go through the list, asking the class to find and highlight the double letters in each word. Also discuss the meaning of any unfamiliar words.
- Point out other spelling features, such as ‹s› saying /s/ and /z/ in *suppose*, the ‹ch› in *attached* (‹tch› usually follows a short vowel sound), the ‹ee› in *committee*, the ‹e› saying /i/ in *equipped, embarrass* and *correspond,* the vowel saying its long sound in *programmed, community* and *communicate,* the ‹ive› saying /iv/ in *aggressive,* the different spellings of /shun/ in *possession* and *interruption,* the prefixes in *interruption, exaggerate* and *recommend,* and the ‹ex› saying /igz/ and soft ‹g› in *exaggerate*.
- It is a good idea to blend and sound out the spelling words quickly every day with the class. Where appropriate, use the *say it as it sounds* strategy, stressing, for example, the pure sound of any schwas (as in *arrive* and *apparent*).

address
arrive
suppose
attached
committee
equipped
programmed
aggressive
apparent
harass
possession
community
interruption
communicate
embarrass
exaggerate
recommend
correspond

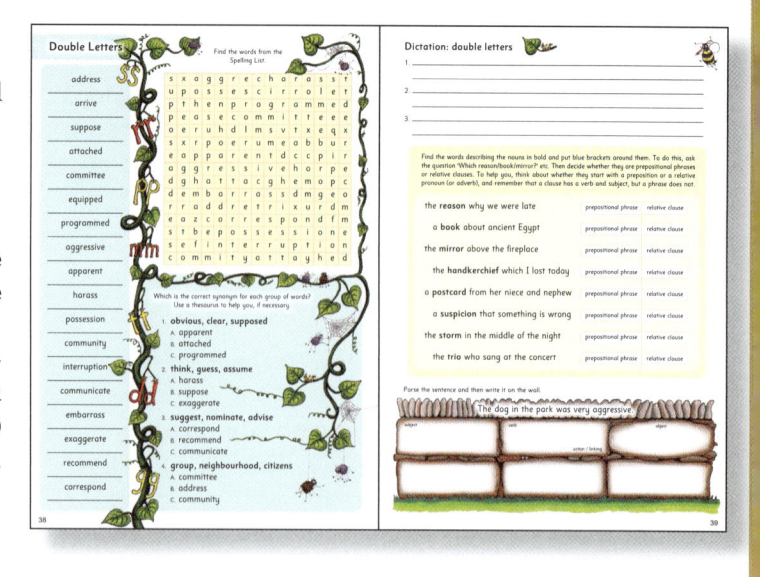

Activity Page 1
- The children split each word into syllables to help remember the spelling *(ad/dress, ar/rive, sup/pose, at/tached, com/mit/tee, e/quipped, pro/grammed, ag/gres/sive, ap/par/ent, har/ass, pos/ses/sion, com/mu/ni/ty, in/ter/rup/tion, com/mu/ni/cate, em/bar/rass, ex/ag/ge/rate, rec/om/mend, cor/re/spond)*.
- They then find the spelling words in the word search, and identify the synonym for each group of words *(1. A, 2. B, 3. B, 4. C)*.

Activity Page 2
- The children identify the words acting as adjectives and decide if they are prepositional phrases or relative clauses *(why we were late [clause], about ancient Egypt [phrase], above the fireplace [phrase], which I lost today [clause], from her niece and nephew [phrase], that something is wrong [clause], in the middle of the night [phrase], who sang at the concert [clause])*.
- Then they parse the sentence and complete the wall:
The dog (in the park) was very aggressive.
Top: dog - was \ aggressive (very) - [blank]
Bottom: The / in the park - [blank] - [blank]
Verb: linking
  - The prepositional phrase *in the park* acts as an adjective describing *dog*, so blue brackets can be put around it.
  - The verb *was* links the adjective complement *aggressive* to the subject *dog* it is describing.

Dictation
- Dictate the following sentences:

  1. We were supposed to arrive before dinner.
  2. "I was so embarrassed!" exclaimed Sam.
  3. There were no interruptions during the lesson.

- Remind the class to use speech marks with the correct punctuation in Sentence 2. *Sam* is a proper noun and needs a capital letter.

Grammar: Coordinating Conjunctions

Aim
- Refine the children's understanding of the conjunctions *for, and, nor, but, or, yet* and *so,* which join together words, phrases or clauses of equal importance. Explain that they are called coordinating conjunctions and can be remembered by the acronym FANBOYS.

Introduction
- Briefly revise conjunctions with the class. Conjunctions are the (usually) small words that join parts of a sentence together, such as *or, but* and *so*.
- Ask the children to think of other conjunctions, such as *because, and, yet, if* and *while,* and how they would put them into sentences.
- Write some of the suggestions on the board and underline the conjunctions in purple.
- Parse one of the simpler sentences to create a grammar action sentence and either use the action cards from earlier lessons (pages 45 and 55) or write each part of speech on the board to show the sequence.
- Ask the class to call out different words each time to make a new sentence: for example, with the sequence pronoun / verb / conjunction / pronoun / verb, the class could create sentences like *He skips and she jumps; I shall go but you will stay; We talked while we waited.*
- Remind the children that many conjunctions can be used to join an independent clause to a dependent (or subordinate) one, but there is a small group of conjunctions – *for, and, nor, but, or, yet* and *so* – which join independent clauses (also known as simple sentences) to form compound sentences.

Main Point
- Using conjunctions in compound sentences helps us avoid having lots of short, repetitive sentences in our writing; it creates a natural flow and helps us digest the information more easily.
- The conjunctions can do this in other ways too. Instead of writing *Joe put on his coat. Joe put on his scarf. Jess put on her coat. Jess put on her scarf,* we are much more likely to write *Joe and Jess put on their coats and scarves,* combining everything in one sentence and using compound subjects and objects joined by *and.*
- Similarly, we could shorten a compound sentence like *Did you leave your book at home, or did you leave it in the car?* to *Did you leave your book at home or in the car?*
- Discuss these examples with the class and look at how the conjunctions can join words *(Joe / Jess, coats / scarves),* phrases *(at home / in the car)* and clauses *(did you leave your book at home / did you leave it in the car).*
- Point out that the joined parts are equally important: Jess is just as much the subject of the sentence as Joe, and the book is as likely to be at home as in the car.
- The conjunctions that join words, phrases and clauses of equal importance are called **coordinating** conjunctions and they can be remembered by the acronym FANBOYS. These conjunctions always go between the parts they are joining and, like other conjunctions, they express meaning:
  - *and* tells us that more information is being added,
  - *or* provides an alternative,
  - *so* shows us the consequences, and
  - *but* and *yet* introduce information that provides a general *(but)* or strong *(yet)* contrast.
- Two other conjunctions are less commonly used:
  - *for* introduces further information as an explanation,
  - and *nor* excludes more information.
- Explain that in a compound sentence using *nor,* the verb in the first clause is always negative and the one in the second clause always goes before the subject, as in *I am not tired, nor am I hungry.*
- *And, nor, but* and *or* are also used in pairs of correlative conjunctions, as in *I am neither tired nor hungry,* but the children can learn about this when they are older.

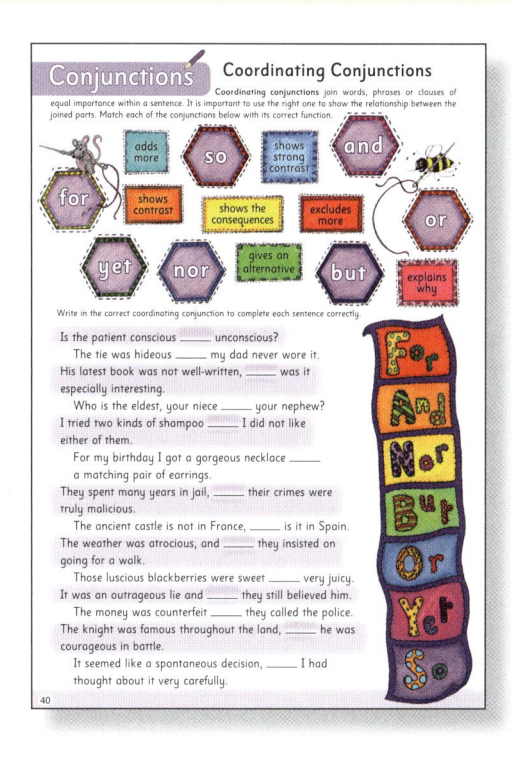

Activity Page
- The children write inside the outlined word *Conjunctions,* using a purple pencil, and match each one to its correct function *(see above).*
- They then read the sentences and decide which of the coordinating conjunctions is needed each time to complete them *(or unconscious; so my dad; nor was it; or your nephew; but I did not; and a matching; for their crimes; nor is it; yet they insisted; and very juicy; yet they still; so they called; for he was; but I had).*

Extension Activity
- The children write a phrase or sentence for each of the conjunctions on a separate sheet of paper.

Rounding Off
- Go over the activity page and extension activity with the children, discussing their answers.

Spelling: ‹cc› for the /k/ Sound

Spelling Test
- The children turn to the backs of their books and find the column labelled *Spelling Test 13*.
- Call out the spelling words learnt last week.

Revision
- Write these words on the board, putting only one consonant letter where there should be two: a*dres*, a*rive*, emba*ras*, inte*ruption*, a*tached*, su*pose*, po*sesion*, *recomend*. Discuss which letters are missing and then ask the children to put the words into sentences.

Spelling Point
- Revise the main ways the /k/ sound can be written; ‹c›, ‹k› and ‹ck› are the most common, but ‹ch› and ‹que› are also used in words with Greek or French origins (see page 96).
- The letter ‹c› can be used for /k/ anywhere in a word, except before ‹e›, ‹i› or ‹y›; then it becomes a soft ‹c› and says /s/, so words like *kept*, *kitten* and *sky* are written with a ‹k›.
- We also tend to use ‹k› after a long vowel sound and ‹c› after a short one (as in *oak* and *act*). This makes ‹c› subject to the doubling rule; it becomes ‹ck› at the end of short words like *stick* (and keeps this spelling when a suffix is added) but it is written as ‹cc› in longer words without a suffix, such as *hiccup*, *soccer* and *raccoon*. The word *soccer* is rather unusual, as ‹cc› before ‹e› usually says /ks/, as in *accept*.

Spelling List
- Go through the list, asking the class to find and highlight the ‹cc› spelling each time. Also discuss the meaning of any unfamiliar words.
- Point out that the spelling always follows a short vowel and discuss other spelling features, such as the ‹ur› spelling of /er/ in *occur*, the ‹i› saying /ee/ at the end of *broccoli*, the ‹y› saying /ie/ in *occupy*, the vowel saying its long sound in *piccolo* and *occasionally*, the ‹eer› spelling of /ear/ in *buccaneer*, and the ‹sion› saying /zhun/ and suffixes ‹-al› and ‹-ly› in *occasionally*.
- It is a good idea to blend and sound out the spelling words quickly every day with the class. Where appropriate, use the *say it as it sounds* strategy, stressing, for example, the pure sound of any schwas (as in *occur* and *accurate*).

hiccup
occur
acclaim
account
raccoon
soccer
broccoli
moccasin
occupy
according
accurate
accomplish
piccolo
buccaneer
occasionally
accommodate
accompany
accordion

Activity Page 1
- The children split each word into syllables to help remember the spelling (*hic/cup, oc/cur, ac/claim, ac/count, rac/coon, soc/cer, broc/co/li, moc/ca/sin, oc/cu/py, ac/cord/ing, ac/cu/rate, ac/com/plish, pic/co/lo, buc/ca/neer, oc/ca/sion/al/ly, ac/com/mo/date, ac/com/pa/ny, ac/cor/di/on*).
- They then write sentences for the first six spelling words and draw pictures of the words in the leaves.

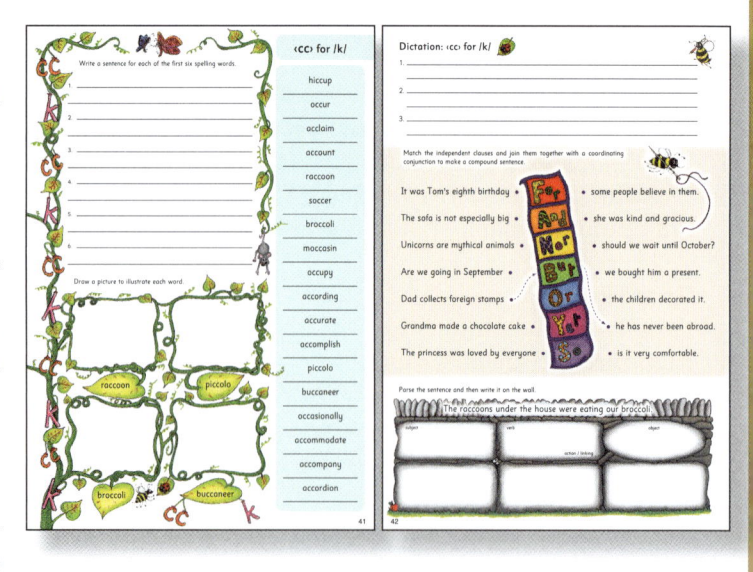

Activity Page 2
- The children match the independent clauses and join them together with a coordinating conjunction to make a compound sentence (*It was Tom's eighth birthday so we bought him a present; The sofa is not especially big nor is it very comfortable; Unicorns are mythical animals yet some people believe in them; Are we going in September or should we wait until October? Dad collects foreign stamps but he has never been abroad; Grandma made a chocolate cake and the children decorated it; The princess was loved by everyone for she was kind and gracious*).
- Then they parse the sentence and complete the wall:
The raccoons (under the house) were eating our broccoli.
Top: raccoons - were eating - broccoli
Bottom: The / under the house - [blank] - our
Verb: action
  – The prepositional phrase *under the house* acts as an adjective describing *raccoons*, so it needs blue brackets.

Dictation
- Dictate the following sentences:

   1. "Is that clock accurate?" asked Ken.
   2. Jill plays the piccolo in the orchestra.
   3. I have a comfortable pair of moccasins.

- Remind the class to use speech marks with the correct punctuation in Sentence 1. *Ken* and *Jill* are proper nouns and need capital letters.

Grammar: Semicolons and Compound Sentences

Aim
- Extend the children's knowledge of punctuation. Introduce them to the semicolon and explain that, like a co-ordinating conjunction, it can be used to join independent clauses in a compound sentence.

Introduction
- Briefly revise sentences with the children. Remind them that:
  – All sentences must make sense, start with a capital letter, contain a verb and subject, and end with a full stop, question mark or exclamation mark. (If the words make sense but there is no verb and subject, it is a phrase.)
  – A simple sentence has one verb and subject (including compound subjects and verbs).
  – A compound sentence has two or more simple sentences (also known as independent clauses) that are joined by a coordinating conjunction *(for, and, nor, but, or, yet* and *so).*
- Write *I stayed at home but you went out* on the board and discuss this compound sentence with the class; underline the conjunction *but* in purple and the verbs *stayed* and *went* in red, and put a box with a small ‹s› in the corner around the subjects *I* and *you*.
- On the board, write a compound sentence for each of the other conjunctions, and look at how they express meaning: *for* explains why, *and* adds more information, *nor* excludes more information, *but* shows contrast, *or* gives an alternative, *yet* shows strong contrast, and *so* shows the consequences.

Main Point
- Remind the children that we often use compound sentences to create a natural flow in our writing. Joining sentences together with a coordinating conjunction allows us to show a connection between ideas: adding or excluding information; giving a choice or an explanation; providing a contrast; or showing the consequences.
- Sometimes this connection is so obvious that we do not need to use the conjunction at all; instead we can join two closely related sentences with a punctuation mark called a semicolon.
- The semicolon looks similar to a colon but has a comma-like mark rather than a bottom dot. Like the colon, it marks a longer pause than a comma, but a shorter one than a full stop, and it indicates a connection between the two parts without interrupting the flow.
- Write a pair of closely related sentences on the board: *It is raining* and *The grass is wet*. Discuss how these sentences could be rewritten as a compound sentence, either with one of the conjunctions *and* or *so,* or by using a semicolon.
- Ask a child to come up and do this with *and*. Make sure (s)he removes the full stop at the end of the first sentence and removes the capital in *The*.
- Now ask another child to come up and rewrite the compound sentence, replacing *and* with a semicolon.
- Write some compound sentences with semicolons on the board and discuss which conjunctions could be used instead.

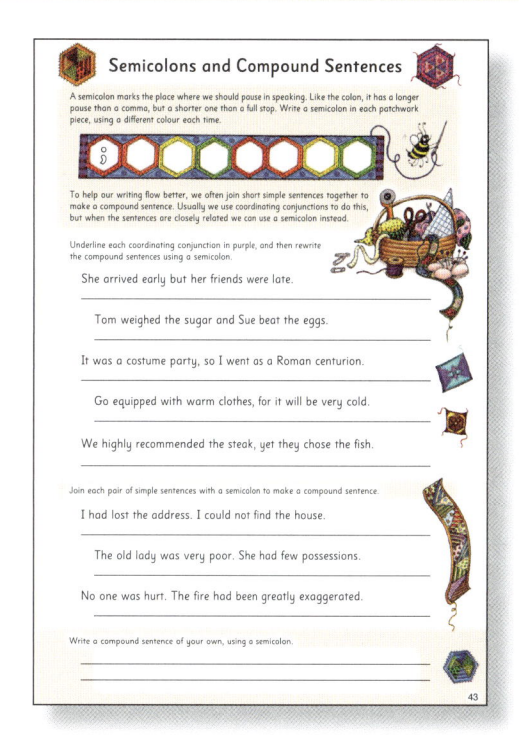

Activity Page
- The children write inside the outlined semicolon in the first patchwork piece and then write one in each of the others, using a different colour every time.
- They then rewrite the compound sentences, replacing the conjunction with a semicolon *(She arrived early; her friends were late / Tom weighed the sugar; Sue beat the eggs / It was a costume party; I went as a Roman centurion / Go equipped with warm clothes; it will be very cold / We highly recommended the steak; they chose the fish).*
- Then the children join each pair of simple sentences with a semicolon to make a compound sentence *(I had lost the address; I could not find the house / The old lady was very poor; she had few possessions / No one was hurt; the fire had been greatly exaggerated).*
- Finally, they write a compound sentence of their own, joining the two clauses with a semicolon.

Extension Activity
- On a separate sheet of paper, the children write more compound sentences with semicolons. They then swap them with a partner, and think of coordinating conjunctions that can be used in place of the hyphens.

Rounding Off
- Go over the activity page with the children, discussing their answers.
- If they have done the extension activity, ask some of the children to read out their sentences.

GRAMMAR 6 PUPIL BOOK: PAGES 44 & 45

Spelling: Doubling Rule for ⟨fer⟩

Spelling Test
- The children turn to the backs of their books and find the column labelled *Spelling Test 14*.
- Call out the spelling words learnt last week.

Revision
- Write these words on the board, putting only one consonant letter where there should be two: *programed, comunity, comitee, exagerate, hicup, ocupy, acompany, ocasion*. Discuss which letters are missing and then ask the children to put the words into sentences.

Spelling Point
- If we stress a syllable, we say it slightly louder to give it more emphasis and to keep the vowel sound pure. Stress is an important feature of the consonant doubling rule.
- Words like *grabbed, wedding, biggest, hotter* and *funny* have a double consonant because this stops the vowel in the suffix influencing the short stressed vowel in the root word; other words do not, either because the vowel in the root word is unstressed (*opened*) or long (*reading*) or because two consonants already form a wall between the vowels (*helper*). The main exception to this rule are words like *travelling* and *pedalled* which double the ⟨l⟩, even though it follows a schwa.
- Verbs ending in ⟨fer⟩ follow the rule in the usual way: we write *referral* when the ⟨fer⟩ is stressed, but *reference* when it is not. The main exception is the word *transferable*, which has a stressed ⟨fer⟩ but only one ⟨r⟩.

Spelling List
- Go through the list, asking the class to find and highlight the ⟨fer⟩ spelling each time. Also discuss the meaning of any unfamiliar words.
- If the word has a suffix, ask the children where the stress is, and point out how the ⟨r⟩ is doubled if ⟨fer⟩ is stressed.
- Point out other spelling features, such as the ⟨e⟩ saying /i/ in *refer, referral, prefer, preferred, defer* and *deferred*, the ⟨a⟩ spelling of /oo/ in *referral*, and the ⟨-ence⟩ suffix with a soft ⟨c⟩ in the abstract nouns *conference, deference, inference* and *reference*.
- Remind the children about the prefixes ⟨re-⟩, ⟨trans-⟩, ⟨pre-⟩ and ⟨de-⟩, and discuss how they add meaning to the words.
- It is a good idea to blend and sound out the spelling words quickly every day with the class. Where appropriate, use the *say it as it sounds* strategy, stressing, for example, the pure sound of any schwas (as in *confer*).

refer
referral
infer
inferred
transfer
transferring
prefer
preferred
defer
deferred
confer
conferring
offer
offered
conference
deference
inference
reference

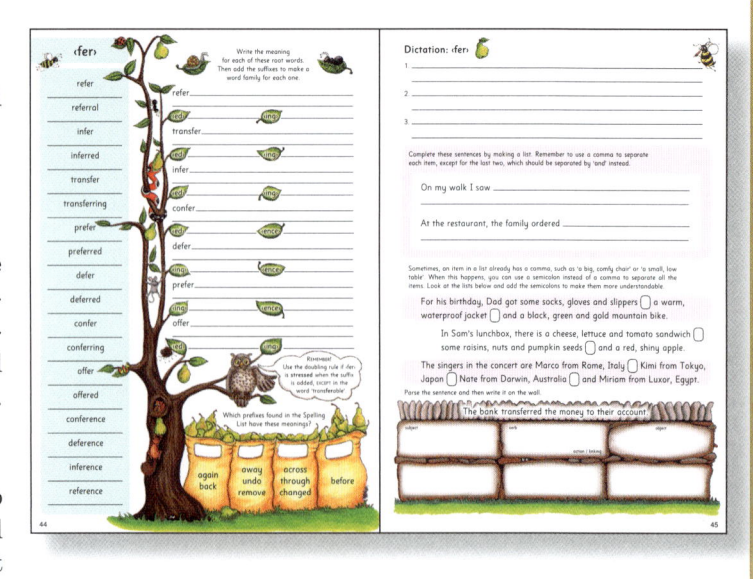

Activity Page 1
- The children split each word into syllables to help remember the spelling (*re/fer, re/fer/ral, in/fer, in/ferred, trans/fer, trans/fer/ring, pre/fer, pre/ferred, de/fer, de/ferred, con/fer, con/fer/ring, of/fer, of/fered, con/fer/ence, def/er/ence, in/fer/ence, ref/er/ence*).
- They then write the meaning for each root word, using a dictionary if needed, and add the suffixes; they should double the ⟨r⟩ each time, except when ⟨fer⟩ is not stressed (*conference, deference, preference, offered, offering*). Lastly, they look at the words in the sacks and identify the prefixes in the spelling words that have these meanings (*Right to left: ⟨re-⟩, ⟨de-⟩, ⟨trans-⟩, ⟨pre-⟩*).

Activity Page 2
- The children complete each sentence by making a list, using commas to separate the items. They then look at the lists below, which have items with commas, and write a semicolon in each box to separate them.
- Then they parse the sentence and complete the wall: The bank transferred the money (to their account).
Top: bank - transferred - money
Bottom: The - to their account - the
Verb: action
  – The prepositional phrase *to their account* is acting as an adverb, so orange brackets can be put around it.

Dictation
- Dictate the following sentences:

  1. The police are offering a reward for any information.
  2. My friends preferred tennis and swimming to soccer.
  3. "I will be at the conference next week," said Miss Beech.

- Remind the class to use speech marks with the correct punctuation in Sentence 3. *Miss Beech* is a proper noun and needs initial capital letters.

Grammar: Colons in Sentences

Aim
- Extend the children's understanding of colons. Demonstrate that, as well as introducing a list of bullet points, a colon can be used in sentences to introduce things like a list of examples, a single idea or an explanation.

Introduction
- Remind the class that punctuation helps us make sense of the words we use. A comma in the wrong place or a missing apostrophe can make our writing confusing or significantly change the meaning.
- Briefly revise the punctuation marks that the children know and discuss when they might be used. These include full stops, question marks, exclamation marks, commas, apostrophes, speech marks, hyphens, parentheses and semicolons (see pages 18 to 20).
- On the board, write *On the farm there were cows, sheep, goats and chickens* and discuss how commas can be used to separate the items in a list.
- Then show how the same list could be presented as bullet points for a presentation or report. Point out the differences, reminding the children that a vertical list always has an introduction that ends in a colon and does not have *and* or *or* before the final item.

Main Point
- Lists like the one above are very straightforward and only need commas to punctuate them in a sentence. Other lists, however, need more of an introduction, usually because they are very long or require more emphasis.
- On the board, write *In our kitchen there are many things,* without any punctuation. Ask the class what goes next and discuss how a full stop can be added, as the words form an independent clause or simple sentence.
- Another option is to expand the sentence by adding a list of what is in the kitchen. Explain that one way to do this is to add a colon, so the words become an introduction for the list. Add the colon, discuss what might be in the kitchen, and ask some children to come and make a long list to complete the sentence.
- Write *In our kitchen there are five pans: a large frying pan, a small frying pan and three saucepans*. This list is not particularly long, but the introduction and colon tell us to expect two things: that there will be more information about the pans and that this information is important.
- Now write *There is only one thing wrong with our kitchen: it is too small*. Here there is no list at all, only a single idea, but the words and colon in the first clause are acting in the same way as before, introducing some more information and emphasising its importance.
- In the example above, the information clarifies or identifies what *the one thing* is, but it could also be an explanation or a set of examples. Tell the children that a colon can be thought of as a little fanfare, announcing the arrival of some important information.
- Write some more examples on the board and point out that the words before a colon always form an independent clause. This means a colon should never separate a verb from its object or complement (so we would never write *I bought: eggs, milk and bread*).

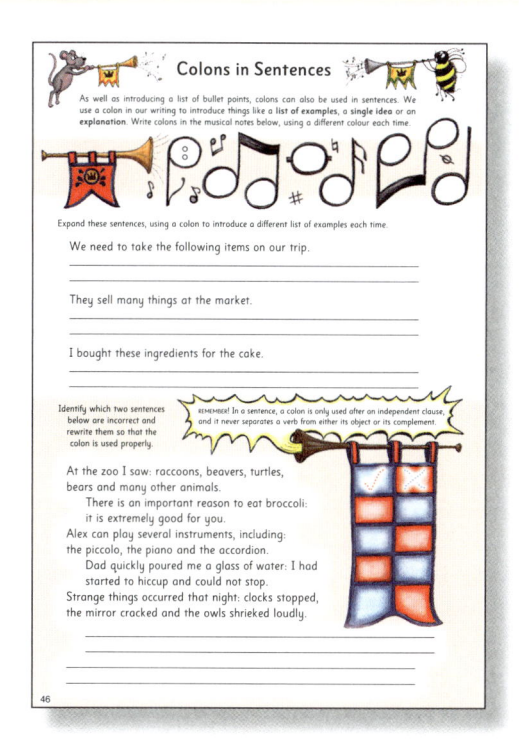

Activity Page
- The children write inside the outlined colon in the first musical note and then write one in each of the others, using a different colour every time.
- They then expand the sentences, adding a list of appropriate items each time, introduced by a colon. Remind the children to punctuate each list properly with commas and to move the full stop to the end.
- Then they decide whether the next set of sentences are using the colon correctly, putting ✓ in the banner for *yes* or ✗ for *no (see below)*.
- Then the children rewrite the two incorrect sentences, making sure that the words in front of the colon can stand alone as a simple sentence (starting, for example, with *At the zoo I saw these creatures:* and *Alex can play several instruments, including these:)*

Extension Activity
- The children write some introductory sentences on a separate sheet of paper and swap them with a partner. They then expand each sentence by adding a list of items introduced by a colon.

Rounding Off
- Go over the activity page with the children, discussing their answers, and ask some of them to read their lists if they have done the extension activity.

GRAMMAR 6 PUPIL BOOK: PAGES 47 & 48

Spelling: Long /oo/ Spellings

Spelling Test
- The children turn to the backs of their books and find the column labelled *Spelling Test 15*.
- Call out the spelling words learnt last week.

Revision
- Ask the children to suggest words that follow the spelling rule: *If you want to say /ee/, it's ‹i› before ‹e›, except after ‹c›.*
- Write the following words on the board and ask the class to identify the sound that the ‹ei›, ‹eir› or ‹eigh› is making in each one: v*ei*l /ai/, rec*ei*ve /ee/, w*eir*d /ear/, th*eir* /air/, f*ei*sty /ie/, count*er*f*ei*t /i/, h*ei*fer /e/, *eigh*th /ai/.

Spelling Point
- Revise the main ways the long /oo/ sound can be written and write them on the board; when the children are young, /oo/ is introduced as one of the sounds made by ‹oo›, as in *moon*, but they soon learn that it can also be represented by the /ue/ spellings, as in bl*ue*, J*u*n*e*, gr*ew* and fl*u*.
- Explain that there are other spelling patterns which are much less common, but which the children will know:
  – Write the words fr*ui*t, s*ou*p, sh*oe* and m*o*v*ie* on the board and discuss which letters are making the /oo/ sound.
  – See if the class can think of other words using these spellings and add them to the board.
- Later, the children will be reminded that long /oo/ can also be written as ‹ough› (see page 84), but this is a rare spelling and they are likely to come across it only in variations of the word *through*.

Spelling List
- Go through the list, asking the class to find and highlight the long /oo/ spelling each time. Also discuss the meaning of any unfamiliar words.
- Point out other spelling features, such as the ‹ie› saying /ee/ in *movie*, the ‹ve› saying /v/ in *prove, disapprove* and *improvement*, the ‹te› saying /t/ in *route*, the soft ‹c› in *juice*, the ‹se› saying /z/ in *bruise*, the ‹e› saying /i/ in *recruit* and *removal*, the prefix in *recruit, removal, disapprove* and *improvement*, and the suffix in *removal, approval* and *improvement*.
- It is a good idea to blend and sound out the spelling words quickly every day with the class. Where appropriate, use the *say it as it sounds* strategy, stressing, for example, the pure sound of any schwas (as in *canoe* and *disapprove*).

fruit
suit
soup
youth
movie
prove
shoe
route
canoe
group
juice
bruise
wound
recruit
removal
approval
disapprove
improvement

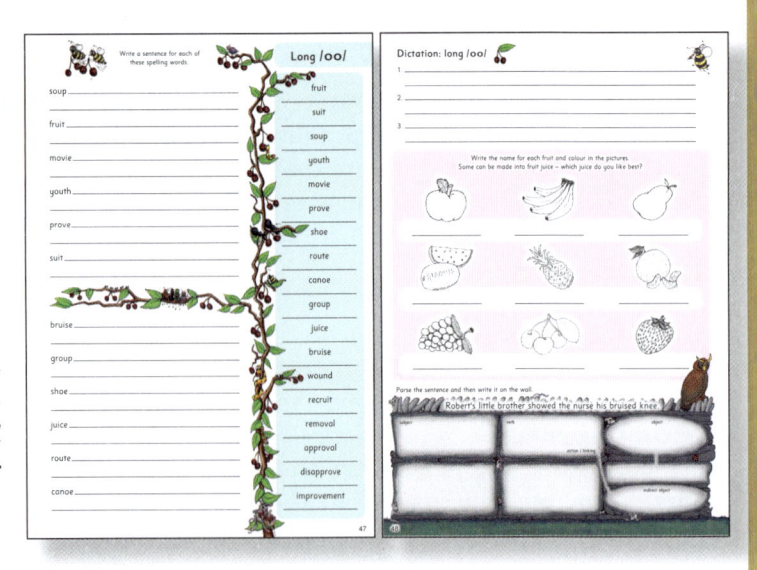

Activity Page 1
- The children split each word into syllables to help remember the spelling *(fruit, suit, soup, youth, mov/ie, prove, shoe, route, ca/noe, group, juice, bruise, wound, re/cruit, re/mov/al, ap/prov/al, dis/ap/prove, im/prove/ment)*.
- They then write sentences for the first twelve spelling words.

Activity Page 2
- The children write the name for each fruit *(Top: apple, banana, pear; Middle: watermelon, pineapple, orange; Bottom: grape, cherry, strawberry)* and colour in the pictures.
- Then they parse the sentence and complete the wall: Robert's little brother showed the nurse his bruised knee.
Top: brother - showed - knee
Bottom: Robert's little - [blank] - his bruised
Indirect object: nurse (the)   Verb: action
  – Possessive nouns always act as adjectives, so *Robert's* should be underlined in blue.

Dictation
- Dictate the following sentences:

1. I lost my shoe as I got out of the canoe.
2. The movie tells the story of a wounded soldier.
3. "I can prove that you stole the suit!" exclaimed Jill.

- Remind the class to use speech marks with the correct punctuation in Sentence 3. *Jill* is a proper noun and needs a capital letter.

Grammar: Subordinating Conjunctions

Aim
- Reinforce the children's knowledge of conjunctions. Explain that those which are used to join a main (or independent) clause to a subordinate (or dependent one) are called subordinating conjunctions.

Introduction
- Briefly revise the coordinating conjunctions (*for, and, nor, but, or, yet* and *so*), which are used to join words, phrases and clauses of equal importance and can be remembered by the acronym FANBOYS.
- These conjunctions always go between the parts they are joining and, like other conjunctions, they express meaning, explaining why *(for)*, adding or excluding more information *(and/nor)*, showing a general or strong contrast *(but/yet)*, giving an alternative *(or)*, or showing the consequences *(so)*.
- Coordinating conjunctions can be used to join two independent clauses in a compound sentence: for example, *I read a book <u>and</u> you wrote a story*. Write this sentence on the board and identify the two clauses, underlining *and* first in purple, and then asking the class to identify the subject and verb on either side of the conjunction (*I read / you wrote*).

Main Point
- Remind the class that not all clauses are independent; some have a subject and verb but cannot stand alone as a simple sentence. These are called *dependent* clauses because they depend on more information for their meaning.
- Write two examples on the board: *which I found in my pocket* and *when the sun shines*. Identify the subject and verb in each clause (*I found / sun shines*) and discuss how they are dependent because we are left to wonder *what* was found in the pocket and *what happens* when the sun shines.
- Remind the class that the first example is a special kind of dependent clause, more commonly known as a relative clause. This is because it starts with a relative pronoun *(which)* that relates the clause to what it is describing.
- However, most dependent clauses are like the second example and start with a **subordinating** conjunction, so called because it joins a main clause to a subordinate one. Remind the class that the prefix ‹sub-› means *below* or *under* and so *subordinate* means *ranked / ordered below*.
- Explain that a subordinating conjunction, unlike a coordinating one, is part of the clause itself. We can see this by putting the clause into a sentence, such as *We play outside when the sun shines*. If we wanted to put the clause at the beginning of the sentence, we would also have to move the conjunction because it is part of the clause: *When the sun shines, we play outside*.
- In the Adverbials lesson on page 73, the children will learn that dependent clauses can be moved in this way because they are acting as adverbs. Point out that we cannot do this in a compound sentence: for example, we would never write *And you wrote a story, I read a book*.
- Call out some subordinating conjunctions, such as *if, because, although, unless, while* and *wherever,* and ask the children to put them into subordinate clauses.

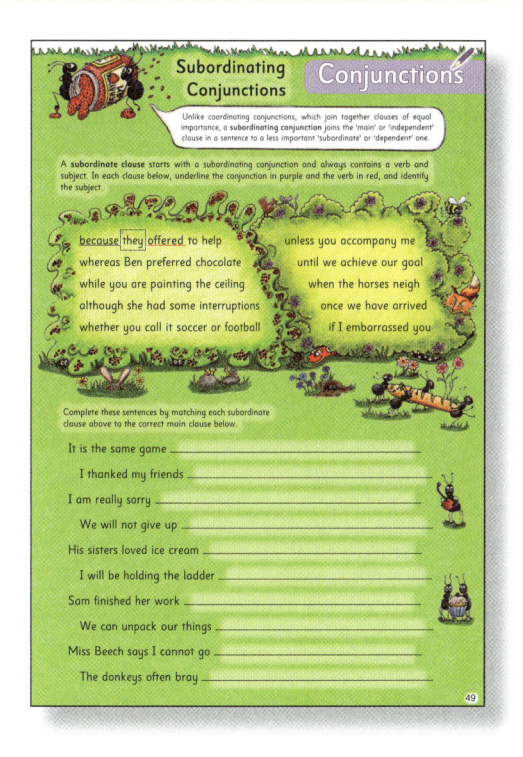

Activity Page
- The children write inside the outlined word *Conjunctions,* using a purple pencil.
- They then parse each subordinate clause, underlining the subordinate conjunction in purple, drawing a box with a small ‹s› around the subject and underlining the verb in red (*because / they / offered; whereas / Ben / preferred; while / you / are painting; although / she / had; whether / you / call; unless / you / accompany; until / we / achieve; when / horses / neigh; once / we / have arrived; if / I / embarrassed*).
- They then match each main clause to the correct subordinate clause, writing it on the line and adding a full stop to complete each sentence (*It is… / whether you…; I thanked… / because they…; I am… / if I…; We will… / until we…; His sisters… / whereas Ben…; I will… / while you…; Sam finished… / although she…; We can… / once we…; Miss Beech… / unless you…; The donkeys… / when the…*).

Extension Activity
- Write on the board the subordinate clauses that the class thought of earlier and ask the children to put them into sentences.

Rounding Off
- Go over the activity page and extension activity with the children, discussing their answers.

GRAMMAR 6 PUPIL BOOK: PAGES 50 & 51

Spelling: /ai/ Spellings

Spelling Test
- The children turn to the backs of their books and find the column labelled *Spelling Test 16*.
- Call out the spelling words learnt last week.

Revision
- Write the following words on the board and ask the class to identify the letters saying /ai/ in each one: expl*ai*n, *A*pr*i*l, Thursd*ay*, decor*a*te, b*ei*ge, n*eigh*.
- Ask the children if they can think of other words with these spelling.

Spelling Point
- Other spelling patterns exist for the /ai/ sound, besides the more common ones. It can be written as ‹ey›, usually at the end of words like *they*, *obey* and *prey*, or as ‹et› in words with a French origin, such as *ballet*, *sorbet* and *cabaret*.
- There are only three common words with the ‹ea› spelling, which can be remembered as *Let's break for a great big steak*, while the spellings in *fete* and *straight* are much rarer.
- See if the children can think of other words with these spellings and write them on the board.

Spelling List
- Go through the list, asking the class to find and highlight the /ai/ spelling each time. Also discuss the meaning of any unfamiliar words.
- Point out other spelling features, such as the ‹k› spelling after the long vowel in *break* and *steak*, the double letters in *ballet* and *buffet*, the different spellings of /ai/ in *heyday*, the ‹o› saying its long vowel sound in *obey*, the ‹ch› saying /sh/ in *sachet*, the ‹ou› spelling for the different vowel sounds in *bouquet* and *gourmet*, the ‹qu› saying /k/ in *bouquet*, and the ‹ur› spelling of /er/ in *survey*.
- Discuss how the words *prey*, *break*, *great* and *steak* have the homophones *pray*, *brake*, *grate* and *stake*.
- Also point out that here *buffet* is a noun, but when it is pronounced /bufit/ it is a verb with a totally different meaning. Ask the class what words that look the same but sound different and have different meanings are called (*heteronyms*).
- It is a good idea to blend and sound out the spelling words quickly every day with the class. Where appropriate, use the *say it as it sounds* strategy, stressing, for example, the pure sound of any schwas (as in c*o*nvey and cabar*e*t).

| they |
| prey |
| break |
| great |
| steak |
| ballet |
| heyday |
| fete |
| buffet |
| convey |
| obey |
| sorbet |
| sachet |
| straight |
| bouquet |
| gourmet |
| survey |
| cabaret |

Activity Page 1
- The children split each word into syllables to help remember the spelling (*they, prey, break, great, steak, bal/let, hey/day, fete, buf/fet, con/vey, o/bey, sor/bet, sach/et, straight, bou/quet, gour/met, sur/vey, cab/a/ret*).
- They then write in the missing letters (*Top: ob*ey*, st*ea*k, pr*ey*; buff*et*, surv*ey*, ball*et* / Middle: gourm*et*, cabar*et*; h*ey*day, bouqu*et* / Bottom: br*ea*k, th*ey*, gr*ea*t; sach*et*, conv*ey*, sorb*et*).
- Then they sort the spelling list words, according to their /ai/ spelling (‹ea›: *break, great, steak*; ‹et›: *ballet, buffet, sorbet, sachet, bouquet, gourmet, cabaret*; ‹ey›: *they, prey, heyday, convey, obey, survey*) and identify the missing words (*fete, straight*).

Activity Page 2
- The children write the meanings for each pair of homophones, using a dictionary to help them if needed.
- Then they parse the sentence and complete the wall:
  The great ballet dancer received a huge bouquet (of lilies).
  Top: dancer - received - bouquet
  Bottom: The great ballet - [blank] - a huge / of lilies
  Verb: action
  – The noun *ballet* is acting as an adjective.
  – The prepositional phrase *of lilies* describes the bouquet, so blue brackets can be put around it.

Dictation
- Dictate the following sentences:

  1. In its heyday, it was a great place for a weekend break.
  2. "The dog obeyed my command straight away!" I exclaimed.
  3. She had a big steak and lemon sorbet at the gourmet restaurant.

- Sentence 1 starts with a prepositional phrase, which is often separated from the rest of the sentence by a comma. Remind the class to use speech marks with the correct punctuation in Sentence 2.

GRAMMAR 6 PUPIL BOOK: PAGE 52

Grammar: Complex Sentences

Aim
- Introduce the term *complex sentence* to describe a sentence with a main clause and a subordinate one. Explain that the main clause always has the important information, while the subordinate one tells us more about it, describing, for example, when, where or why it happened.

Introduction
- Briefly revise clauses with the class:
  – A clause is a group of words that makes sense and contains a subject and verb.
  – If it can stand alone as a simple sentence, it is called an *independent* or *main* clause.
  – If it depends on more information for its meaning, it is called a *dependent* or *subordinate* one.
  – Relative clauses, which are a special kind of dependent clause, begin with a relative pronoun *(who, which, that, whom, whose)* or adverb *(where, when, why)* that relates the clause to what it is describing.
  – Most dependent clauses, however, start with a subordinating conjunction, so called because it tells us that the clause it belongs to is *ranked below* the main clause in terms of importance.
- Call out some subordinating conjunctions, such as *if, because, although, unless, while* and *wherever,* and ask the children to put them into sentences.

Main Point
- Ask the children what kinds of sentence they know; they should be able to name **simple** sentences, which have only one (independent) clause, and also **compound** sentences, where two independent clauses are joined together with either a coordinating conjunction or a semicolon.
- Point out that they know another type of sentence: one which has both an independent clause and a dependent clause. Explain that this is called a **complex** sentence and it can usually be written by starting with either clause (but not when there is a relative clause).
- Also explain that when the dependent clause comes first we separate the clauses with a comma. Show this on the board, using some of the sentences suggested earlier by the class, and identify which clause is which each time.
- Ask some children to come up and put square brackets around the independent clauses. Point out that these always contain the most important information, which is why they are called main clauses.
- The dependent clauses, which provide extra information that cannot be used alone, are not so important and this is why they are described as subordinate.
- Discuss what each subordinate clause on the board is telling us about the main clause. Some **explain** it (using conjunctions like *because, since* and *as*), some provide a **contrast** to it (with conjunctions like *though, while* and *although*), others make the clause **conditional** (using *if* and *unless*); many indicate **time** (with *as, while, when, after, before, until, since* and *whenever*) and a few indicate **place** (with *where, wherever* and *everywhere*).

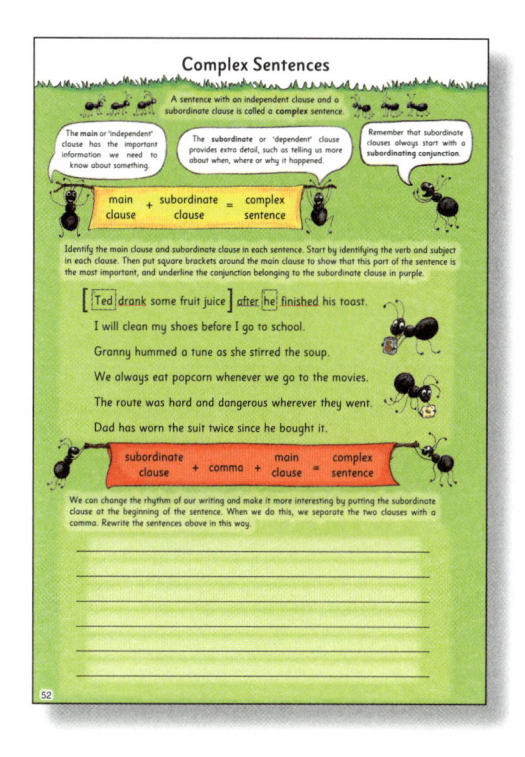

Activity Page
- The children look at the two clauses in each sentence, draw a box with a small ‹s› around the subjects and underline the verbs in red *(Ted drank/he finished; I will clean/I go; Granny hummed/she stirred; We eat/we go; route was/they went; Dad has worn/he bought)*.
- They then put square brackets around the main clause and underline the conjunction at the beginning of the subordinate clause in purple: [Ted drank some fruit juice] *after* he finished his toast; [I will clean my shoes] *before* I go to school; [Granny hummed a tune] *as* she stirred the soup; [We always eat popcorn] *whenever* we go to the movies; [The route was hard and dangerous] *wherever* they went; [Dad has worn the suit twice] *since* he bought it].
- Then the children rewrite the sentences, putting the subordinate clause first. They should remember to add the comma and make sure that the main clause no longer starts with a capital letter (unless it is a proper noun).

Extension Activity
- The children look at the six sentences on the activity page and think about what kind of extra information the subordinate clause is giving *(All the sentences say something about **when** the main clause happens, except for the fifth one, which says **where**)*.

Rounding Off
- Go over the activity page and extension activity with the children, discussing their answers.

GRAMMAR 6 PUPIL BOOK: PAGES 53 & 54

Spelling: Silent ⟨h⟩ Digraphs

Spelling Test
- The children turn to the backs of their books and find the column labelled *Spelling Test 17*.
- Call out the spelling words learnt last week.

Revision
- Write the following words on the board and ask the class to identify the silent letter in each one: *plum**b**er, **w**riting, **k**nuckle, **r**hythmic, **w**holesome, **s**cissors, **s**ignpost, sand**c**astle*.
- Ask the children if they can think of other words that have silent letters.

Spelling Point
- Remind the class that a silent letter often goes with a particular consonant to form a silent letter digraph. Common pairings include ⟨mb⟩, ⟨wr⟩, ⟨kn⟩, ⟨rh⟩, ⟨wh⟩, ⟨sc⟩, ⟨gn⟩ and ⟨st⟩.
- As we can see from ⟨wh⟩ and ⟨wr⟩, sometimes the same silent letter can be used in different digraphs. This is particularly true of silent ⟨h⟩, which is often paired with ⟨r⟩ but is also found with ⟨w⟩ and ⟨g⟩ in words like **wh**isper and **gh**ostly.
- There are less common silent ⟨h⟩ digraphs too, such as ⟨kh⟩ and ⟨dh⟩ which – like ⟨rh⟩ – are found in words that have been borrowed from other languages. For example, words like *khaki*, *Buddhism* and *jodhpurs* come from India: *khaki* means *dust-coloured* in Urdu, *Buddha* means *enlightened* in Sanskrit and a pair of *jodhpurs* takes its name from the Indian city of Jodhpur; other words come from Arabic (*sheikh*) and Egyptian (*ankh*), while ⟨rh⟩ words come from Greek.

Spelling List
- Go through the list, asking the class to find and highlight the silent ⟨h⟩ digraph each time. Also discuss the meaning of any unfamiliar words.
- Point out other spelling features, such as the initial capital letter in the proper nouns *Sikh* and *Buddhism*, the ⟨i⟩ saying /ee/ in *Sikh*, *khaki* and *dhoti*, the ⟨n⟩ saying /ng/ in *ankh*, the way *magic* ⟨e⟩ influences ⟨y⟩ to say /ie/ in *rhyme* (whereas in *rhythm*, *rhythmically* and *gymkhana* it says /i/), the ⟨u⟩ spelling in *Buddhism*, *rhubarb* and *sadhu*, the vowel making its long sound in *rhino*, *dhoti* and *rhinoceros*, the ⟨ur⟩ in *jodhpurs*, the ⟨ei⟩ saying /ai/ or /ee/ in *sheikh*, the soft ⟨g⟩ in *gymkhana* and soft ⟨c⟩ in *rhinoceros*, and the ⟨eu⟩ saying /oo/ in *rheumatism*.
- It is a good idea to blend and sound out the spelling words quickly every day with the class. Where appropriate, use the *say it as it sounds* strategy, stressing,

Sikh
ankh
khaki
rhyme
rhythm
Buddhism
rhino
jodhpurs
rhubarb
rhombus
rhapsody
sheikh
dhoti
sadhu
gymkhana
rhinoceros
rheumatism
rhythmically

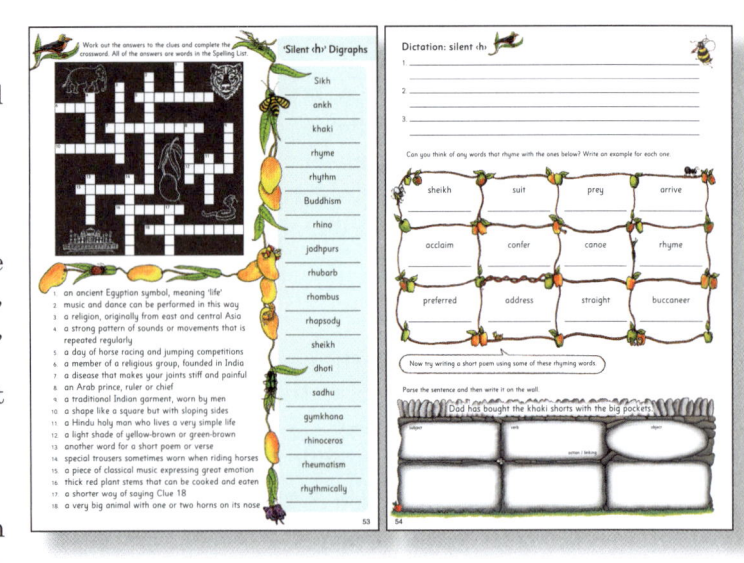

for example, the pure sound of any schwas (as in *rhinoceros*).

Activity Page 1
- The children split each word into syllables to help remember the spelling *(Sikh, ankh, kha/ki, rhyme, rhyth/m, Bud/dhis/m, rhi/no, jodh/purs, rhu/barb, rhom/bus, rhap/so/dy, sheikh, dho/ti, sa/dhu, gym/kha/na, rhi/noc/er/os, rheu/ma/tis/m, rhyth/mi/cal/ly)*.
- They then work out the answers to the crossword clues and write them in *(1. ankh, 2. rhythmically, 3. Buddhism, 4. rhythm, 5. gymkhana, 6. Sikh, 7. rheumatism, 8. sheikh, 9. dhoti, 10. rhombus, 11. sadhu, 12. khaki, 13. rhyme, 14. jodhpurs, 15. rhapsody, 16. rhubarb, 17. rhino, 18. rhinoceros)*.

Activity Page 2
- The children think of words that rhyme with those given. If there is time, they can then use some of them to write a short poem on a separate sheet of paper.
- Then they parse the sentence and complete the wall: Dad has bought the khaki shorts (with the big pockets).
Top: Dad - has bought - shorts
Bottom: [blank] - [blank] - the khaki / with the big pockets
Verb: action
  – The prepositional phrase *with the big pockets* describes the shorts, so it needs blue brackets.

Dictation
- Dictate the following sentences:

1. "Can I wear my jodhpurs to the gymkhana?" she asked.
2. My book on ancient Egypt has a great picture of an ankh.
3. Our grandfather showed us the best way to grow rhubarb.

- Remind the class to use speech marks with the correct punctuation in Sentence 1. *Egypt* is a proper noun and needs a capital letter.

Grammar: Simple, Compound & Complex Sentences

Aim
- Reinforce the children's understanding of sentences, and enable them to recognise simple, compound and complex sentences more easily.

Introduction
- Remind the class that several things are needed to make a group of words a sentence. A sentence must make sense, start with a capital letter, contain a verb and subject, and end with a full stop, question mark or exclamation mark.
- Write *a chocolate cake* on the board and ask if this is a sentence. Although the words make sense, there is no verb or subject. Instead, all the words describe (or *modify*) the noun *cake* and so we can identify them as a noun phrase.
- Now expand the phrase, adding a verb and subject to make it a sentence: for example, *Tom made a chocolate cake.* Underline the verb *(made)* in red and ask the children to identify the subject *(Tom)* and object *(cake)*. Remind them that the subject does the verb action and the object (if there is one) receives the verb action.
- Now add the word *Anna* after the verb and ask the class what this word is doing. Anna is the person for whom Tom made the cake, so she is the indirect object.
- Another thing that a sentence must have is at least one clause. Ask the children what the different clauses are called *(independent/main clauses, dependent/subordinate clauses and relative clauses)*.
- Remind them that a sentence can be called simple, compound or complex, depending on which clauses are used and how many there are.

Main Point
- It is important to use different kinds of sentences in our writing to provide variety and interest. Write on the board *Tom made a chocolate birthday cake for his friend Anna,* and ask the class what kind of sentence it is. There is only one verb *(made)* with a subject *(Tom)* so the words form an independent clause which, when used on its own, is known as a **simple** sentence.
- Now write *It is Anna's birthday, so Tom made her a chocolate cake* and discuss what kind of sentence this is. There are two clauses *(It is Anna's birthday/Tom made her a chocolate cake)* joined by a coordinating conjunction, *so.* Both are equally important and could stand alone as simple sentences, but together they form a **compound** sentence.
- Now write *Tom made Anna a chocolate cake because it is her birthday.* Again, there are two clauses and a conjunction, but this time the clause *because it is her birthday* is subordinate, or ranked below the main clause, making this a **complex** sentence.
- Remind the class that most subordinate clauses start with a subordinating conjunction and can go at the start of the sentence; however, relative clauses (which are a special kind of subordinate clause) start with a pronoun or an adverb and do not work in this way.

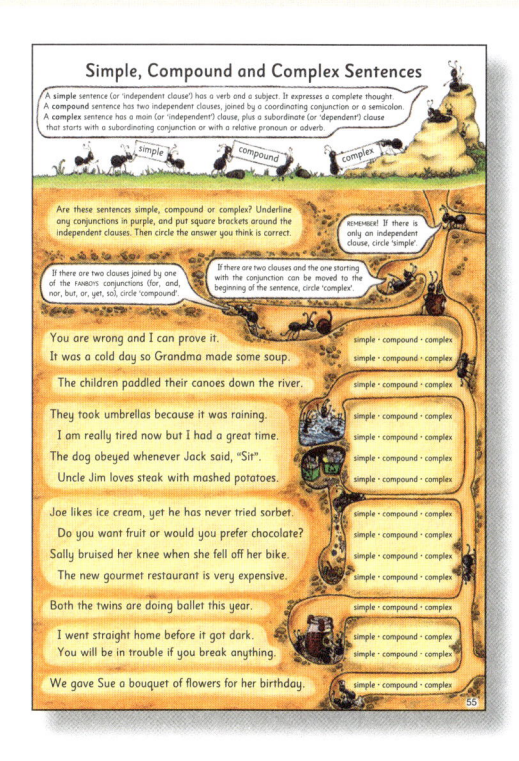

Activity Page
- In each sentence, the children underline the conjunction in purple and put square brackets around any independent clauses, before deciding what kind of sentence it is: [You are wrong] and [I can prove it] COMPOUND; [It was a cold day] so [Grandma made some soup] COMPOUND; [The children paddled their canoes down the river] SIMPLE; [They took umbrellas] because it was raining COMPLEX; [I am really tired now] but [I had a great time] COMPOUND; [The dog obeyed] whenever Jack said, "Sit" COMPLEX; [Uncle Jim loves steak with mashed potatoes] SIMPLE; [Joe likes ice cream,] yet [he has never tried sorbet] COMPOUND; [Do you want fruit] or [would you prefer chocolate?] COMPOUND; [Sally bruised her knee] when she fell off her bike COMPLEX; [The new gourmet restaurant is very expensive] SIMPLE; [Both the twins are doing ballet this year] SIMPLE; [I went straight home] before it got dark COMPLEX; [You will be in trouble] if you break anything COMPLEX; [We gave Sue a bouquet of flowers for her birthday] SIMPLE.

Extension Activity
- On a separate sheet of paper, the children write three sentences: one simple, one compound and one complex. They then swap sentences with a partner and identify which kinds they are.

Rounding Off
- Go over the activity page and extension activity with the children, discussing their answers.

GRAMMAR 6 PUPIL BOOK: PAGES 56 & 57

Spelling: /t/ Spellings

Spelling Test
- The children turn to the backs of their books and find the column labelled *Spelling Test 18*.
- Call out the spelling words learnt last week.

Revision
- Write the following words on the board and ask the class to identify the silent ⟨h⟩ digraph in each one: din**gh**y, shei**kh**, **rh**ino, jo**dh**purs, **wh**eel, **rh**ombus, **kh**aki, Bud**dh**ism.
- Ask the children if they can think of other words that have a silent ⟨h⟩ digraph.

Spelling Point
- The letter ⟨t⟩ is often paired with different silent letters to make the /t/ sound in words with a foreign origin. Common pairings include ⟨bt⟩, ⟨te⟩, ⟨tte⟩ and ⟨th⟩:
  – The silent letter digraph ⟨bt⟩ is found in words with a Latin origin, as are some words ending in ⟨te⟩ (although others are Germanic).
  – The ⟨tte⟩ spelling is found in words borrowed from French and usually indicates a smaller version of the root word, so a rosette is a small rose and a statuette is a small statue. (The word *silhouette* is named after the French author and politician Étienne de Silhouette).
  – The ⟨th⟩ digraph often appears in proper nouns, such as Es**th**er, **Th**omas, **Th**ailand and the **Th**ames.
- There is also a highly unusual spelling for /t/, which is the ⟨cht⟩ found in *yacht*. This derives from *jaghtschip*, the Dutch word for a fast pirate ship.

Spelling List
- Go through the list, asking the class to find and highlight the silent letter digraph (or trigraph) saying /t/ each time. Also discuss the meaning of any unfamiliar words.
- Point out other spelling features, such as the vowel making its long sound in *paste*, *baste*, *rosette* and *favourite*, the way magic ⟨e⟩ influences ⟨y⟩ to say /ie/ in *thyme*, the initial capital letter in the proper noun *Thailand* and its ⟨ai⟩ saying /ie/, the ⟨a⟩ saying /o/ in *yacht*, the ⟨le⟩ saying /ool/ at the end of *subtle* and *redoubtable*, the ⟨s⟩ saying /z/ in *rosette*, the ⟨e⟩ saying /i/ in *palette* and *redoubtable*, the ⟨ui⟩ saying /wee/ in *suite*, the silent letters in *baguette* and *silhouette*, the ⟨u⟩ and ⟨ou⟩ saying /oo/ in *brunette* and *silhouette*, and the suffix in *redoubtable*.
- It is a good idea to blend and sound out the spelling words quickly every day with the class. Where appropriate, use the *say it as it sounds* strategy, stressing,

debt
doubt
paste
baste
thyme
Thailand
yacht
subtle
rosette
palette
definite
favourite
suite
baguette
statuette
brunette
silhouette
redoubtable

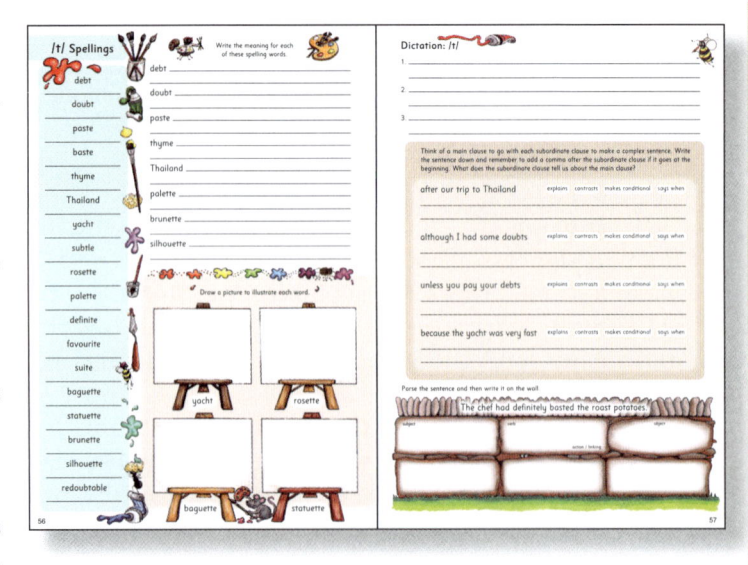

for example, the pure sound of any schwas (as in *definite*, *favourite* and *redoubtable*).

Activity Page 1
- The children split each word into syllables to help remember the spelling (debt, doubt, paste, baste, thyme, Thai/land, yacht, sub/tle, ro/sette, pal/ette, def/i/nite, fa/vour/ite, suite, ba/guette, stat/u/ette, bru/nette, sil/hou/ette, re/doubt/a/ble).
- They then write the meanings for the spelling words shown, using a dictionary if needed.
- Finally, they draw a picture for each of the words shown under the four easels.

Activity Page 2
- The children think of a main clause to go with each subordinate clause and write it down. (They should add a comma after the subordinate clause if it is at the beginning.)
- They then decide whether the subordinate clause explains or provides a contrast to the main clause, states a condition of it, or places it in a particular time (after...[says when], although...[contrasts], unless... [makes conditional], because...[explains]).
- Then they parse the sentence and complete the wall: The chef had definitely basted the roast potatoes.
Top: chef - had basted - potatoes
Bottom: The - definitely - the roast
Verb: action

Dictation
- Dictate the following sentences:

1. Granny grows mint and thyme in her herb garden.
2. The winner of the talent show got a golden statuette.
3. "Would you like a cheese and tomato baguette?" I asked.

- *Granny* is a proper noun and needs a capital letter. Remind the class to use speech marks with the correct punctuation in Sentence 3.

Grammar: Adverbials

Aim
- Introduce the term *adverbial*, which is used to describe any word, phrase or clause that acts as an adverb in a sentence. An adverbial placed at the beginning of a sentence is called a *fronted* adverbial, and it is usually separated from the rest of the sentence by a comma.

Introduction
- On the board, write the adverbs *loudly, here, today* and *sometimes* and give the class the following grammar action sequence: definite article / noun / verb / adverb. (If action cards were used in earlier lessons, they could be put on the board or held by some children).
- Using this sequence, ask the class to think of a sentence for each adverb. Possible examples are *The baby is crying loudly; The family moved here; The sale ends today; The boys argue sometimes*).
- Discuss how each adverb tells us more about how (*loudly*), where (*here*), when (*today*) or how often (*sometimes*) the verb is done. Also remind the class that some adverbs tell us how much or to what extent the verb is done, as in *The plan almost worked*.
- Discuss how most adverbs can go in several different positions, but ones like *almost* always go between the subject and verb or after the auxiliary verb (*The plan had almost worked*).
- Remind the class that some adverbs like *really, very* and *too* can also describe adverbs and adjectives.

Main Point
- With the class, parse one of the earlier sentences and put it into sentence wall boxes on the board (see pages 21 and 22): for example, The family moved here. (Top: family - moved - [blank] / Bottom: The - here - [blank]).
- Remind the children that *here* goes in the box underneath the verb because it is an adverb telling us more about where the family moved.
- Ask them what else can go in this box (prepositional phrases acting as adverbs) and replace *here* with *in a hurry* on the sentence wall. Point out that if we parsed the new sentence, we would put orange brackets around this phrase because it tells us more about how the family moved.
- Now write *The family moved because the house was too small* on the board. Identify the two clauses in this complex sentence and discuss what the subordinate clause tells us about the verb in the main clause (*it tells us why the family moved*). Put orange brackets around *because the house was too small* and write it in the box under the verb in the sentence wall.
- Explain that any word, phrase or clause that acts as an adverb in a sentence is called an **adverbial**. Adverbials tell us more about the main verb (and also sometimes about the whole sentence), such as how, where, when or why it happened.
- The most common adverbials are adverbs, noun phrases, prepositional phrases and subordinate clauses. Adverbial noun phrases express time, telling us when (*next Sunday, this month, tomorrow afternoon*), how often (*every week, each year*), or how long (*all day, the whole time*) something happens.
- Write *The family moved last week* on the board and put orange brackets around *last week*. Then put the sentence into the wall, with the noun phrase in the box under the verb.
- Tell the class that when adverbials go at the start of a sentence, they are called **fronted adverbials**, which we usually follow with a comma.

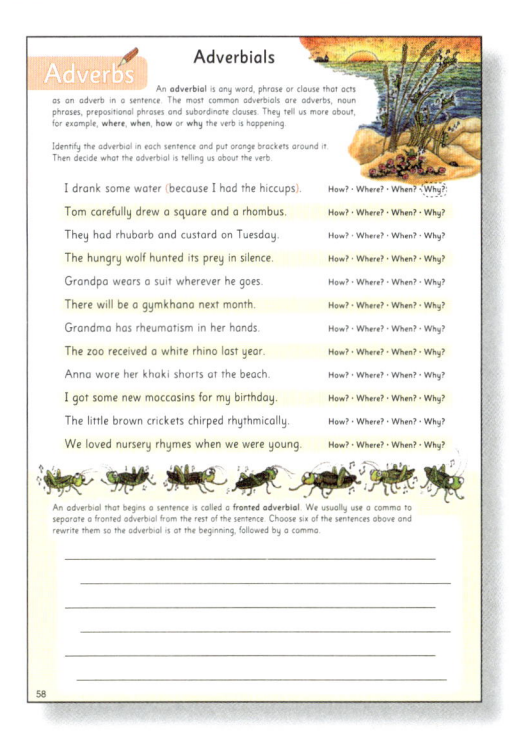

Activity Page
- The children write inside the outlined word *Adverbs*, using an orange pencil, and find the adverbial in each sentence. They put orange brackets around it and decide what it is telling them about the verb: *because I had the hiccups* (WHY); *carefully* (HOW); *on Tuesday* (WHEN); *in silence* (HOW); *wherever he goes* (WHERE); *next month* (WHEN); *in her hands* (WHERE); *last year* (WHEN); *at the beach* (WHERE); *for my birthday* (WHY); *rhythmically* (HOW); *when we were young* (WHEN).
- They then rewrite six of the sentences, so each has a fronted adverbial, followed by a comma.

Extension Activity
- Write some adverbials on the board, such as *across the room, as it was late, this morning* and *suddenly* for the children to put into sentences. Remind the children that if they use a fronted adverbial, they should separate it from the rest of the sentence with a comma.

Rounding Off
- Go over the activity page and extension activity with the children, discussing their answers.

GRAMMAR 6 PUPIL BOOK: PAGES 59 & 60

Spelling: /m/ Spellings

Spelling Test
- The children turn to the backs of their books and find the column labelled *Spelling Test 19*.
- Call out the spelling words learnt last week.

Revision
- Write the following words on the board and ask the class to identify the silent letter digraph (or trigraph) saying /t/ in each one: dou**bt**, ya**cht**, pas**te**, su**btle**, pale**tte**, sui**te**, brune**tte**, **th**yme.
- Ask the children if they can think of other words that have these spellings.

Spelling Point
- The letter ‹m› is often paired with different silent letters to make the /m/ sound. Common pairings include ‹m**b**›, ‹m**e**› and ‹m**n**›:
  – The silent letter digraphs ‹m**b**› and ‹m**e**› are found in words derived from Old and Middle English, some of which (such as *tomb* and *bomb*) go further back to Latin and Greek, as do the words ending in ‹m**n**›.
  – There is also a rarer spelling of /m/, sometimes used in British English, which is found in words like *gra***mm****e* and *progra***mm****e*. These words come from Latin and Greek via French and have kept the French spelling. They can also be spelt *gram* and *program*.

Spelling List
- Go through the list, asking the class to find and highlight the silent letter digraph saying /m/ each time. Also discuss the meaning of any unfamiliar words.
- Point out other spelling features, such as the ‹o› saying /u/ in c**o**me, s**o**me, inc**o**me, outc**o**me and honey-c**o**mb, the ‹y› saying /i/ in h**y**mn, the ‹au› spelling in **au**tumn, the silent ‹d› in han**d**some, the ‹o› saying /oo/ in t**o**mbstone and the ‹ey› saying /ee/ and ‹o› saying its long vowel sound in hon**ey**c**o**mb.
- It is a good idea to blend and sound out the spelling words quickly every day with the class. Where appropriate, use the *say it as it sounds* strategy, stressing, for example, the pure sound of any schwas (as in welc**o**me and sol**e**mn).

numb
bomb
come
some
hymn
autumn
welcome
column
dumb
solemn
condemn
gruesome
income
outcome
handsome
thumbnail
tombstone
honeycomb

Activity Page 1
- The children split each word into syllables to help remember the spelling (numb, bomb, come, some, hymn, au/tumn, wel/come, col/umn, dumb, sol/emn, con/demn, grue/some, in/come, out/come, hand/some, thumb/nail, tomb/stone, hon/ey/comb).

- They then write a sentence for each of the spelling words shown, using a dictionary to check the meaning if needed.
- Finally, they find the compound words in the spelling list *(income, outcome, thumbnail, tombstone, honeycomb)* and write three of them in the compound birds, putting the first part of the word in the bird's body and the second part in the tail. *Handsome* is not really a compound word as ‹-some› is a suffix added to words to make adjectives.

Activity Page 2
- The children think of an antonym and a synonym for each word. *(Possible answers include: pleasant, lovely / ghastly, hideous [gruesome]; trust, believe / distrust, suspect [doubt]; tiny, ordinary, unpleasant / enormous, magnificent, enjoyable [great]; unpleasant, discouraging, unpopular / pleasing, encouraging, desirable [welcome]; leave, depart, retreat / approach, arrive, reach [come]; wrong, incorrect / correct, exact [accurate]; carefree, lively / serious, stern [solemn]; ugly, hideous / attractive, gorgeous [handsome]).*
- Then they parse the sentence and complete the wall: The committee gave the musicians a courteous welcome.
  Top: committee - gave - welcome
  Bottom: The - [blank] - a courteous
  Indirect object: musicians (the)   Verb: action

Dictation
- Dictate the following sentences:

  1. The Roman temple had handsome marble columns.
  2. "Come and try some lovely honeycomb," called the lady.
  3. The gruesome monsters appeared among the tombstones.

- *Roman* is a proper adjective and needs a capital letter. Remind the class to use speech marks with the correct punctuation in Sentence 2.

Grammar: Past Participles as Adjectives

Aim
- Refine the children's knowledge of participles, and develop their awareness that past participles, like present participles, can act as adjectives in a sentence.

Introduction
- Remind the class that present participles (used in the continuous tenses) are completely regular, but past participles (used in the perfect tenses) can be regular or irregular, depending on the verb.
- If a verb is regular, its past participle is formed in the same way as the simple past tense, by adding the suffix ‹-ed›, but if the verb is irregular, the past participle can be formed in a variety of ways.
- Write the verbs *climb, paste, slip, play* and *hurry* on the board and discuss the spelling rules that are applied when making the past participles *climbed, pasted, slipped, played* and *hurried* (see page 30).
- Then look at two common patterns for irregular verbs: *ring / rang / rung* (where a change in vowel letter indicates a change in tense) and *fall / fell / fallen* (where the vowel letter changes in the past tense, but the past participle is formed by adding ‹-n› or ‹-en› to the root verb).
- Ask the class to put some of these verbs into the perfect tenses *(for example: He has climbed the mountain three times; Someone will have rung the doorbell; Several people had slipped and fallen on the ice).*

Main Point
- As well as being used in the continuous and perfect tenses, participles can also be used as adjectives.
- Call out some present participles, ask the children to put each one into a noun phrase and write them on the board *(possible examples include: a crawling crab, the missing button, an annoying whine, a burning match, their flashing swords, some floating petals, a marching band).*
- Now do the same with some past participles *(examples include: piles of fallen leaves, a worried look, the hidden cave, two sliced onions, three beaten eggs, buried treasure, some stolen cars).*
- Look at some of the examples and compare the way that present and past participles act as adjectives:
  – Present participles: When these act as adjectives, they indicate an action that is still happening or that happens regularly, so that a missing button stays missing until it is found, and a marching band usually marches along as it plays. The action described is also usually done by the head noun (the main person or thing in the phrase).
  – Past participles: These usually indicate an action that has already happened and that is often done to the head noun, so the onions have already been sliced by someone and the treasure has already been buried by somebody.
- Past and present participles also differ when they concern feelings: for example, a story might be *boring, interesting* or *frightening* and we, in turn, can be *bored, interested* or *frightened* by the story. The present participles describe the thing that makes us feel a certain way and the past participles describe the way it makes us feel.

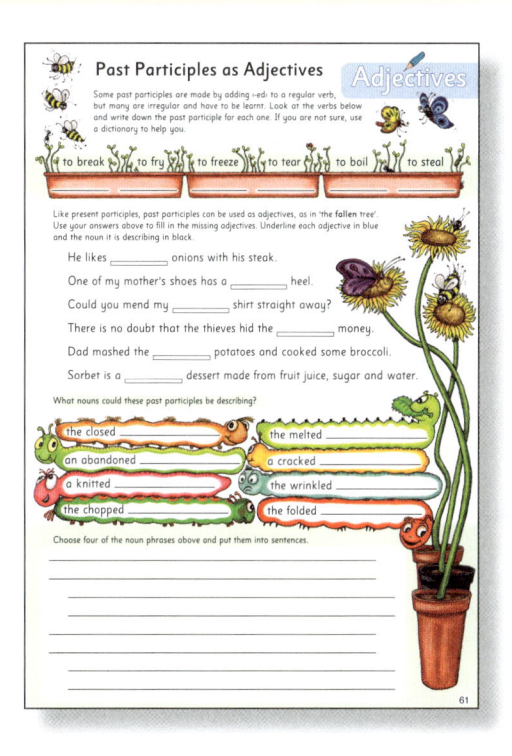

Activity Page
- The children write inside the outlined word *Adjectives*, using a blue pencil, and write down the past participles *(broken, fried, frozen, torn, boiled, stolen)*, applying the spelling rules for adding ‹-ed› and using a dictionary, if needed, to check any irregular verbs.
- Then they use the past participles to complete six sentences, deciding which adjective goes where (<u>fried</u> onions; <u>broken</u> heel; <u>torn</u> shirt; <u>stolen</u> money; <u>boiled</u> potatoes; <u>frozen</u> dessert). They should also underline these words in blue and the nouns they are describing in black.
- Finally, the children complete eight noun phrases by deciding what the past participles could be describing and expand four of them into sentences.

Extension Activity
- Write the verbs *to freeze, to boil, to beat, to fall, to tire* and *to terrify* on the board and ask the children to write down their present and past participles *(freezing / frozen; boiling / boiled; beating / beaten; falling / fallen; tiring / tired; terrifying / terrified)*. They then use them as adjectives in some noun phrases or sentences.

Rounding Off
- Go over the activity page with the children, discussing their answers.
- If they have done the extension activity, ask some children to read out their sentences or phrases.

Grammar 6 Pupil Book: Pages 62 & 63

Spelling: Silent ‹p› Digraphs

Spelling Test
- The children turn to the backs of their books and find the column labelled *Spelling Test 20*.
- Call out the spelling words learnt last week.

Revision
- Write the following words on the board and ask the class to identify the silent letter digraph saying /m/ in each one: cli**mb**, aweso**me**, hy**mn**book, beco**me**, sole**mn**ly, cru**mb**, overco**me**, co**mb**.
- Ask the children if they can think of other words that have these spellings.

Spelling Point
- Remind the class that a silent letter often goes with a particular consonant to form a silent letter digraph, such as ‹mb›, ‹wr›, ‹kn›, ‹rh›, ‹wh›, ‹sc›, ‹gn› and ‹st›.
- Sometimes, the same silent letter can be used in different digraphs: for example, silent ‹p› is often paired with ‹s›, ‹t› or ‹n› in words like **p**salm, attem**p**t and **p**neumonia. Words with these spellings are usually derived from other languages: ‹ps› and ‹pn› come from Greek, while ‹pt› comes from Latin.

Spelling List
- Go through the list, asking the class to find and highlight the silent ‹p› digraph each time. Also discuss the meaning of any unfamiliar words.
- Point out other spelling features, such as the ‹a› saying /ar/ in psalm, the ‹y› saying /ie/ and the ‹ch› spelling of /k/ in *psyche, psychiatry, psychology, psychiatrist* and *psychological,* the vowel saying its long sound in *psyche, pseudo, pneumonia, psychiatry, psychiatrist, psoriasis* and *psi*, the ‹eu› saying /ue/ in *pseudo, pneumonia, pneumatic* and *pseudonym,* the ‹e› saying /i/, soft ‹c› and ‹ei› saying /ee/ in *receipt,* the suffix in *pneumatic, psychology, psychiatrist* and *psychological,* the ‹y› saying /ee/ at the end of *psychiatry* and *psychology,* the soft ‹g› in *psychology* and *psychological,* and the ‹y› saying /i/ in *pterodactyl* and *pseudonym.*
- It is a good idea to blend and sound out the spelling words quickly every day with the class. Where appropriate, use the *say it as it sounds* strategy, stressing, for example, the pure sound of any schwas (as in *a*ttempt and psychol*o*gy).

psalm	
psyche	
pseudo	
tempt	
prompt	
attempt	
receipt	
pneumonia	
pneumatic	
psychiatry	
psychology	
pterodactyl	
psychiatrist	
pseudonym	
ptarmigan	
psoriasis	
psi	
psychological	

Activity Page 1
- The children split each word into syllables to help remember the spelling *(psalm, psy/che, pseu/do, tempt, prompt, at/tempt, re/ceipt, pneu/mo/ni/a, pneu/mat/ic, psy/chi/a/try, psy/chol/o/gy, pter/o/dac/tyl, psy/chi/a/trist, pseu/do/nym, ptar/mi/gan, pso/ri/a/sis, psi, psy/cho/log/i/cal).*
- They then put the spelling words into alphabetical order (1. attempt, 2. pneumatic, 3. pneumonia, 4. prompt, 5. psalm, 6. pseudo, 7. pseudonym, 8. psi, 9. psoriasis, 10. psyche, 11. psychiatrist, 12. psychiatry, 13. psychological, 14. psychology, 15. ptarmigan, 16. pterodactyl, 17. receipt, 18. tempt).

Activity Page 2
- The children look up the word *psychological* in the dictionary to check its meaning and make as many other words as they can with its letters.
- Then they parse the sentence and complete the wall: The psoriasis (on the patient's arm) looked rather sore.
Top: psoriasis - looked \ sore (rather) - [blank]
Bottom: The / on the patient's arm - [blank] - [blank]
Verb: linking
  – The prepositional phrase *on the patient's arm* describes the psoriasis, so it needs blue brackets.
  – The verb *looked* links the adjective complement *sore* to the subject *psoriasis* it is describing.

Dictation
- Dictate the following sentences:

  1. "A psalm is a hymn of praise," explained Miss Beech.
  2. The psychiatrist will attempt some psychological tests.
  3. The doctor had some doubts that the man had pneumonia.

- Remind the class to use speech marks with the correct punctuation in Sentence 1. *Miss Beech* is a proper noun and needs initial capital letters.

Grammar: The Active and Passive Voice

Aim
- Introduce the idea that a sentence can be written in either an active or a passive voice. When the subject of the sentence **does** the verb action, we are writing in the active voice, but if the subject **receives** the verb action, we are writing in the passive voice.

Introduction
- Remind the class that a sentence always has a verb and subject and, if the verb is transitive, it will also have an object.
- Discuss how the subject and object are identified by deciding who or what is **doing** the verb action *(the subject)* and who or what is **receiving** it *(the object)*.
- Point out that sometimes the subject or object is compound, and that most simple subjects and objects are part of a longer noun phrase.
- Also remind the class that the verb action has either a direct or an indirect effect on an object: the person or thing receiving the verb action is called the **direct object** and the person or thing for whom or to whom the verb action is done is called the **indirect object**.
- Write on the board *Granny and Grandpa sent their eldest grandchildren cards and presents* and discuss it with the class. Point out:
  - the transitive verb *sent,*
  - the compound subjects *(Granny/Grandpa),*
  - the compound direct objects *(cards/presents),* and
  - the indirect object *(grandchildren),* which is part of a longer noun phrase *(their eldest grandchildren).*

Main Point
- Not all sentences have a subject that performs the verb action. Sometimes the *doer* of the verb is not known, or is considered less important, so the focus is put on the person or thing that receives the verb action instead.
- Write on the board *The cars were stolen by the thieves last night* and ask the children to find the subject of the sentence. They will probably identify it correctly, because *cars* appears before the verb and is the main focus of the sentence.
- However, they may also recognise that this subject is unusual, because it is not doing the stealing. Instead, the *doer* or *agent* of the verb action appears in the prepositional phrase *by the thieves,* which comes after the verb. In fact, this phrase could be removed and the sentence would still make sense.
- Explain that when the subject of a sentence is actively doing the verb, we say it is written in the **active voice**, but when the subject is passive and receives the verb action, it is written in the **passive voice**.
- Write some more examples on the board, such as *The thieves have been arrested; Our bikes are kept in the garage; The cake was baked by Sue yesterday;* and *The fence will be painted today,* and identify the verb and subject each time, along with the agent, if there is one.

- Look at the verb in each sentence and point out that it is formed in a special way in the passive voice, using the verb *to be* as an auxiliary with the past participle of the main verb.

Activity Page
- The children look at each pair of sentences, deciding which is written in the active voice and which is written in the passive (*yacht was sailed* PASSIVE/ *crew sailed* ACTIVE; *Bees store* ACTIVE/*Honey is stored* PASSIVE; *We welcomed* ACTIVE/*guests were welcomed* PASSIVE; *seeds will be planted* PASSIVE/*gardener will plant* ACTIVE).
- They then look at each sentence below, identify the verb and subject, and decide whether it is written in the active or passive voice (*hymn was sung* PASSIVE; *Sam bruised* ACTIVE; *Rhinos come* ACTIVE; *chicken was basted* PASSIVE; *leaves fell* ACTIVE; *rosette was awarded* PASSIVE; *toothpaste is kept* PASSIVE; *Lucy went* ACTIVE; *baguettes are made* PASSIVE; *Granny gave* ACTIVE).

Extension Activity
- On a seperate sheet of paper, the children put some passive sentences from the activity page into six sentence wall boxes: for example, *The* yacht was sailed (by the crew). *(Top: yacht - was sailed - [blank] / Bottom: The - by the crew - [blank]).*

Rounding Off
- Go over the activity page with the children, discussing their answers.
- If they have done the extension activity, make sure the children have filled in the six boxes correctly.

Spelling: ⟨ui⟩ and ⟨u⟩ for the /i/ Sound

Spelling Test
- The children turn to the backs of their books and find the column labelled *Spelling Test 21*.
- Call out the spelling words learnt last week.

Revision
- Write the following words on the board and ask the class to identify the silent ⟨p⟩ digraph in each one: **p**neumonia, **p**salm, recei**p**t, **p**syche, prom**p**t, **p**neumatic, **p**seudo, **p**tarmigan.
- Ask the children if they can think of other words that have a silent ⟨p⟩ digraph.

Spelling Point
- The short vowel sound /i/ is usually represented by the letter ⟨i⟩, although sometimes it is spelt ⟨y⟩ (as in *hymn* and *rhythm*) and occasionally ⟨e⟩ (as in *pretty* and *English*).
- There are two less common spellings: ⟨u⟩, as in *busy*, and – as a silent letter digraph – ⟨ui⟩, as in b**ui**lding. These spellings are usually found in words originating from Old English, such as *busy* and *build,* or Middle English (via Old French and based on Latin), such as *biscuit, lettuce, minute* and *circuit*. The word *cuisine* is borrowed directly from French and so the ⟨u⟩ is not silent, but rather makes a /w/ sound, followed by the /i/.

Spelling List
- Go through the list, asking the class to find and highlight the ⟨ui⟩ or ⟨u⟩ saying /i/ each time. Also discuss the meaning of any unfamiliar words.
- Point out other spelling features, such as the ⟨s⟩ saying /z/ in *busy, busily, cuisine, business, busybody* and *businesslike*, the ⟨y⟩ saying /ee/ in *busy, busily, busybody* and *bodybuilder*, the suffix in *busi**ly**, (body)build**er**, (out)build**ing*** and *busin**ess** (**like**)*, the prefix in **re**built, the soft ⟨c⟩ in *lettuce* and *circuit*, the ⟨te⟩ saying /t/ in *minute*, the ⟨i⟩ saying /ee/ and ⟨ne⟩ saying /n/ in *cuisine*, the silent ⟨i⟩ in *business(like)*, the compound words *built-in* (with its hyphen), *busybody, outbuilding* and *bodybuilder*, and the ⟨ir⟩ spelling of /er/ in *circuit*.
- It is a good idea to blend and sound out the spelling words quickly every day with the class. Where appropriate, use the *say it as it sounds* strategy, stressing, for example, the pure sound of any schwas (as in *business*).

build
built
busy
busily
biscuit
rebuilt
lettuce
minute
builder
building
cuisine
business
built-in
circuit
busybody
businesslike
outbuilding
bodybuilder

Activity Page 1
- The children split each word into syllables to help remember the spelling (*build, built, bus/y, bus/i/ly, bis/cuit, re/built, let/tuce, min/ute, build/er, build/ing, cui/sine, busi/ness, built-/in, cir/cuit, bus/y/bod/y, busi/ness/like, out/build/ing, bod/y/build/er*).
- They then find the eighteen spelling words in the word search.
- Finally, the children identify the four spelling words that are in the same word family as *busy* (*busily, business, busybody, businesslike*).

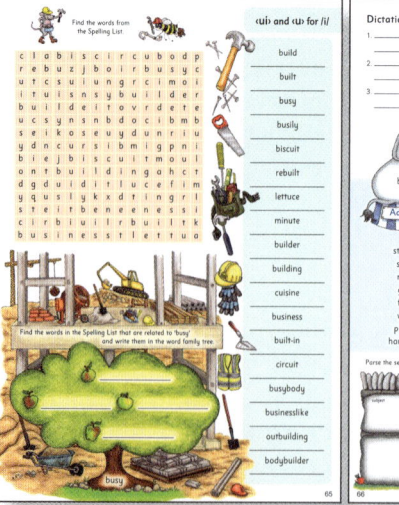

Activity Page 2
- The children look at the adjective *busy* and write its comparative *(busier)* and superlative *(busiest)* in the elephants. They then write the comparative and the superlative for each of the other adjectives (*straighter/straightest, subtler/subtlest, number/numbest, greater/greatest, feistier/feistiest, weirder/weirdest, prompter/promptest, handsomer/handsomest*).
- Then they parse the sentence and complete the wall: The ancient buildings were built (in the twelfth century).
Top: buildings - were built - [blank]
Bottom: The ancient - in the twelfth century - [blank]
Verb: passive
  – The passive verb uses the auxiliary *were* with the irregular past participle *built*.
  – The prepositional phrase *in the twelfth century* is acting as an adverb, so it needs orange brackets.

Dictation
- Dictate the following sentences:

  1. The rabbit was busily munching a juicy lettuce.
  2. The bodybuilder was flexing his huge muscles.
  3. "The biscuits will be ready in five minutes," said Dad.

- Remind the class to use speech marks with the correct punctuation in Sentence 3. *Dad* is a proper noun and needs a capital letter.

Grammar: The Passive Voice

Aim
- Reinforce the children's understanding of sentences that are written in the passive voice, and develop their ability to rewrite them in the active voice, turning the agent back into the subject.

Introduction
- Remind the children that not all sentences are written in the active voice (when the subject is **doing** the verb action); sometimes, the subject is the person or thing who **receives** the verb action, and this is called the passive voice.
- Write on the board, *Granny's lettuces are being eaten by a rabbit* and discuss whether it is written in the active or passive voice:
  – The subject *lettuces* **receives** the action of the verb *to eat*.
  – The actual *doer* of the verb *(rabbit)* appears as an agent in a prepositional phrase.
  – The verb has an auxiliary *(are being,* which is the present continuous of the verb *to be)* followed by the past participle *eaten*.
  All this tells us that it is written in the **passive** voice.
- Discuss how writing it in the passive voice has put the main focus on the lettuces, rather than the rabbit, and remind the class that sometimes we do not know who is performing the action of the verb or might consider the information less important or even irrelevant.
- Underline the verb *(are being eaten)* in red, and draw boxes around the subject *lettuces* and agent *rabbit*, with a small ‹s› and ‹a› in the corner, respectively.

Main Point
- We usually use the active voice in our writing as it is generally considered to have a more direct and powerful effect on the reader. However, there are times when the passive is more appropriate, so the children have to be able to write in both voices.
- Ask the children how they would write the sentence on the board in the active voice. Remind them that, in the active voice, the subject of the verb is the *doer* of the verb action, so they must turn the agent *rabbit* back into the subject.
- Write *A rabbit* on the board and then ask the children what form of the verb *to eat* should follow. Explain that they need to use the same tense in the active as in the passive, and must make sure that the verb agrees with the subject.
- Remind the children that the verb *to be* is in the present continuous and ask them what the present continuous of *to eat* is *(am/are/is eating)*. As the subject is *rabbit,* the verb that follows must be in the third person singular, so add *is eating* to the board, along with *Granny's lettuces,* to make the sentence *A rabbit is eating Granny's lettuces.*
- Compare the two sentences and ask what role *lettuces* plays in both sentences *(it is the subject in the passive voice and the direct object in the active voice).* Point out that the auxiliary verb *to be* is in the third person plural in the passive, but that it is in the third person singular in the active.

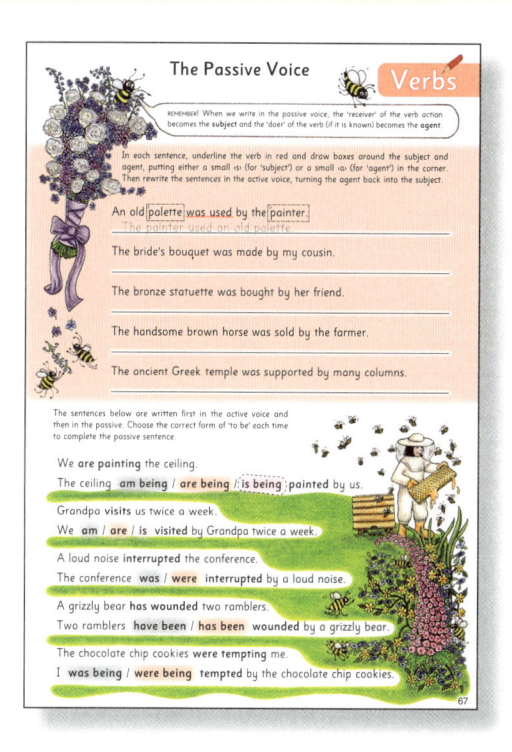

Activity Page
- The children write inside the outlined word *Verbs* in red and then look at the sentences, identifying the subject, verb and agent in each one. They underline the verb in red and draw a box around the subject and agent, with either a small ‹s› or ‹a› in the corner *(palette / was used / painter; bouquet / was made / cousin; statuette / was bought / friend; horse / was sold / farmer; temple / was supported / columns).*
- They then rewrite the sentences in the active voice *(The painter used an old palette; My cousin made the bride's bouquet; Her friend bought the bronze statuette; The farmer sold the handsome brown horse; Many columns supported the ancient Greek temple).*
- Lastly, the children identify the correct form of the auxiliary verb *to be* to complete each sentence *(<u>is being</u> painted; <u>are</u> visited; <u>was</u> interrupted; <u>have been</u> wounded; <u>was being</u> tempted).*

Extension Activity
- On a seperate sheet of paper, the children put some passive sentences from the activity page into six sentence wall boxes: for example, An old palette was used (by the painter). *(Top: palette - was used - [blank] / Bottom: An old - by the painter - [blank]).*

Rounding Off
- Go over the activity page with the children, discussing their answers.
- If they have done the extension activity, ask the children to write some of their answers on the board.

GRAMMAR 6 PUPIL BOOK: PAGES 68 & 69

Spelling: ⟨gh⟩, ⟨gue⟩

Spelling Test
- The children turn to the backs of their books and find the column labelled *Spelling Test 22*.
- Call out the spelling words learnt last week.

Revision
- Write the following words on the board and ask the class to identify the ⟨u⟩ or silent letter digraph saying /i/ in each one: b*u*sy, bisc*ui*t, min*u*te, b*ui*lder, lett*u*ce, circ*ui*t, b*u*siness, c*ui*sine. (As *cuisine* is borrowed directly from French, the ⟨u⟩ is not silent, but says /w/).
- Ask the children if they can think of other words with these spellings for /i/.

Spelling Point
- The ⟨gh⟩ spelling is used in several ways in English:
  – It is found in some vowel-sound spellings, as in h*igh*, h*eigh*t, *eigh*t, c*augh*t and b*ough*t (the other pronunciations of ⟨ough⟩ are taught shortly on page 84).
  – It also says /f/ in words like *tough* and *laugh*.
  – As a silent ⟨h⟩ digraph it says /g/ in words like *ghost*. Words with this silent letter digraph are often Germanic in origin, although *spaghetti* is borrowed from Italian, *ghoul* comes from Arabic and *dinghy* is from Hindi.
- As well as ⟨g⟩ and ⟨gh⟩, another spelling of the /g/ sound is ⟨gue⟩, as in *vague* and *intrigue*, although ⟨gue⟩ also makes the /ng/ sound when it is preceded by ⟨n⟩, as in *meringue*. This spelling is usually found in words that come from Latin via French, except for *tongue*, which is Germanic in origin.

Spelling List
- Go through the list, asking the class to find and highlight the ⟨gh⟩ or ⟨gue⟩ spelling each time. Also discuss the meaning of any unfamiliar words.
- Point out other spelling features, such as the way the ⟨g⟩ in *dinghy* helps say /ng/, but sometimes also makes its own sound (depending on how it is said), the ⟨y⟩ saying /ee/ at the end of *dinghy, ghastly* and *ghoulishly,* the vowel saying its long sound in *rogue, plague, vague, ghostwriter, dialogue* and *prologue,* the ⟨ea⟩ in *league* and *colleague,* the suffix in *ghastly, ghostwriter* and *ghoulishly,* the ⟨i⟩ saying /a/ in *meringue,* the ⟨i⟩ saying /ee/ in *intrigue, fatigue* and *spaghetti,* the ⟨o⟩ saying /u/ in *tongue,* the silent letter digraph in *ghostwriter,* and the ⟨ou⟩ saying /oo/ in *ghoulishly.*
- It is a good idea to blend and sound out the spelling words quickly every day with the class. Where appropriate, use the *say it as it sounds* strategy, stressing,

dinghy
rogue
plague
vague
league
ghastly
meringue
intrigue
tongue
fatigue
spaghetti
ghostwriter
colleague
dialogue
prologue
epilogue
harangue
ghoulishly

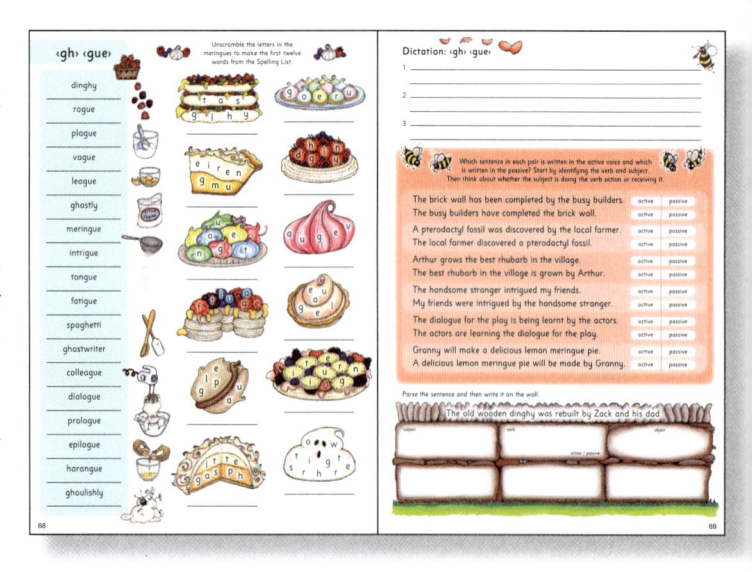

for example, the pure sound of any schwas (as in *meringue* and *fatigue*).

Activity Page 1
- The children split each word into syllables to help remember the spelling *(din/ghy, rogue, plague, vague, league, ghast/ly, me/ringue, in/trigue, tongue, fa/tigue, spa/ghet/ti, ghost/writ/er, col/league, di/a/logue, pro/logue, ep/i/logue, ha/rangue, ghoul/ish/ly)*.
- They then unscramble the letters in the meringues to make the first twelve spelling words *(ghastly, rogue, meringue, dinghy, tongue, vague, fatigue, league, plague, intrigue, spaghetti, ghostwriter)*.

Activity Page 2
- In each sentence, the children identify the verb and subject and then decide whether it is written in the active or passive voice *(brick wall: passive/active; pterodactyl: passive/active; rhubarb: active/passive; stranger: active/passive; dialogue: passive/active; pie: active/passive)*.
- Then they parse the sentence and complete the wall: The old wooden dinghy was rebuilt (by Zac and his dad).
Top: dinghy - was rebuilt - [blank]
Bottom: The old wooden - by Zac and his dad - [blank]
Verb: passive
  – The passive verb uses the auxiliary *was* with the irregular past participle *rebuilt*.

Dictation
- Dictate the following sentences:

1. Spaghetti is an extremely popular pasta in Italian cuisine.
2. "A good meringue should melt on the tongue," said the chef.
3. The ghostwriter added a prologue and an epilogue to the story.

- Remind the class to use speech marks with the correct punctuation in Sentence 2. *Italian* is a proper adjective and needs a capital letter.

Grammar: Gerunds

Aim
- Introduce gerunds, which are a special kind of noun, made by adding ‹-ing› to a verb. Rather than people or objects, gerunds name activities like *reading* or *camping*, and they function like other nouns in a sentence, acting as the subject, object or complement, for example.

Introduction
- Remind the class that the suffix ‹-ing› is added to verbs to make the present participle.
- Call out the verbs *to fish, to skate, to lie, to jog, to cry* and *to sway* and ask the children to use the present participle of each one in a sentence.
- Write their suggestions on the board, revising the spelling rules applied to make *fishing, skating, lying, jogging, crying* and *swaying* (see page 30).
- Then discuss whether the participle is being used, along with the auxiliary *to be,* to form the continuous tenses (as in *The children were fishing on the lake*), or whether it is acting as an adjective (as in *the swaying branches of the tree*).

Main Point
- Now write on the board the sentence *They were enjoying the singing*. Identify the ‹-ing› words, *enjoying* and *singing*, and discuss what each word is doing in the sentence.
- The children should be able to identify *enjoying* as the present participle used with the auxiliary *were* to form the past continuous of the verb *to enjoy*. However, the word *singing* is not a participle, as it is not acting as a verb or as an adjective.
- Ask the children *Who or what were enjoying the singing?* to find the subject of the sentence *(They)* and *They were enjoying what?* to find the direct object of the sentence *(the singing)*.
- Remind the children that the object of a sentence is usually a noun or pronoun and that words that can have *the* in front of them are usually nouns, so *singing* in this sentence is acting as a noun.
- Explain that nouns that are formed in this way are called *gerunds* and instead of naming people or objects, they name activities.
- Gerunds act in the same way as other nouns in a sentence, so they can be the subject or object of a sentence, or a subject complement following a linking verb, for example. Write the following sentences on the board and ask the children what role the gerund is playing in each one:
  - Smiling makes me happy *(subject)*
  - We love jogging *(object)*
  - My best subject is reading *(complement)*
- Also point out that a gerund, like other nouns, can be used with adjectives, including articles and other determiners, to make a noun phrase, such as *her baby's loud crying*, or *the rhythmic swaying of the branches*.

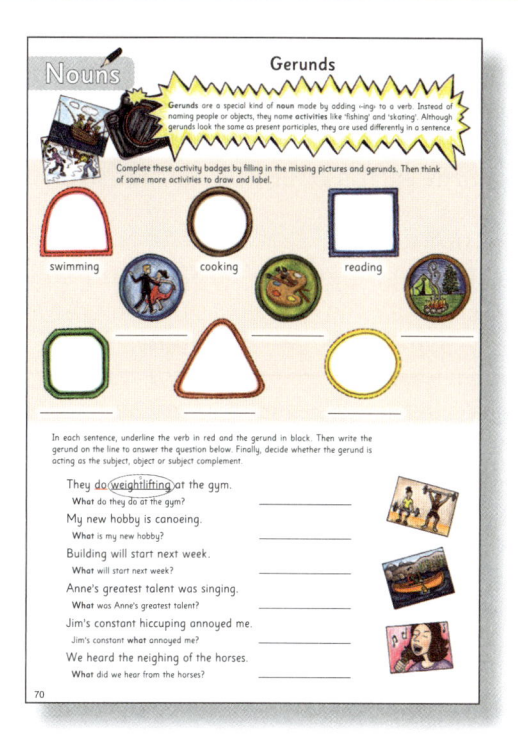

- Gerunds can also be used in gerund phrases, where the whole phrase acts, for example, as the subject, object or complement, as in *Learning to swim is an important skill; I like playing the guitar;* or *Her new pastime is collecting stamps;* however, the children can learn more about this when they are older.

Activity Page
- The children write inside the outlined word *Nouns*, using a black pencil.
- Then they complete the activity badges by drawing pictures to represent the gerunds *swimming, cooking* and *reading;* by labelling the middle badges correctly *(dancing, painting, camping);* and by choosing three other activities to label and illustrate.
- They then read the sentences and underline each verb in red and gerund in black, before answering each question and deciding whether the gerund is acting as a subject, object or complement *(do weightlifting OBJECT; is canoeing COMPLEMENT; Building will start SUBJECT; was singing COMPLEMENT; hiccuping annoyed SUBJECT; heard neighing OBJECT)*.

Extension Activity
- Write the following verbs on the board and ask the children to make some of them into gerunds and use them in a sentence: *to walk, to bake, to dig, to fly, to draw, to drive, to knit, to study, to sail, to hike, to run, to play, to work, to race, to chat, to bully.*

Rounding Off
- Go over the activity page with the children, discussing their answers.
- If they have done the extension activity, ask some of the children to read out their sentences.

GRAMMAR 6 PUPIL BOOK: PAGES 71 & 72

Spelling: ‹gu›

Spelling Test
- The children turn to the backs of their books and find the column labelled *Spelling Test 23*.
- Call out the spelling words learnt last week.

Revision
- Write the following words on the board and ask the class to identify the ‹gh› or ‹gue› spelling in each one: din**gh**y, va**gue**, spa**gh**etti, lea**gue**, **gh**ost, ton**gue**, **gh**oul, merin**gue**.
- Discuss whether the spellings say /g/ or /ng/ in each one (if either spelling follows ‹n›, it usually says /ng/).
- Ask the children if they can think of other words with these spellings.

Spelling Point
- As well as ‹g› and ‹gh›, another spelling of the /g/ sound is the silent letter digraph ‹gu›, which is found in words like **gu**ide and **gu**ess.
- Write the above examples on the board and explain that words with this spelling originate from different languages, but usually come via Old or Middle English, when the ‹u› was added.
- Now write *penguin* and *language* on the board and ask what sound(s) ‹gu› is making now. In words like this, the ‹gu› says /gw/, which often reflects the pronunciation of the original word from which it is derived.
- In the middle six words of the spelling list – *language, penguin, iguana, anguish, extinguish* and *distinguished* – ‹gu› says /gw/.

Spelling List
- Go through the list, asking the class to find and highlight the ‹gu› spelling each time. Also discuss the meaning of any unfamiliar words.
- Point out other spelling features, such as the double ‹s› after the short, stressed vowel in *guess*, the way the ‹g› in *language, penguin, anguish, extinguish* and *distinguished* helps say /ng/ as well as making its own sound, the ‹age› saying /ij/ at the end of *language*, the ‹e› saying /i/ in *extinguish* and *beguile*, the ‹ed› saying /t/ in *distinguished*, the ‹ee› in *guarantee*, the compound word *lifeguard*, the ‹s› saying first /s/ and then /z/ in *disguise* and the ‹i_e› saying /ee/ in *guillotine*.
- It is a good idea to blend and sound out the spelling words quickly every day with the class. Where appropriate, use the *say it as it sounds* strategy, stressing, for example, the pure sound of any schwas (as in *igua**n**a, guara**n**tee, guard**i**an* and *guill**o**tine*).

guide
guard
guess
guest
guilt
guitar
language
penguin
iguana
anguish
extinguish
distinguished
guarantee
lifeguard
disguise
beguile
guardian
guillotine

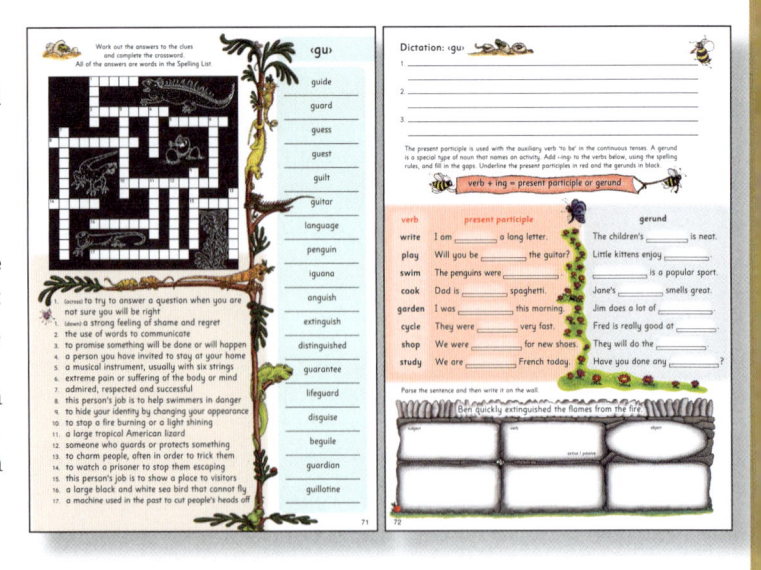

Activity Page 1
- The children split each word into syllables to help remember the spelling (*guide, guard, guess, guest, guilt, gui/tar, lan/guage, pen/guin, i/gua/na, an/guish, ex/tin/guish, dis/tin/guished, guar/an/tee, life/guard, dis/guise, be/guile, guard/i/an, guil/lo/tine*).
- They then work out the answers to the crossword clues and write them in (1. *guess* (across) *guilt* (down), 2. *language*, 3. *guarantee*, 4. *guest*, 5. *guitar*, 6. *anguish*, 7. *distinguished*, 8. *lifeguard*, 9. *disguise*, 10. *extinguish*, 11. *iguana*, 12. *guardian*, 13. *beguile*, 14. *guard*, 15. *guide*, 16. *penguin*, 17. *guillotine*).

Activity Page 2
- The children add ‹-ing› to each verb, using the spelling rules. They then write in the missing word in each pair of sentences, underlining it in red when it is a present participle and in black when it is a gerund (*writing, playing, swimming, cooking, gardening, cycling, shopping, studying*).
- Then they parse the sentence and complete the wall:
Ben quickly extinguished the flames (from the fire).
Top: Ben - extinguished - flames
Bottom: [blank] - quickly - the / from the fire
Verb: active
  – The adverb *quickly* is made by adding ‹-ly› to the adjective *quick*.
  – The prepositional phrase *from the fire* describes the flames, so it needs blue brackets.

Dictation
- Dictate the following sentences:

1. "Welcome!" exclaimed Miss Beech to her guests.
2. The ghastly rogue was cleverly disguised as a guard.
3. The children saw the penguins and iguanas at the zoo.

- Remind the class to use speech marks with the correct punctuation in Sentence 1. *Miss Beech* is a proper noun and needs initial capital letters.

Grammar: Idioms

Aim
- Introduce idioms, which are common expressions that have a special meaning that is not conveyed by the actual words used (so they have a *figurative* meaning that is different to the *literal* meaning). Idioms help us to describe events vividly and are especially used in stories and speech.

Introduction
- Briefly revise sentences and phrases:
  - A sentence must make sense, start with a capital letter, contain a subject and verb, and end in a full stop, question mark or exclamation mark.
  - When a group of words makes sense but has no verb and subject, it is called a phrase.
- Ask the children what kinds of phrases they know *(noun phrases* and *prepositional phrases):*
  - Noun phrases consist of a main (or *head*) noun, together with all the words that describe it. They often represent the 'complete' subject or object of a sentence, as in <u>The big blue ball</u> landed in the muddy puddle or they can be part of a prepositional phrase, like *in* <u>the muddy puddle</u>.
  - Prepositional phrases often act as adverbs in a sentence (in the example above, the phrase tells us **where** the ball landed) but they can also be used as adjectives in bigger noun phrases, such as *the dog* <u>with the long tail</u>.
- Ask the children to suggest some more phrases and then put them into sentences.

Main Point
- Now write the phrase *at the drop of a hat* on the board and ask the children what they notice about it.
- They may recognise that this long prepositional phrase is made up of two smaller prepositional phrases *(at the drop/of a hat)*, but they may also notice that it is not like the other phrases discussed so far.
- Ask them to put it into a sentence, such as *Dan is happy to go swimming at the drop of a hat,* and discuss what the phrase actually means: Is Dan waiting for someone to drop a hat before he can go swimming? No, Dan loves swimming so much that he will go immediately, given the chance.
- Explain that there are many phrases or expressions like this in English that are used to describe something in a lively, vivid way. They are called *idioms* and are usually old sayings with meanings that have become less obvious over time *(at the drop of a hat,* for example, probably comes from the time when a hat was used to signal the start of a fight or race).
- Call out some more examples that the children will know, or ask them to suggest some examples of their own. Discuss them with the class, comparing what the words actually say with what the idioms really mean.
- Draw a picture on the board, showing the literal meaning of an idiom and see if the class can guess which expression it represents. Then ask some children to come and draw pictures of their own on the board for the rest of the class to guess.
- There are many examples of idioms, including *a pain in the neck; a tall story; to beat about the bush; by the skin of your teeth; to cost an arm and a leg; down in the dumps; to get cold feet; to have a bee in your bonnet; in a nutshell; in the doghouse; to kick the bucket; to lend a hand; to play it by ear; to pull your leg; to rain cats and dogs; to rock the boat.*

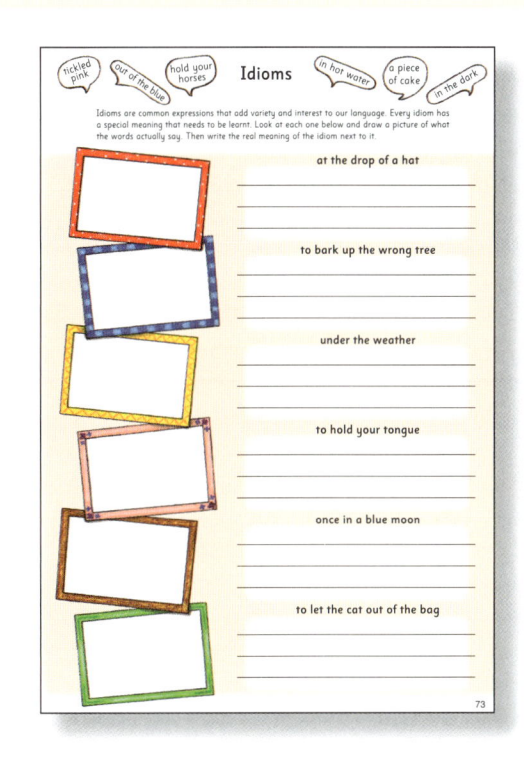

Activity Page
- The children read each idiom, draw a picture of what the words actually say, and then write the real meaning next to it. Answers should indicate the following meanings in the children's own words *(at the drop of a hat: immediately/without delay; to bark up the wrong tree: to be mistaken; under the weather: unwell/ill/sick; to hold your tongue: to keep quiet; once in a blue moon: very rarely/not very often; to let the cat out of the bag: to reveal someone's secret).*

Extension Activity
- The children think of some idioms and draw the literal meanings on a separate sheet of paper. They then swap with a partner, who has to guess which idioms the pictures represent.
- The children should also be encouraged to start collecting idioms in their Spelling Word Books or to create a class book of illustrated idioms.

Rounding Off
- Go over the activity page with the children, discussing their answers.
- If they have done the extension activity, show the class some pictures and see if they can guess the idioms.

Spelling: ‹ough›

Spelling Test
- The children turn to the backs of their books and find the column labelled *Spelling Test 24*.
- Call out the spelling words learnt last week.

Revision
- Revise the spelling rule: **If you want to say /ee/, it's ‹i› before ‹e›, except after ‹c›.** Write these words on the board and ask the class whether ‹ei› or ‹ie› is needed each time: shr(ie)k, n(ie)ce, rec(ei)ve, f(ie)nd, ach(ie)ve, conc(ei)ted, handkerch(ie)f, perc(ei)ve.

Spelling Point
- Recently (see page 80), the children were reminded that ‹gh› is used in several spelling patterns, either to represent the consonant sound /f/ in words like *rough* and *laughter* or /g/ in *yoghurt*, or as part of a vowel spelling in words like l<u>igh</u>t, h<u>eigh</u>t, w<u>eigh</u>, d<u>augh</u>ter and t<u>hough</u>t.
- Write *rough* and *thought* on the board and point out how the ‹ough› says /uff/ in the first word and /or/ in the second. Explain that there are several other ways ‹ough› can be pronounced, including:
  – /ou/ (as in *bough*),
  – the schwa (as in *thorough*),
  – /oa/ (as in *dough*),
  – /off/ (as in *cough*) and
  – /oo/ (as in *through*).
  It can even say /up/ in *hiccough*, the alternative spelling of *hiccup*.
- There are no rules to help us work out when these spellings are used, so they have to be learnt, but there are only a limited number of common words that use it for each of these sounds. This is why, when mastered, they can be remembered as **oh you get happy** words!

Spelling List
- Go through the list, asking the class to find and highlight ‹ough› each time. As they do so, the children should say the sound that ‹ough› is making. Also discuss the meaning of any unfamiliar words.
- Point out other spelling features, such as the different spellings of /c/ in *cough* and *breakthrough* the ‹e› saying /i/ in *enough*, the alternative spelling in *although* and *breakthrough* (and the way the ‹l› in *although* also says its own sound), the compound words *doughnut, throughout, overwrought, breakthrough* and *afterthought* and the silent letter digraph in *over<u>w</u>rought*.
- It is a good idea to blend and sound out the spelling words quickly every day with the class. Where appropriate, use the *say it*

cough
dough
bough
rough
tough
bought
though
through
enough
drought
although
doughnut
sought
thorough
throughout
overwrought
breakthrough
afterthought

as it sounds strategy, stressing, for example, the pure sound of any schwas (as in *th<u>o</u>rough*).

Activity Page 1
- The children split each word into syllables to help remember the spelling (*cough, dough, bough, rough, tough, bought, though, through, e/nough, drought, al/though, dough/nut, sought, thor/ough, through/out, o/ver/wrought, break/through, af/ter/thought*).
- They then write them in the nests, grouped by sound (/ou/: *bough, drought*; /uff/: *rough, tough, enough*; /or/: *bought, sought, overwrought, afterthought*; /oa/ or schwa: *dough, though, although, doughnut/thorough*; /off/: *cough*; /oo/: *through, throughout, breakthrough*).
- Then they write the present tense (*buy, bring, fight, seek, think*) for each of the tricky past tenses shown on the tree.

Activity Page 2
- The children write the meanings for each pair of homophones, using a dictionary to help them if needed.
- Then they parse the sentence and complete the wall:
  The thoughtless man coughed loudly (throughout the play).
  Top: man - coughed - [blank]
  Bottom: The thoughtless - loudly/throughout the play - [blank]
  Verb: active
  – The adverb *loudly* is made by adding ‹-ly› to the adjective *loud*.
  – The prepositional phrase *throughout the play* is acting as an adverb, so it needs orange brackets.

Dictation
- Dictate the following sentences:

  1. The drought has damaged the bough of the tree.
  2. "Have we bought enough doughnuts?" asked Dad.
  3. The scientists will make a breakthrough very soon.

- Remind the class to use speech marks with the correct punctuation in Sentence 2. *Dad* is a proper noun and needs a capital letter.

GRAMMAR 6 PUPIL BOOK: PAGE 76

Grammar: Irregular Verb 'To Do'

Aim
- Ensure the children can conjugate the irregular verb *to do* in the past, present and future tenses (simple, continuous and perfect), and develop their understanding of how it can be used as a main verb.

Introduction
- Remind the class that some verbs do not form the past tense and past participle by adding ‹-ed› to the root. Such verbs are irregular or *tricky* and have to be learnt.
- The verb *to do* is one of these verbs: it has the tricky past *did*; its past participle is *done;* and the third person singular in the simple present tense – *does* – has the ‹-es› suffix rather than ‹-s›.
- Draw a simple grid of nine boxes on the board, fill in the tenses with the class (as shown on the activity page), and discuss how each one is formed (see pages 10 and 11), pointing out the regular and irregular parts.
- The children need to be able to conjugate *to do* properly, as – like *to be* and *to have* – it is one of the most commonly used verbs in English, both as a main verb and as an auxiliary.
- Unlike *to be* and *to have*, however, the auxiliary is not used to form tenses, but to add emphasis to a sentence, to make it negative, or to form a question, and the children learn more about this in the following two lessons.

Main Point
- The verb *to do* has a number of meanings, mostly related to:
  – The idea of performing or taking part in an action (*What are you doing?*)
  – Achieving/completing an activity or task (*I did... the crossword/my homework/some drawing/the ironing*)
  – Studying (*We do French at school*)
  – Inquiring about someone's job (*What does Anna do?*)
- Often it is used instead of another verb, particularly when the action described is obvious or routine, or when it includes several different tasks. For example, we can say that we *do* our teeth and hair in the morning instead of using the verbs *clean* and *brush,* or we will often say that we *did* the gardening or cleaning, meaning that we undertook various activities like digging, weeding, mowing the lawn and watering the plants or dusting, polishing, vacuuming and tidying up.
- Point out that this list of activities is made up of gerunds (nouns formed by adding ‹-ing› to the root verb), which the children learnt about recently (see page 81); *to do* is often used with gerunds, as the verb action is already obvious from the noun itself, as in *to do the... cooking/sewing/shopping* and so on.
- Write some other *to do* phrases on the board, discuss them with the children and see if they can think of other verbs to use instead. Possible examples include the following: *to do ...the dishes (wash/clean), ...our hair (brush/tidy/style), ...their teeth (brush/clean),* ...the laundry (wash/dry/iron), ...the shopping (buy), ...breakfast/lunch/dinner (cook/make/prepare), ...sums (work out/solve), ...a cartwheel/handstand (perform), ...some damage (cause/result in).

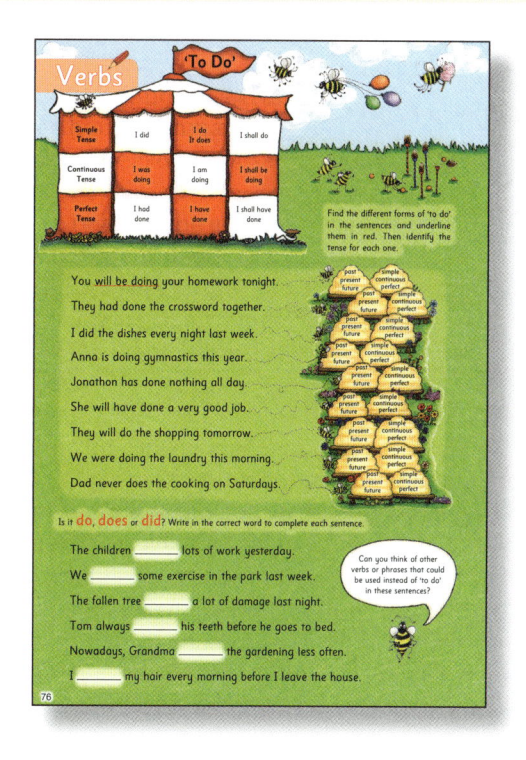

Activity Page
- The children write inside the outlined word *Verbs,* using a red pencil.
- They then find the different forms of the verb *to do* in the sentences, underline them in red and identify the tense used each time (*will be doing/future continuous; had done/past perfect; did/simple past; is doing/present continuous; has done/present perfect; will have done/future perfect; will do/simple future; were doing/past continuous; does/simple present*).
- Then they complete each sentence by writing the correct form of the verb (*children did; we did; tree did; always does; Grandma does; I do*) and think about what other verbs might be used instead (for example: completed lots of work; took part in some exercise; caused a lot of damage; brushes/cleans his teeth; undertakes the gardening; brush my hair).

Extension Activity
- On a separate sheet of paper, the children rewrite some sentences from the activity page in the other eight tenses.
- Alternatively, they can create their own sentences using *to do,* swap them with a partner, and then rewrite them in the other tenses.

Rounding Off
- Go over the activity page with the children, discussing their answers.
- If they have done the extension activity, ask some of the children to read out their sentences.

85

GRAMMAR 6 PUPIL BOOK: PAGES 77 & 78

Spelling: Schwa ‹ure›

Spelling Test
- The children turn to the backs of their books and find the column labelled *Spelling Test 25*.
- Call out the spelling words learnt last week.

Revision
- Write these words on the board and ask the class to identify the sound made by ‹ough› in each one: *tough* /uff/, *cough* /off/, *drought* /ou/, *thorough* (schwa), *through* /oo/, *doughnut* /oa/, *afterthought* /or/.
- Ask the children to use one of these words in a sentence.

Spelling Point
- Revise the ‹ure› spelling, which is often preceded by ‹t› or ‹s›, but can follow other letters as well.
- Remind the class that in monosyllabic words like *pure* and *cure,* and in most words where the ‹ure› is stressed, it keeps its pure sound, /ue-r/, as in *impure, secure* and *manicure.*
- It can make other sounds too, such as a stressed /or/ in *sure* and other words in that family (for example, *unsure, ensure, insure* and *reassure*),
- More commonly, however, it is unstressed and the vowel becomes a schwa. It is often added to words as a suffix to make abstract nouns indicating action or a group (as in *failure* and *legislature*) but is also found in other types of word.

Spelling List

| picture |
| nature |
| injure |
| lecture |
| texture |
| pasture |
| sculpture |
| creature |
| stature |
| torture |
| rupture |
| cultured |
| manufacture |
| adventurer |
| procedure |
| treasurer |
| acupuncture |
| disfigurement |

- Go through the list, asking the class to find and highlight the ‹ure› spelling each time. Also discuss the meaning of any unfamiliar words.
- Point out other spelling features, such as the ‹t› saying /ch/ in *picture* and all the other ‹ture› words, the vowel saying its long sound in *nature* and *procedure,* the alternative spelling in *creature,* the /y/ sound before the schwa in *manufacture* and *acupuncture,* the ‹d› saying /j/ and soft ‹c› in *procedure,* the ‹ea› saying /e/ and ‹s› saying /zh/ in *treasurer,* the ‹n› saying /ng/ in *acupuncture* and the prefix and suffix in **dis**figure**ment**.
- It is a good idea to blend and sound out the spelling words quickly every day with the class. Where appropriate, use the *say it as it sounds* strategy, stressing, for example, the pure sound of any schwas (as in *adventur**er*** and *procedure*).

Activity Page 1
- The children split each word into syllables to help remember the spelling (*pic/ture, na/ture, in/jure, lec/ture, tex/ture, pas/ture, sculp/ture, crea/ture, stat/ure, tor/ture, rup/ture, cul/tured, man/u/fac/ture, ad/ven/tur/er, pro/ce/dure, trea/sur/er, ac/u/punc/ture, dis/fig/ure/ment*).
- They then put the spelling words into alphabetical order (*1. acupuncture, 2. adventurer, 3. creature, 4. cultured, 5. disfigurement, 6. injure, 7. lecture, 8. manufacture, 9. nature, 10. pasture, 11. picture, 12. procedure, 13. rupture, 14. sculpture, 15. stature, 16. texture, 17. torture, 18. treasurer*).

Activity Page 2
- The children decide whether each word is a noun or verb, or whether it can act as both. They then write in the correct outlined word(s), using the appropriate colour(s): black for nouns and red for verbs (*Nouns only: creature, nature, mixture, procedure; Verbs only: injure, conjure; Both: treasure, lecture, rupture, fracture, puncture*).
- Then they parse the sentence and complete the wall: Sculptures (from ancient cultures) were bought (by the museum).
Top: Sculptures - were bought - [blank]
Bottom: from ancient cultures - by the museum - [blank]
Verb: passive
  – The prepositional phrase *from ancient cultures* describes the sculptures, so it needs blue brackets.
  – The passive verb uses the auxiliary *were* with the irregular past participle *bought.*

Dictation
- Dictate the following sentences:

1. Daisy took a picture of the cows in the pasture.
2. The adventurer gave a lecture about her travels.
3. "The poor creature is badly injured!" exclaimed the vet.

- *Daisy* is a proper noun and needs a capital letter. Remind the class to use speech marks with the correct punctuation in Sentence 3.

Grammar: Using the Verb 'To Do' in Statements

Aim
- Develop the children's understanding of auxiliary verbs, which can help to emphasise a positive verb or to make it negative. If there is no auxiliary, we use the irregular verb *to do* instead, along with the infinitive form of the main verb.

Introduction
- Briefly revise sentences:
  - Remind the class that all sentences must make sense, start with a capital letter, contain a verb and subject, and end with a full stop, question mark or exclamation mark.
  - Sentences that state some information and end in a full stop are called statements.
  - Sentences that ask for more information and end in ⟨?⟩ are called questions.
  - Sentences that express something very strongly and end in ⟨!⟩ are called exclamations.
- Explain that sentences can be **positive**, expressing what **is**, or **negative**, expressing what **is not**.
- Write the positive statement *The cows were grazing in the pasture* and ask the children how they would turn this into a negative statement: the children should know how to put the adverb *not* between the main verb and the auxiliary so that it becomes *The cows were not grazing in the pasture*.
- Explain that if we wanted to add emphasis to this in our speech, we would stress *not*, but if we wanted to emphasise the positive statement we would stress the auxiliary, as in *The cows **were** grazing in the pasture*.
- Call out some other positive statements in the continuous or perfect tenses (such as *The painting is hanging on the wall* or *They had buried the treasure*) and ask the class to say them with emphasis or to make them negative.

Main Point
- Now write on the board *The cows grazed in the pasture* and ask the children how this can be turned into a negative statement.
- Explain that the verb *grazed* is in the simple past tense so *not* cannot go in its usual place between the auxiliary and the main verb.
- Instead, we make the verb *to do* the auxiliary, use the infinitive form of the main verb and put *not* in between, so the sentence becomes *The cows did not graze in the pasture*.
- Similarly, if we wanted to add emphasis to the positive statement, we would have to add *to do* in the same way and stress the auxiliary, as in *The cows **did** graze in the pasture*.
- Write some more positive statements on the board (in the simple past and present tenses) and rewrite them, firstly to show emphasis, and then as negative statements. Possible examples include: *We like the sculpture (We do [not] like the sculpture); The adventurer returned safely (The adventurer did [not] return safely); The factory manufactures cars (The factory does [not] manufacture cars)*. Make sure the children use the correct form of *to do* each time and revise the irregular parts of the verb if necessary.

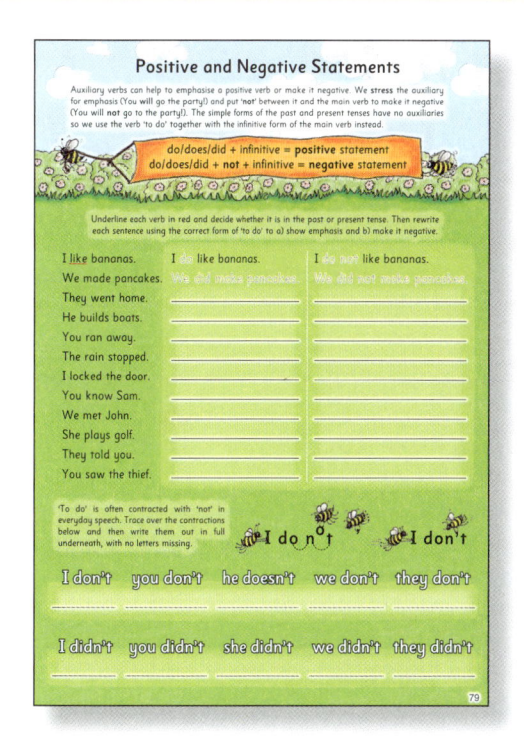

Activity Page
- The children look at each sentence and underline the verb in red *(like; made; went; builds; ran; stopped; locked; know; met; plays; told; saw)*.
- They then add emphasis to the positive statement by adding *do* or *does* in the present tense, or by adding *did* in the past tense, along with the infinitive form of the main verb (see below).
- Then they add *not* between the auxiliary and the main verb to turn it into a negative statement *(I do [not] like bananas; We did [not] make pancakes; They did [not] go home; He does [not] build boats; You did [not] run away; The rain did [not] stop; I did [not] lock the door; You do [not] know Sam; We did [not] meet John; She does [not] play golf; They did [not] tell you; You did [not] see the thief)*.
- Lastly, the children write inside the outlined contractions and write them out in full underneath, writing *don't* as *do not*, *doesn't* as *does not* and *didn't* as *did not*.

Extension Activity
- The children rewrite some of their negative statements, using the correct contraction each time, such as *They didn't go home,* for example.

Rounding Off
- Go over the activity page with the children, discussing their answers.
- If they have done the extension activity, ask some of the children to read out their sentences.

GRAMMAR 6 PUPIL BOOK: PAGES 80 & 81

Spelling: Schwa ‹our›

Spelling Test
- The children turn to the backs of their books and find the column labelled *Spelling Test 26*.
- Call out the spelling words learnt last week.

Revision
- Write these words on the board and ask the class to identify the schwa ‹ure› in each one: *figure, structure, future, measure, feature, furniture, moisture, vulture*.
- Ask the children to use one of these words in a sentence.

Spelling Point
- The ‹our› spelling can be pronounced in several ways in stressed syllables, such as /er/ in *journey*, /or/ in *four*, the little /oo/ followed by a schwa in *tour*, or the /ou/ and schwa in *flour*.
- However, ‹our› is often found in a final, unstressed syllable, where it becomes a schwa sound, as in *colour*, *flavour* and *neighbour*. Ask the children to clap the syllables in each of these words and listen for the stress in the first syllable.
- Many words like this are derived from Latin nouns ending in ‹or›, but they have come via French, which uses the ‹our› spelling instead.

Spelling List
- Go through the list, asking the class to find and highlight the ‹our› spelling each time. Also discuss the meaning of any unfamiliar words.
- Point out other spelling features, such as the vowel saying its long sound in *favour, flavour, humour, odour, labourer, savoury* and *behaviour*, the ‹u› saying /oo/ in *rumour*, the ‹o› saying /u/ in *colourful*, the suffix in *colourful, labourer, savoury* and *honourable*, the ‹eigh› in *neighbour*, the ‹e› saying /i/ in *behaviour* and *endeavour*, the ‹i› saying /y/ when it goes before ‹our› in *behaviour*, the ‹ea› saying /e/ in *endeavour*, and the silent ‹h› in *honourable*.
- It is a good idea to blend and sound out the spelling words quickly every day with the class. Where appropriate, use the *say it as it sounds* strategy, stressing, for example, the pure sound of any schwas (as in *labourer*) or syllables that are almost swallowed, as in *honourable*).

armour
favour
flavour
humour
harbour
rumour
odour
clamour
colourful
neighbour
labourer
vigour
valour
savoury
splendour
behaviour
endeavour
honourable

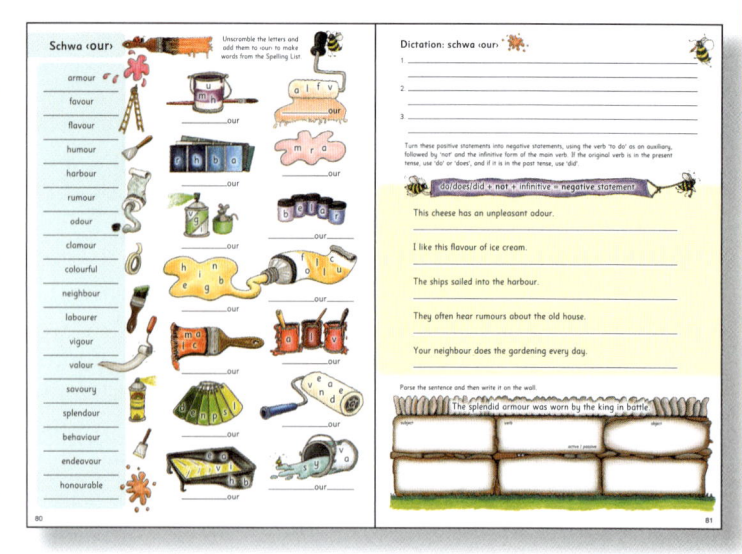

Activity Page 1
- The children split each word into syllables to help remember the spelling (*arm/our, fa/vour, fla/vour, hu/mour, har/bour, ru/mour, o/dour, clam/our, col/our/ful, neigh/bour, la/bour/er, vig/our, val/our, sa/vour/y, splen/dour, be/hav/iour, en/deav/our, hon/our/a/ble*).
- They then unscramble the letters and add them to ‹our› to make some of the spelling words (*humour, flavour, harbour, armour, vigour, labourer, neighbour, colourful, clamour, valour, splendour, endeavour, behaviour, savoury*).

Activity Page 2
- The children turn the positive statements into negative ones by using the auxiliary verb *to do*, followed by *not* and the infinitive form of the main verb (*This cheese **does not have** an unpleasant odour; I **do not** like this flavour of ice cream; The ships **did not sail** into the harbour; They **do not** often hear rumours about the old house; Your neighbour does **not do** the gardening every day*).
- Then they parse the sentence and complete the wall: The splendid armour was worn (by the king) (in battle).
Top: armour - was worn - [blank]
Bottom: The splendid - by the king / in battle - [blank]
Verb: passive
  – The passive verb uses the auxiliary *was* with the irregular past participle *worn*.
  – The prepositional phrases *by the king* and *in the battle* are acting as adverbs, so they needs orange brackets.

Dictation
- Dictate the following sentences:

1. "Can you do me a favour?" I asked my neighbour.
2. Always reward your pet for good behaviour.
3. The sorbet had an interesting colour and flavour.

- Remind the class to use speech marks with the correct punctuation in Sentence 1.

Grammar: Using the Verb 'To Do' in Questions

Aim
- Develop the children's ability to turn statements into questions when the main verb is not *to be* and it has no auxiliary. Explain that when this happens, we make *to do* the auxiliary, put it at the beginning of the question and use the infinitive form of the main verb.

Introduction
- Briefly revise the ways that the children know how to form a question or turn a statement into a question:
  - They could use one of the ‹wh› question words *(what, why, when, where, who, which, whose)*.
  - Alternatively, if *to be* is the main verb, it can be moved to the beginning to form a question *(The armour is heavy/Is the armour heavy?)*
  - Similarly, if the verb has an auxiliary, this too can be moved to the beginning *(Her neighbours are moving soon/Are her neighbours moving soon?)*
- Ask the children to think of some questions using the ‹wh› words and discuss them with the class.
- Then write some statements on the board in the continuous and perfect tenses and ask the children to turn them into questions by moving the auxiliary to the beginning and putting a question mark at the end, instead of a full stop.

Main Point
- Now write *Her neighbours moved away* on the board, and ask the children how they think this statement could be rewritten as a question.
- Unlike the previous examples, this statement is written in the simple past *(moved)* and has no auxiliary to put at the beginning.
- Remind the class that when we want to add emphasis to a verb like this, we make *to do* the auxiliary and use the infinitive form of the main verb, as in *Her neighbours did move away*.
- Now explain that we can do the same thing to turn the statement into a question, only this time the auxiliary goes at the beginning and the full stop is replaced by a question mark, as in *Did her neighbours move away?*
- Write some more statements on the board in the simple past or present tense and ask the class to turn them into questions, such as *We like the sculpture (Do we like the sculpture?); The adventurer returned safely (Did the adventurer return safely?); The factory manufactures cars (Does the factory manufacture cars?).*
- Each time, ask the children to answer their own question: they may say, for example, *Yes, we do like the sculpture* or *Yes, the adventurer did return safely,* but they may also say *Yes, we do* or *Yes, he did.* Point out how, in these examples, *to do* is used on its own as a substitute for the rest of the sentence.
- In addition, the verb is also used in what are called *question tags* or *tag questions* (*We like the sculpture, don't we? The factory doesn't manufacture cars, does it?*).

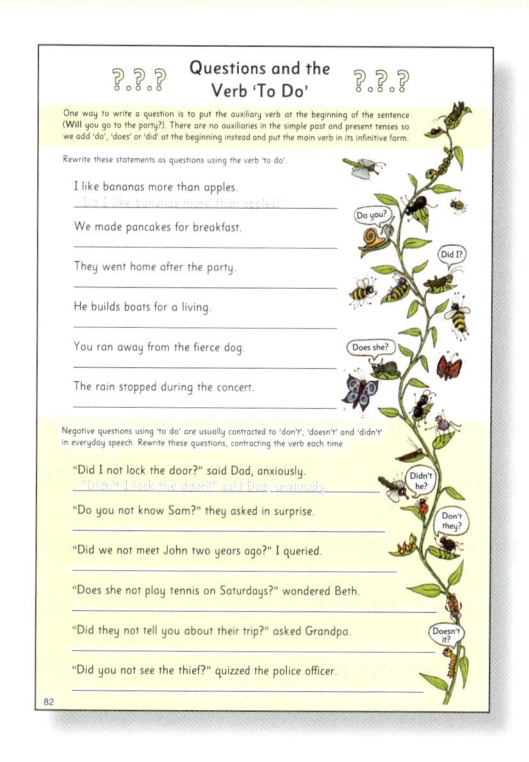

Activity Page
- The children turn each statement into a question:
  - First they add *do* or *does (present tense)* or *did (past tense)* to the beginning of the sentence.
  - Then they use the infinitive form of the main verb.
  - They then replace the full stop with a question mark. (*Do I like bananas more than apples? Did we make pancakes for breakfast? Did they go home after the party? Does he build boats for a living? Did you run away from the fierce dog? Did the rain stop during the concert?*) Those children who need extra support can refer back to page 79 in their *Pupil Book* as a prompt.
- Then they rewrite the negative questions, using the contractions *don't, doesn't* or *didn't* (*Didn't I lock the door? Don't you know Sam? Didn't we meet John two years ago? Doesn't she play tennis on Saturdays? Didn't they tell you about their trip? Didn't you see the thief?*).

Extension Activity
- The children write some questions of their own on a separate piece of paper, starting with, for example, *Do you...? Did I...? Does she...? Didn't we...? Don't they...? Doesn't he...?*

Rounding Off
- Go over the activity page with the children, discussing their answers.
- If they have done the extension activity, ask some of the children to read out their questions.

GRAMMAR 6 PUPIL BOOK: PAGES 83 & 84

Spelling: ‹-ity›, ‹-ety›

Spelling Test
- The children turn to the backs of their books and find the column labelled *Spelling Test 27*.
- Call out the spelling words learnt last week.

Revision
- Write these words on the board and ask the class to identify the schwa ‹our› in each one: *colour, labour, humour, savoury, honour, favour, clamour, vigour*.
- Ask the children to use one of these words in a sentence.

Spelling Point
- Write the words *security* and *safety* on the board and ask the children what they have in common. These words are synonyms (words with the same, or similar, meaning), and they also have similar suffixes: ‹-ity› and ‹-ety›.
- These suffixes are always unstressed and have a swallowed vowel that makes either the schwa or /i/ sound, so the spellings have to be learnt.
- They are found in abstract nouns with the quality or condition of the root word (so if there is a possibility of rain, for example, it is possible this will happen, or if there is a variety of choices, there are various options to consider).
- The less common suffix ‹-ety› is usually added to root words ending in ‹e› or is used to avoid having a double ‹i› in words like *variety* and *anxiety*. However, words with roots ending in ‹e› can also have the ‹-ity› suffix, as in *activity* and *security*.

Spelling List
- Go through the list, asking the class to find and highlight the suffix ‹-ity› or ‹-ety› each time. Also discuss the meaning of any unfamiliar words.
- Point out other spelling features, such as the way the final ‹e› of the root word has been removed before adding the suffix in *activity, purity, security, safety, entirety, subtlety* and *opportunity*, the ‹e› saying /i/ in *security, entirety* and *responsibility*, the vowel saying its long sound in *reality, identity, anxiety, variety, society* and *opportunity*, the way the ‹e› in *safety* and *subtlety* is not pronounced, the ‹nx› saying /ng-z/ in *anxiety*, the soft ‹c› in *society*, the silent letter digraph in *sub**b**tlety*, and the soft ‹g› in *generosity*.
- It is a good idea to blend and sound out the spelling words quickly every day with the class. Where appropriate, use the *say it as it sounds* strategy, stressing, for example, the pure sound of any schwas (as in *ability*).

activity
ability
purity
reality
security
identity
safety
anxiety
variety
society
entirety
subtlety
opportunity
possibility
curiosity
familiarity
generosity
responsibility

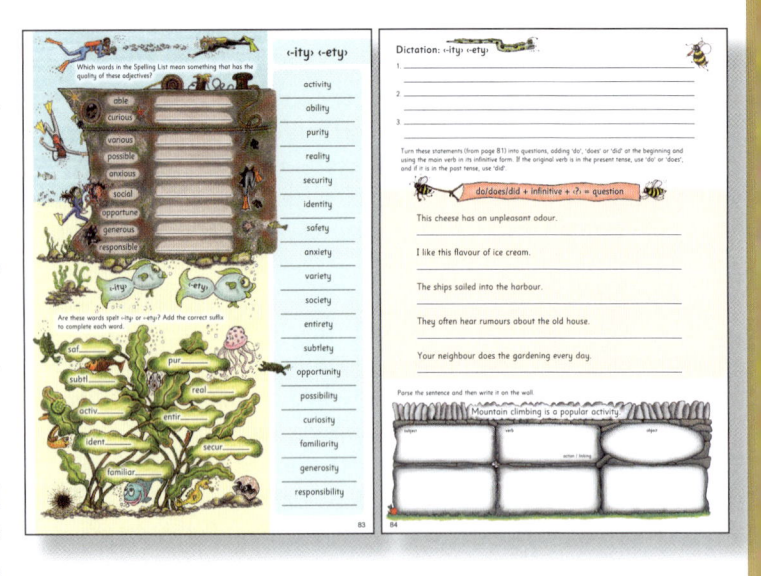

Activity Page 1
- The children split each word into syllables to help remember the spelling (*ac/tiv/i/ty, a/bil/i/ty, pu/ri/ty, re/al/i/ty, se/cu/ri/ty, i/den/ti/ty, safe/ty, anx/i/e/ty, va/ri/e/ty, so/ci/e/ty, en/tir/e/ty, sub/tle/ty, op/por/tu/ni/ty, pos/si/bil/i/ty, cu/ri/os/i/ty, fa/mil/i/ar/i/ty, gen/e/ros/i/ty, re/spon/si/bil/i/ty*).
- They then write the spelling words that belong to the same word family as the adjectives (*ability, curiosity, variety, possibility, anxiety, society, opportunity, generosity, responsibility*)
- Then they add the correct suffix to the spelling words.

Activity Page 2
- The children turn the statements into questions (***Does** this cheese **have** an unpleasant odour? **Do** I like this flavour of ice cream? **Did** the ships **sail** into the harbour? **Do** they often hear rumours about the old house? **Does** your neighbour **do** the gardening every day?*).
- Then they parse the sentence and complete the wall: *Mountain climbing is a popular activity.*
Top: climbing - is \ activity (a popular) - [blank]
Bottom: Mountain - [blank] - [blank]
Verb: linking
  – The noun *mountain* is acting as an adjective and should be underlined in blue.
  – *Climbing* is a gerund made by adding ‹-ing› to the verb *climb*.

Dictation
- Dictate the following sentences:

  1. They had a responsibility to ensure our safety.
  2. We have the opportunity to create a better society.
  3. "I will now reveal your true identity!" exclaimed the detective.

- Remind the class to use speech marks with the correct punctuation in Sentence 3.

Grammar: Modal Verbs

Aim
- Introduce modal verbs, which are a special kind of auxiliary verb. They are used with the infinitive of the main verb to help express things like certainty, obligation, permission or ability. The most common modal verbs are *will, shall, can, could, may, might, should, would* and *must*.

Introduction
- Briefly revise auxiliary verbs and the different ways that they can 'help' the main verb in a sentence:
  - They are often used to form different tenses: for example, *shall* and *will* help to indicate the future (*She will arrive soon / I shall go tomorrow*); *to be* forms part of the continuous tenses (*I am/was/will be doing the shopping*); and *to have* is used in the perfect tenses (*He had/has/will have lost his keys*).
  - Auxiliary verbs are also moved to the beginning of a sentence when we want to turn a statement into a question (*Are you going now?*).
  - If there is no auxiliary to move, we use *to do* instead, along with the infinitive form of the main verb (*They went home / Did they go home?*).
  - Similarly, *to do* can be used to add emphasis to a positive statement (*We do like ice cream!*) or to make it negative (*We don't like ice cream!*).
  - Finally, *to be* is paired with the past participle of the main verb when we want to write in the passive voice (*They were seen by the doctor*).
- Write the examples on the board, identify the auxiliary verb each time, and make sure the children understand how each one is used.

Main Point
- We can also use auxiliary verbs to help us express how certain we are about something. For example:
  - If we are very sure that we will go somewhere we can say *I will/shall go tomorrow*.
  - However, if we are not entirely certain, we could say *I might/may go tomorrow*.
  - *I can go tomorrow* suggests that it is possible and also likely.
  - *I could go tomorrow* suggests that although it is possible it may not happen.
  - If we feel it is important to go but there is some uncertainty, we can say *I should go tomorrow*.
  - If it depends on something else, we can say *I would go tomorrow*.
  - Also, if it is absolutely necessary to go, we can say *I must go tomorrow*, which rules out any uncertainty.
- Explain that *will, shall, can, could, may, might, should, would* and *must* belong to a special group of auxiliaries called *modal verbs*. As well as expressing degrees of certainty and obligation, they can:
  - Indicate ability: *She can ride a horse* (present tense) / *She could ride a horse* (past tense).
  - Be used to ask or give permission: *Can/May/Could I go next? You can/may*.
  - Be used to give advice or make suggestions: *You should rest / We could go swimming*.
- Modal verbs are always used with the infinitive form of the main verb and, unlike other auxiliary verbs, do not change depending on the grammatical person (so the verb stays the same, whichever pronoun is used).
- Ask the children to suggest their own sentence for each of the modal verbs and discuss how it affects the meaning each time.

Activity Page
- The children write inside the outlined word *Verbs*, using a red pencil.
- They then read the definitions for each sentence and decide which one is correct (*You could draw...* A; *She can speak...* B; *He must polish...* A; *If your tongue...* B; *We shall find...* A; *I said that...* B; *You may leave...* A; *I will have...* A; *They might see...* B).

Extension Activity
- Working in pairs, the children think of some more sentences using the modal verbs *will, shall, can, could, may, might, should, would* and *must*.
- They then discuss what they think the modal verb is doing in each sentence.

Rounding Off
- Go over the activity page with the children, discussing their answers.
- If they have done the extension activity, ask some of the children to read out their sentences and discuss what the modal verb is doing each time.

GRAMMAR 6 PUPIL BOOK: PAGES 86 & 87

Spelling: ‹-ial›

Spelling Test
- The children turn to the backs of their books and find the column labelled *Spelling Test 28*.
- Call out the spelling words learnt last week.

Revision
- Write these words on the board and ask the class to identify the suffix in each one: s*afety*, r*eality*, so*ciety*, a*bility*, va*riety*, curi*osity*, anx*iety*, possi*bility*.
- Ask the children to use one of these words in a sentence.

Spelling Point
- Revise the suffix ‹-ial› – a variant of ‹-al› – often used when the root word ends in ‹y› or ‹ce›. When it appears in words ending in ‹tial›, ‹cial› and ‹sial›, the ‹i› helps make the /sh/ sound and the unstressed ‹a› becomes a schwa.
- However, when other letters precede it, the ‹i› usually makes a sound somewhere between /i/ and /ee/, as in *burial* and *trivial*, and can also say /ie/, as in *denial*.
- Remind the children that ‹-ial› often appears in adjectives that describe something as relating to or having the qualities of the (root) noun (so secretarial work is done by a secretary and a ceremonial uniform is worn at special ceremonies).
- Look again at the words *denial* and *burial* and point out that ‹-ial› is also found in nouns that name the action or practice of the root verb.
- Look at some more spelling words and identify the root word where possible.

Spelling List
- Go through the list, asking the class to find and highlight the suffix ‹-ial› each time. Also discuss the meaning of any unfamiliar words.
- Point out other spelling features, such as the ‹e› saying /i/ in *denial* and *secretarial*, the ‹i› saying /ie/ in *denial*, the ‹u› saying /e/ in *burial*, the ‹o› saying its long sound in *jovial* and *ceremonial*, the ‹er› saying /ear/ in *material* and *imperial*, the double ‹r› in *territorial*, the ‹ar› saying /air/ in *secretarial*, the soft ‹c› in *ceremonial* and *celestial*, the spoken ‹i› in *celestial* (rather than ‹tial› saying /shul/), and ‹u› saying /oo/ in *marsupial*.
- It is a good idea to blend and sound out the spelling words quickly every day with the class. Where appropriate, use the *say it as it sounds* strategy, stressing, for example, the pure sound of any schwas (as in *material* and *memorial*).

denial
trivial
burial
jovial
material
imperial
memorial
territorial
editorial
industrial
secretarial
ceremonial
celestial
sacrificial
substantial
marsupial
prejudicial
controversial

Activity Page 1
- The children split each word into syllables to help remember the spelling *(de/ni/al, triv/i/al, bur/i/al,*

jo/vi/al, ma/te/ri/al, im/pe/ri/al, me/mo/ri/al, ter/ri/to/ri/al, ed/i/to/ri/al, in/dus/tri/al, sec/re/tar/i/al, cer/e/mo/ni/al, ce/les/ti/al, sac/ri/fi/cial, sub/stan/tial, mar/su/pi/al, prej/u/di/cial, con/tro/ver/sial).
- They then work out the answers to the crossword clues and write them in *(1. denial, 2. ceremonial, 3. substantial, 4. industrial, 5. sacrificial, 6. trivial, 7. burial, 8. marsupial, 9. secretarial, 10. prejudicial, 11. celestial, 12. editorial, 13. jovial, 14. imperial, 15. memorial, 16. territorial, 17. material).*

Activity Page 2
- The children write the spelling word that belongs to the same word family as each noun or verb *(Left-hand column: prejudicial, material, burial, trivial, sacrificial, ceremonial, controversial; Right-hand column: secretarial, memorial, denial, editorial, imperial, territorial, substantial).*
- Then they parse the sentence and complete the wall:
A memorial service was held (for their uncle).
Top: service - was held - [blank]
Bottom: A memorial - for their uncle - [blank]
Verb: passive
   – The passive verb uses the auxiliary *was* with the irregular past participle *held*.
   – The prepositional phrase *for their uncle* is acting as an adverb, so it needs orange brackets.

Dictation
- Dictate the following sentences:

1. The referee's decision was extremely controversial.
2. "The kangaroo is an Australian marsupial," she explained.
3. The imperial guards were wearing their ceremonial swords.

- Remind the class to use speech marks with the correct punctuation in Sentence 2. The proper adjective *Australian* needs a capital letter.

GRAMMAR 6 PUPIL BOOK: PAGE 88

Grammar: Modal Adverbs

Aim
- Introduce modal adverbs, which modify main verbs and modal verbs to express different degrees of certainty. They range from **very certain** (as in *surely, certainly, clearly, definitely, obviously* and *absolutely*) to **quite certain** (usually expressed by *probably*) to **less certain** (as in *apparently, possibly, perhaps* and *maybe*).

Introduction
- Revise adverbs with the class:
  - Adverbs are words that usually describe or *modify* a verb, telling us more about how, where, when, how much or how often something happens (as in *quickly, away, yesterday, almost* and *sometimes*).
  - Although many adverbs – like *quickly* – are made by adding ‹-ly› to an adjective, many others are not; in fact, some words that do end in ‹-ly› – such as *lovely, silly* and *friendly* – are not adverbs, but adjectives.
  - Adverbs can also modify other adverbs and adjectives, as in **really** *quickly* and **really** *sad*.
  - A few adverbs *(when, where* and *why)* are used in relative clauses to replace the more formal phrases *in which, on which, at which* and *for which*.
- Remind the class that any word, phrase or clause that acts as an adverb is called an adverbial:
  - When adverbials are at the beginning of a sentence they are usually followed by a comma.
  - The most common are adverbs, noun phrases, prepositional phrases and subordinate clauses.
  - Adverbial noun phrases always express time, telling us more about when *(next week)*, how often *(every day)*, or how long *(all year)* something occurs.
  - Prepositional phrases and subordinate clauses sometimes tell us the reason *why* something occurred *(I got a bike <u>for my birthday</u> / I was running <u>because I was late</u>)*.

Main Point
- Remind the children that in the last lesson they learnt about the modal verbs *will, shall, can, could, may, might, should, would* and *must*.
- Modal verbs are a special kind of auxiliary which are used to express degrees of certainty and obligation; indicate ability; give or ask permission; offer advice; or make suggestions.
- They are always used with the main verb's infinitive and stay the same whichever pronoun is used.
- Write *Jane can sing* on the board and look at how the modal verb *can* expresses certainty about Jane's ability to sing.
- Now write *Jane can probably sing* and ask the class how this changes the meaning: it suggests that we do not know for sure whether Jane can sing but that we think it is quite likely.
- Change *probably* to *definitely* and look at the meaning again: now there is no doubt that Jane can sing.
- Finally, change the sentence to *Perhaps Jane can sing* and ask the class whether it expresses a high or low degree of certainty: *perhaps* suggests that while it is possible that Jane can sing, we are not really sure and so our degree of certainty is low.
- Ask the class what part of speech *probably, definitely* and *perhaps* are *(adverbs)* and explain that modal adverbs, like modal verbs, can be used to express degrees of certainty.
- They are used with modal verbs like *can* (as in the example on the board) or with main verbs, as in *I definitely like ice cream*. Replace *definitely* in this sentence with some other modal adverbs and discuss how it affects the meaning each time.
- Point out that not all modal adverbs go so well with some modal verbs: for example, *perhaps*, which expresses a low degree of certainty, is not usually used with *must*, which expresses a high level of certainty.

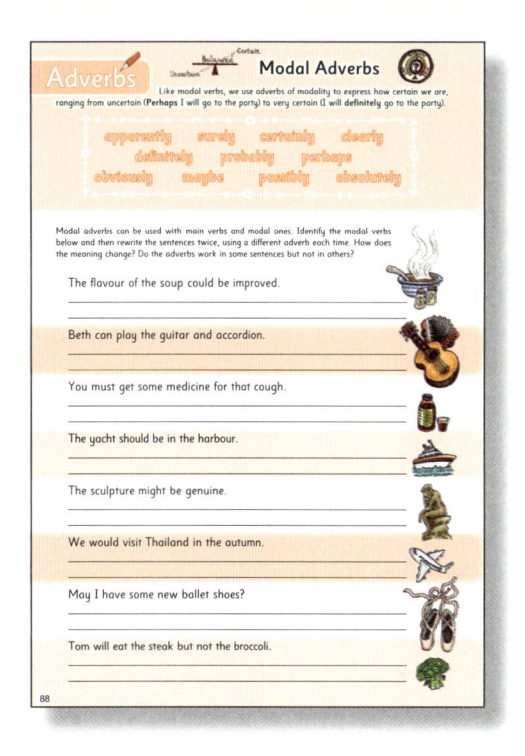

Activity Page
- The children write inside the outlined word *Adverbs* in orange and then identify the modal verbs, underlining them in red (<u>could</u> be improved; <u>can</u> play; <u>must</u> get; <u>should</u> be; <u>might</u> be; <u>would</u> visit; <u>May</u> I have; <u>will</u> eat).
- They then rewrite each sentence twice, using a different adverb. There is no wrong or right answer, as long as the sentence makes sense.

Extension Activity
- Working in pairs, the children look at their sentences and discuss what effect the different modal adverbs have on them.

Rounding Off
- Go over the activity page with the children, discussing their answers. If any modal adverbs do not work in a sentence, discuss the reasons why.

93

GRAMMAR 6 PUPIL BOOK: PAGES 89 & 90

Spelling: ‹-able›

Spelling Test
- The children turn to the backs of their books and find the column labelled *Spelling Test 29*.
- Call out the spelling words learnt last week.

Revision
- Write these words on the board and ask the class to identify the suffix ‹-able› or ‹-ible› in each one: *controllable, sensible, valuable, forcible, changeable, flexible, variable, enjoyable*. Revise the rules for adding a suffix that starts with a vowel as you do so (see page 30).

Spelling Point
- Revise the suffixes ‹-able› and ‹-ible›, which are found in adjectives that mean *capable or worthy of being the root (word)*. (The adjectives' Latin roots determine which suffix is used):
  - The suffix ‹-able› is more common; it is often added to an identifiable root word, and always comes after words ending in a hard ‹c› or ‹g›.
  - The suffix ‹-ible› is less common, and it is less likely to follow a whole root word; *horrible*, for example, comes from the Latin *horrere* (to tremble or shudder) and is part of the same word family as *horrid, horrify, horrifying and horrific*.
- Sometimes we can use our existing knowledge to help us decide which suffix to use: knowing *adoration, toleration* and *application*, for example, tells us that ‹-able› should be used in *adorable, tolerable* and *applicable*. (The same strategy can be used for other suffixes, as in *applicant* and *tolerance*.) There will always be exceptions, of course, and the children should use a dictionary if they are not sure.

Spelling List
- Go through the list, asking the class to find and highlight the suffix ‹-able› each time. Also discuss the meaning of any unfamiliar words.
- Point out other spelling features, such as the ‹e› saying /i/ in *enjoyable* and *reliable*, the alternative spellings in *enjoyable* and *reasonable*, the vowel saying its long sound in *notable, reliable* and *recognisable*, the ‹o› saying /u/ in *comfortable*, the ‹ui› saying /oo/ in *suitable*, the ‹s› saying /z/ in *recognisable*, the ‹su› saying /sw/ in *persuadable*, the double ‹p› in *applicable* and – in *knowledgeable* – the silent ‹k›, the ‹ow› saying /o/ and ‹edge› saying /ij/.
- It is a good idea to blend and sound out the spelling words quickly every day with the class. Where appropriate, use the *say it as it sounds* strategy, stressing, for example, the pure sound of any schwas (as in *adorable*) or syllables that

enjoyable
adorable
avoidable
available
notable
reasonable
comfortable
valuable
reliable
suitable
fashionable
understandable
considerable
recognisable
persuadable
tolerable
applicable
knowledgeable

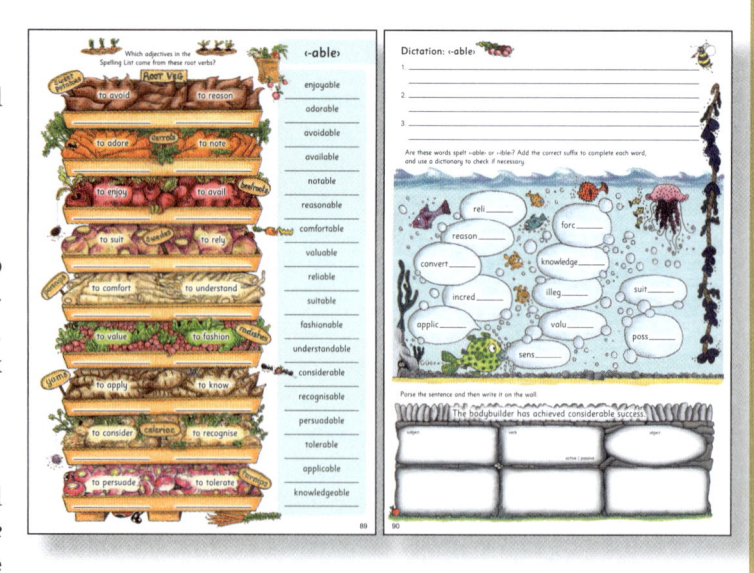

are sometimes almost swallowed (as in *comfortable, valuable* and *fashionable*).

Activity Page 1
- The children split each word into syllables to help remember the spelling (*en/joy/a/ble, a/dor/a/ble, a/void/a/ble, a/vail/a/ble, no/ta/ble, rea/son/a/ble, com/fort/a/ble, val/u/a/ble, re/li/a/ble, suit/a/ble, fash/ion/a/ble, un/der/stand/a/ble, con/sid/er/a/ble, rec/og/nis/a/ble, per/suad/a/ble, tol/e/ra/ble, ap/plic/a/ble, knowl/edge/a/ble*).
- They then match the spelling words to the root verbs (Left-hand column: *avoidable, adorable, enjoyable, suitable, comfortable, valuable, applicable, considerable, persuadable*; Right-hand column: *reasonable, notable, available, reliable, understandable, fashionable, knowledgeable, recognisable, tolerable*).

Activity Page 2
- The children add the correct suffix to complete each word (Left: *reliable, reasonable, convertible, incredible, applicable*; Middle: *forcible, knowledgeable, illegible, valuable, sensible*; Right: *suitable, possible*).
- Then they parse the sentence and complete the wall: The bodybuilder has achieved considerable success.
Top: bodybuilder - has achieved - success
Bottom: The - [blank] - considerable
Verb: active

Dictation
- Dictate the following sentences:

  1. "The puppy is adorable!" exclaimed Beth.
  2. Playing the guitar is an enjoyable activity.
  3. The variety of material available is notable.

- Remind the class to use speech marks with the correct punctuation in Sentence 1. *Beth* is a proper noun and needs a capital letter.

Grammar: Imperatives

Aim
- Introduce the imperative, which is a special form of the verb that is used to give commands, warnings, instructions and advice or to make suggestions, invitations and requests. An imperative sentence usually ends in a full stop, unless it is a forceful command or warning, when it ends in an exclamation mark.

Introduction
- Revise the different types of sentence that the children know:
  – They have learnt, for example, that sentences can be **simple** (having a subject and verb), **compound** (consisting of two simple sentences joined by a coordinating conjunction or a hyphen) or **complex** (containing a main clause and a dependent clause).
  – They also know that sentences can state facts, ask for information or make an exclamation and that these **statements**, **questions** and **exclamations** have their own punctuation, ending in a full stop, question mark or exclamation mark.
  – Sentences can also be **positive**, expressing what is, or they can be **negative**, expressing what is not. Sentences are usually made negative by putting the adverb *not* between the auxiliary verb and the main verb, as in *The baby will not sleep*. If there is no auxiliary, we add the verb *to do* and use the infinitive form of the main verb, as in *I do not swim every week*.

Main Point
- Ask the class if they know the game *Simon Says,* the children's game where one player gives instructions (such as *Stand up, Sit down, Jump in the air, Clap your hands* and *Stamp your feet*) and the other players obey, as long as the instruction begins with *Simon says...*.
- Write some of these instructions on the board and ask the children what is unusual about them. The sentences make sense and have a verb, but the verb is in the infinitive form and the subject is not stated.
- Explain that these are imperative sentences. The word *imperative* comes from the Latin verb *imperare* meaning to *command,* but actually, imperatives are used to give more than orders and commands.
- They can be used to give:
  – Warnings *(Beware of the dog!)*
  – Instructions *(Stir in the flour gradually)*
  – Advice *(Use a sharp knife)*
- They can also be used to make:
  – Suggestions *(Try the apple pie)*
  – Invitations *(Come and see us soon)*
  – Requests *(Help me, please)*
- Remind the class that when we talk directly to someone we use the second person, *you,* but this is not the case in imperative sentences. Instead, the *you* is implied, although it can be used to add emphasis, as in *You be quiet*. (We can tell that this is in the imperative form and not in the simple present tense, because the verb is *be* rather than *are*.)
- We make negative imperatives by using the auxiliary *to do,* as in *Do not disturb,* although they are often contracted in speech, as in *Don't say anything!* or *Don't go yet,* for example.
- Also explain that imperative sentences usually end in a full stop, unless they are forceful commands or warnings, when an exclamation mark is used instead.

Activity Page
- The children write some positive and negative imperatives in the blank spaces, which could be similar to the existing instructions or could include some actions that can be done in the classroom, like *Turn around three times*.

Extension Activity
- The children play the game in small groups. Each group will need a die and some counters, as well as a completed activity page.
- The players take it in turns to throw the die and move their counter accordingly. When they land on a space with an imperative, they have to follow the instruction. The first person to finish is the winner.

Rounding Off
- Go over the activity page with the children, and ask them to read out some of their instructions.

Spelling: ‹que› for the /k/ Sound

Spelling Test
- The children turn to the backs of their books and find the column labelled *Spelling Test 30*.
- Call out the spelling words learnt last week.

Revision
- Write *knowledgeable* on the board and discuss how the suffix ‹-able› has been added to the noun *knowledge* to make an adjective.
- Point out the silent letter digraph ‹kn› and ‹edge› saying /ij/ and revise the ‹dge› spelling, which always follows a short vowel.
- Explain that these words are in the same word family as *know*; ask the class to think of some others (such as *unknown, unknowingly, unacknowledged, acknowledge* and *acknowledgement*) and identify their parts of speech.

Spelling Point
- The main ways of writing the /k/ sound are ‹c›, ‹k› and ‹ck›:
  – The letter ‹c› usually follows a short vowel, as in *fact* and *hectic*.
  – This means that ‹c› is subject to the doubling rule and is written as ‹ck› at the end of short words like *clock* or as ‹cc› in longer words without a suffix, like *occasion*.
  – The letter ‹k› usually follows vowels that are not short, as in *book* and *walk*, and is used with ‹n› to make the /ng-k/ sound in words like *bank* and *sink* (although other spellings of /k/ are sometimes used, as in *anchor* and *conquer*); it is also used instead of ‹c› in words like *kettle, kilt* and *sky* to avoid the soft ‹c› spellings.
- Two less commonly used ways to write /k/ are ‹ch› and ‹que›. These spellings both have foreign origins: words with ‹ch›, like *chorus* and *echo*, are derived from Greek, but words with ‹que›, such as *technique* and *boutique,* have often been 'borrowed' from French.
- The ‹que› spelling is usually found at the end of a word, although *queue* is a notable exception.

Spelling List
- Go through the list, asking the class to find and highlight the ‹que› spelling each time. Also discuss the meaning of any unfamiliar words.
- Point out other spelling features, such as the vowel saying its long sound in *unique, opaque* and *grotesque,* the ‹i› saying /ee/ in *unique, antique, boutique, physique, mystique, pique* and *technique,* the ‹n› saying /ng/ in *conquer,* the way the first ‹e› in *marquee* is part of both the ‹que› spelling and the /ee/ sound, the ‹ou› saying /oo/ in *boutique,* the

unique
antique
queue
mosque
plaque
conquer
marquee
boutique
physique
mystique
opaque
pique
grotesque
picturesque
masquerade
statuesque
technique
arabesque

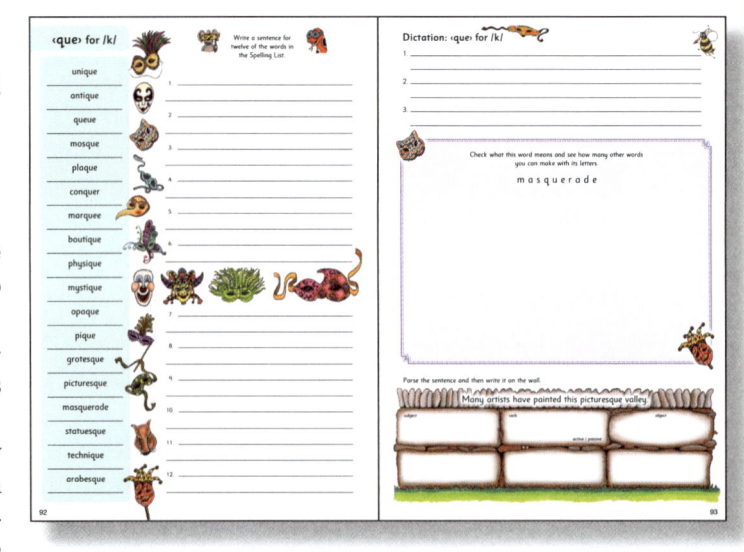

alternative /f/ spelling and ‹s› saying /z/ in *physique,* the ‹y› saying /i/ in *physique* and *mystique,* the ‹ture› saying /cher/ in *picturesque,* and the ‹ch› spelling of /k/ in *technique.*
- It is a good idea to blend and sound out the spelling words quickly every day with the class. Where appropriate, use the *say it as it sounds* strategy, stressing, for example, the pure sound of any schwas (as in *arabesque*).

Activity Page 1
- The children split each word into syllables to help remember the spelling (*u/nique, an/tique, queue, mos/que, plaque, con/quer, mar/quee, bou/tique, phy/sique, mys/tique, o/paque, pique, gro/tesque, pic/tur/esque, mas/que/rade, stat/u/esque, tech/nique, ar/a/besque*).
- They then write sentences for twelve of the spelling words.

Activity Page 2
- The children look up *masquerade* in the dictionary, check its meaning, and make as many words as they can with its letters.
- Then they parse the sentence and complete the wall: Many artists have painted this picturesque valley.
Top: artists - have painted - valley
Bottom: Many - [blank] - this picturesque
Verb: active

Dictation
- Dictate the following sentences:

  1. The sculpture is a valuable antique.
  2. "This technique is unique," said the scientist.
  3. She bought her dress in a fashionable boutique.

- Remind the class to use speech marks with the correct punctuation in Sentence 2.

Grammar: Using Paragraphs and Cohesion

Aim
- Introduce the children to the idea that a paragraph needs a beginning, a middle and an end. Also encourage them to use **cohesion** in their writing by using adverbs and conjunctions to link their ideas both within and between paragraphs.

Introduction
- Revise paragraphs with the children. Remind them that paragraphs do the following:
  - Break down a longer piece of text into smaller sections so that it is easier to read and understand.
  - Start on a new line, which is usually indented.
  - Are made up of sentences that describe one idea or topic.
- Show the children a page of writing (for example, part of a story, a magazine article, a letter, or a newspaper story) and identify the paragraphs with the class.
- Read some of them out. Decide what each one is about and look at the order that they have been put in: could this be changed and, if so, what affect would it have?
- Look at some of the vocabulary used to move the story or argument along, and discuss how these words and phrases link ideas within a paragraph or link one paragraph to another.

Main Point
- Explain that, just like a story, a paragraph has a beginning, a middle and an end:
  - The first sentence usually explains what the whole paragraph is about and is called the ***topic*** sentence.
  - The sentences that follow provide the **evidence** to support the main idea.
  - The final sentence usually acts as a **conclusion**, summing up what the paragraph is about (although not all paragraphs do this).
- Look again at some of the paragraphs from the piece of writing and find the topic, evidence and conclusion in each one. Explain that writing paragraphs in this way will help the children avoid repeating or contradicting themselves and allow their ideas to flow more naturally.
- Another way they can do this is to use *cohesion*, which means *sticking together* in Latin and describes the use of words and phrases to link ideas and paragraphs together. Many adverbs and conjunctions (and phrases acting as these parts of speech) are used in this way and are often referred to as *connectives*.
- Connectives can be categorised by function and include words that indicate:
  - Time or sequence (*meanwhile, next, then, firstly, secondly, thirdly*)
  - An opening (*at first, to begin with, initially*)
  - A summing-up (*finally, after all, in conclusion*)
  - Place (*nearby, around the corner, down the road*)
  - Cause and effect (*because, since, therefore, as a result*)
  - Additional information (*also, as well as, moreover*)
  - Contrast (*instead, although, however, unless*)
- Tell the children that they are going to think about something they would like to invent and then write about it. Remind them how to plan their work:
  - Start by deciding what type of invention it will be.
  - Then organise ideas into three main paragraphs about what the invention will do, how it can be made, and how it will make life easier.
  - Put these ideas down in note form first.
  - Then expand them into proper sentences, which can be put together to make paragraphs, using cohesion where appropriate.
- Ask the children to suggest some ideas for inventions and write them on the board.

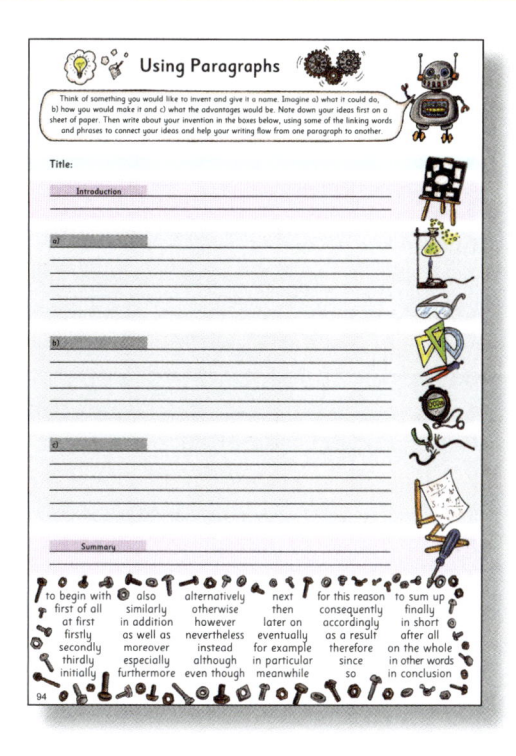

Activity Page
- The children note down their ideas first on a separate sheet of paper, organising them under three different headings: what the invention will do; how it will be made; and what its advantages are.
- They then expand these ideas into sentences, writing them in the three boxes and using some of the linking words and phrases shown.
- They should also put the invention's name at the top and write an introductory paragraph and a closing paragraph.

Extension Activity
- The children draw a picture of their invention or create a diagram and label the different parts.

Rounding Off
- Go over the activity page with the children, and ask them to read out some of their paragraphs. Identify any connectives used and make sure each paragraph has a beginning, a middle and an end.

Spelling: ‹ne› for the /n/ Sound

Spelling Test
- The children turn to the backs of their books and find the column labelled *Spelling Test 31*.
- Call out the spelling words learnt last week.

Revision
- Write *mystique* on the board and revise words ending in ‹que›, which are often 'borrowed' from French.
- Point out the ‹y› saying /i/, the ‹i› saying /ee/ and the ‹que› saying /k/.
- Explain that *mystique* belongs to the same word family as *mystery*; ask the class to think of some other examples (such as *mystic, mystical, mysterious, mysteriously, mystify, mystified, mystifying* and *demystify*) and identify their part(s) of speech.

Spelling Point
- It is not unusual for words in English to end in a silent ‹e›. For example:
  - In the spelling lessons on pages 72 and 74, the children learnt the silent letter digraphs (and trigraph) found at the end of words like *taste, palette* and *awesome*.
  - In previous years, they also learnt that silent ‹e› often appears in words ending in /s/, /z/, /v/ or /iv/, as in *horse, cheese, bronze, twelve* and *massive*.
- Silent ‹e› also appears sometimes in words ending in /n/; write some of the words from the spelling list on the board and underline the silent letter digraph ‹ne› in each one.
- Remind the class that these examples are different from *magic* ‹e› words because the ‹e› at the end has no influence on any other vowel. For example, in the words *gone* and *examine*, the preceding vowels ‹o› and ‹i› keep their short sounds, whereas in *bone* and *line* the influence of *magic* ‹e› makes the vowels say their long sounds.

Spelling List
- Go through the list, asking the class to find and highlight the silent letter digraph ‹ne› each time. Also discuss the meaning of any unfamiliar words.
- Point out other spelling features, such as the ‹o› saying /wu/ in *one* and *anyone* (but /u/ in *none* and *undone*), the soft ‹g› in *engine, imagine* and *genuine*, the prefix in *undone*, the ‹a› saying /e/ and ‹y› saying /ee/ in *anyone*, the vowel saying its long sound in *heroine, genuine, masculine* and *migraine*, the ‹ex› saying /igz/ in *examine*, the ‹y› saying /ie/ in *bygone*, the soft ‹c› in *medicine*, the silent letter digraph in *discipline*, and the ‹e› saying /i/ in *determined*.

one
none
gone
engine
imagine
undone
anyone
famine
heroine
examine
bygone
genuine
medicine
feminine
masculine
discipline
migraine
determined

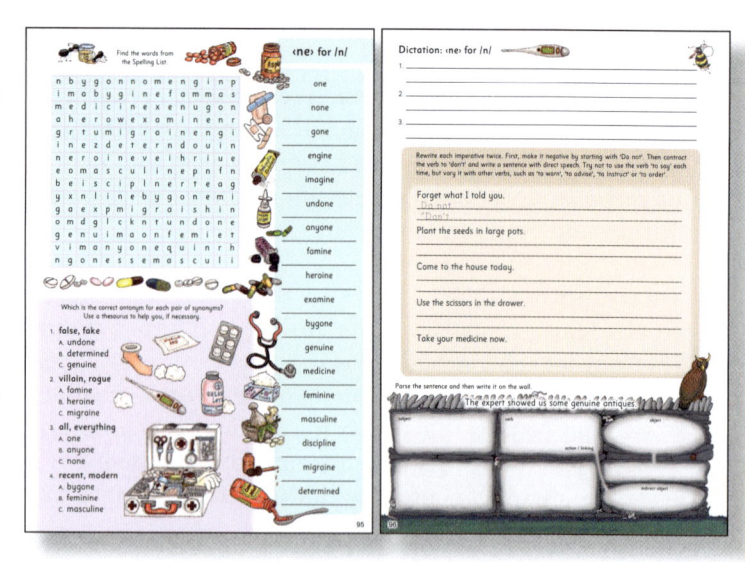

- It is a good idea to blend and sound out the spelling words quickly every day with the class. Where appropriate, use the *say it as it sounds* strategy, stressing, for example, the pure sound of any schwas (as in *feminine* and *discipline*) or swallowed syllables (as in *medicine*).

Activity Page 1
- The children split each word into syllables to help remember the spelling *(one, none, gone, en/gine, im/ag/ine, un/done, an/y/one, fam/ine, her/o/ine, ex/am/ine, by/gone, gen/u/ine, medi/cine, fem/i/nine, mas/cu/line, dis/ci/pline, mi/graine, de/ter/mined)*.
- They then find the eighteen spelling words in the word search.
- Then they identify the correct antonym for each pair of synonyms *(1. C, 2. B, 3. C, 4. A)*.

Activity Page 2
- The children rewrite each imperative twice: first they make it negative by starting the sentence with *Do not* (as in *Do not forget what I told you*); then they contract the negative imperative and put it in direct speech, (as in *"Don't forget what I told you," warned Dad*).
- Then they parse the sentence and complete the wall: The expert showed us some genuine antiques.
Top: expert - showed - antiques
Bottom: The - [blank] - some genuine
Indirect object: us   Verb: action

Dictation
- Dictate the following sentences:

  1. "Imagine that!" exclaimed the heroine.
  2. We were determined to examine the engine.
  3. He took some medicine to cure his migraine.

- Remind the class to use speech marks with the correct punctuation in Sentence 1.

Grammar: Formal and Informal Writing

Aim
- Introduce the children to the idea that writing can be formal or informal. Develop their ability to write in both styles and refine their understanding of when to use each one.

Introduction
- Remind the children that a sentence can be written in the first, second or third person, with the person being singular or plural:
  - *First person* refers to the author and uses *I* and *we*.
  - *Second person* addresses someone directly with *you*.
  - *Third person* refers to someone else and uses *he, she, it* and *they*.

  I, we, you, he, she, it and *they* are personal pronouns, so called because they relate mostly to people.
- We use the first and second person when we communicate directly with someone either in speech or in writing, and the third person is used to describe something from another person's point of view or to keep things impersonal.
- Call out a few sentences and ask the children to identify the grammatical person each time.

Main Point
- Write *c u l8ter* on the board and ask what kind of writing this is and when it might be used. Would the children write this in class, for example? Explain that it is *text speak*, which we only really use when sending a text or chatting online with someone we know very well.
- Show the children some examples of writing that include things like slang, idioms, contractions and words like *well, like* and *anyway* that are often added unnecessarily.
- Discuss when this kind of writing is appropriate. For example, we may write in this relaxed, informal style in notes to ourselves or in a letter to a friend, but we would use a more formal style when addressing someone we do not know or when it concerns something more serious, like a letter of complaint.
- Show the class a more formal piece of writing, such as a report or an instruction manual, and compare the styles: the tone is more polite in the formal writing; standard punctuation is used; the vocabulary is more sophisticated; there are no contractions; and there is a greater use of the third person and the passive voice.
- Now ask the children what differences there might be between a formal and an informal letter. Write two short messages on the board, one in each style:
  - The informal one could read something like: *Hi Zack! Is it OK if I stop by on Saturday to chat about that stuff you've decided to chuck out? Cheers! Sam.*
  - The other should be a more formal request: *Dear Zack, I am writing to ask if I can visit you on Saturday, 12th May, to talk about the items that you wish to throw away. Many thanks, Sam.*
- Discuss them with the class, asking what makes the second one more formal, and compare the punctuation, the tone, and the synonyms chosen, like *hi/dear; stop by/visit; chat/talk; stuff/items; chuck out/throw away;* and *cheers/many thanks*.
- Look at synonyms that are even more formal, like *discuss* for *talk, discard* for *throw away* and *kind regards* instead of *many thanks*, and remind the children that a thesaurus can help them to vary the words they write.
- Look at some more examples, such as those used in the extension activity, and discuss them with the class.

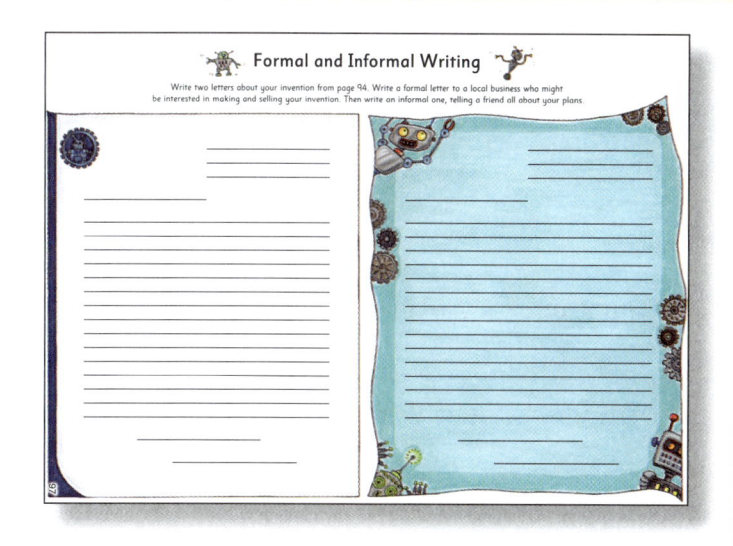

Activity Page
- The children write a formal letter to a business, asking whether it would like to make and sell the invention they wrote about in the previous lesson (see page 97).
- Then they write an informal letter to a friend, telling them about the invention and their plans to sell it.
- Before they start, remind the children where to write the date and their address, and make sure they know when to use *Dear Sir or Madam, Yours sincerely* and *Yours faithfully*.
- Remind them to use paragraphs and cohesion, and make sure they refer back to their essay on page 94 of their Pupil Books.

Extension Activity
- The children turn to page 116 in their Pupil Books and match the formal words and phrases in the list with the informal ones in the pyramid *(you'd/you would; get/obtain; help/assist; find out/discover; I don't/I do not; try/endeavour; ask/enquire; tell/inform; set up/establish; show/demonstrate; think about/consider; in the end/finally; letters/correspondence; start/commence; point out/indicate; need/require; say sorry/apologise; OK/satisfactory).*

Rounding Off
- Ask some children to read out a paragraph from one of their letters, and discuss whether it is written in a formal or informal style. Also check the children's answers if they have done the extension activity.

Spelling: Commonly Confused Words

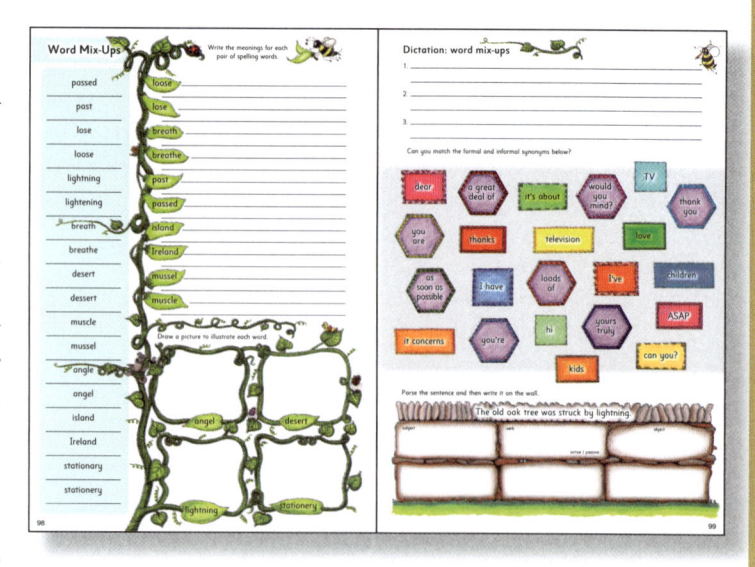

Spelling Test
- The children turn to the backs of their books and find the column labelled *Spelling Test 32*.
- Call out the spelling words learnt last week.

Revision
- Write *imagine* on the board and point out the soft ‹g› spelling and silent letter digraph ‹ne›.
- Explain that this word belongs to the same word family as *image* and ask the class to think of some other examples (such as *imagery, imaginary, imagination, (un)imaginative(ly)* and *unimaginable*).
- Identify the part(s) of speech for each word.

Spelling Point
- Revise the word *homophone*, which means *same* (homos) *sound* (phone) in Greek. Homophones sound similar to one another but have different spellings and meanings and include words like *our*, *hour* and *are* and *where*, *wear* and *were*.
- Explain that *are* and *our* and *were* and *where* – which are not strictly homophones but sound similar enough to cause confusion – are called near homophones.
- Look at the near homophones *lose/loose, lightning/lightening, breath/breathe, desert/dessert, angle/angel* and *island/Ireland* and discuss how they differ in pronunciation and meaning.
- Point out that the verb *desert* (to abandon) and the noun *dessert* (a sweet course at the end of a meal) are homophones, as they both stress the second syllable, but that the noun *desert* (a dry, arid region) is a near homophone, because its stress is on the first syllable.

Spelling List
- Go through the list, and look at the differences in meaning and spelling between each pair of words.
- Point out other spelling features, such as the suffix saying /t/ in *passed*, the ‹o› saying /oo/ in *lose*, the ‹s› and ‹ss› saying /z/ in *lose, desert* and *dessert*, the silent letter digraph (or trigraph) in *lose, loose, breathe, muscle* and *island*, the ‹igh› in *lightning* and *lightening*, the ‹ea› saying /e/ in *breath* but /ee/ in *breathe*, the ‹e› saying /i/ in *desert* (to abandon) and *dessert*, but /e/ in *desert* (a dry arid region), the different spellings of /ool/ in *muscle, mussel, angle* and *angel*, the way the ‹g› in ‹ng› also says /g/ in *angle*, the vowel saying its long sound in *angel, island, stationary* and *stationery*, the soft ‹g› in *angel*, and the suffixes in *stationary* and *stationery* and the ‹tion› saying /shun/.
- It is a good idea to blend and sound out the spelling words quickly every day with the class. Where appropriate, use the *say it as it sounds* strategy, stressing, for example, the pure sound of any schwas (as in *lightening* and *Ireland*) or saying /is-land/ for *island*).

| passed |
| past |
| lose |
| loose |
| lightning |
| lightening |
| breath |
| breathe |
| desert |
| dessert |
| muscle |
| mussel |
| angle |
| angel |
| island |
| Ireland |
| stationary |
| stationery |

Activity Page 1
- The children split each word into syllables to help remember the spelling (*passed, past, lose, loose, light/ning, light/en/ing, breath, breathe, des/ert (noun), de/sert (verb), des/sert, mus/cle, mus/sel, an/gle, an/gel, is/land, Ire/land, sta/tion/a/ry, sta/tion/e/ry*).
- They then write the meanings for each pair of spelling words, using a dictionary to help them if needed.
- Then the children read the four words below and draw pictures to illustrate them.

Activity Page 2
- The children match the synonyms (*thanks/thank you, TV/television, kids/children, loads of/a great deal of, you're/you are, ASAP/as soon as possible, hi/dear, love/yours truly, I've/I have, it's about/it concerns, can you?/would you mind?*).
- Then they parse the sentence and complete the wall: The old oak tree was struck (by lightning).
Top: tree - was struck - [blank]
Bottom: The old oak - by lightning - [blank]
Verb: passive
— The passive verb has the irregular past participle *struck*.

Dictation
- Dictate the following sentences:

  1. The ship sailed past the desert island.
  2. How many angles are there in a triangle?
  3. "Don't lose that key," warned my mother.

- Sentence 2 needs a question mark. Remind the class to use speech marks with the correct punctuation in Sentence 3.

Grammar: Alliteration

Aim
- Introduce the children to the idea of *alliteration:* the use of repeated sounds in a series of words, which can be used to grab our attention and make the words more memorable.

Introduction
- Say the alphabet with the class and write it on the board in capital letters.
- Remind the children that when we say the alphabet we use the letter **names**, but when we want to read and write words, we use the letter **sounds**.
- Point to various letters in the alphabet and ask the class to say the sounds. Then take one of those sounds and go around the class, asking each child to think of a word that begins with that sound. Write the words on the board and repeat the activity with other sounds from the alphabet.
- Now write *The knowledgeable naughty knight knew a lot about knives* and read it with the children. Ask them what they notice about it *(most of the words begin with the /n/ sound)* and discuss the effect this has on them. Some children may find it a bit of a tongue twister, others might think it is funny, while others in the class might like the way it makes the silent ‹k› words memorable.

Main Point
- Explain that when we repeat a sound like this, it is called *alliteration,* and the effect is used in writing to grab our attention, make something memorable or to create a particular mood.
- Look again at the words that the class called out earlier and ask the children to make some alliterative sentences of their own. Remind them that:
  – It is the initial sound that matters, and not the way the sound is spelt, so not all the words have to start with the same letter.
  – Not all the words have to start with the same sound: smaller words like articles, pronouns and prepositions can be used regardless of their initial sound.
- Look at some of the children's suggestions and discuss the effect the alliteration has:
  – Some sentences may seem quite poetic.
  – Others might sound like a line from a song or nursery rhyme.
  – Others could be quite catchy, like a newspaper headline, advertising slogan or an idiom (as in *curiosity killed the cat*).
  – Some might resemble well-known tongue twisters like *Peter Piper picked a peck of pickled peppers* or *She sells seashells on the seashore* (in this last example there are two repeated sounds – /s/ and /sh/ – which do not always come at the beginning of the word).
- Alliteration is not just used in sentences and long phrases: it is used in brand names and television shows, and many characters in children's literature, television, film, cartoons and video games have alliterative names. Ask the children if they can think of any examples and discuss them with the class.

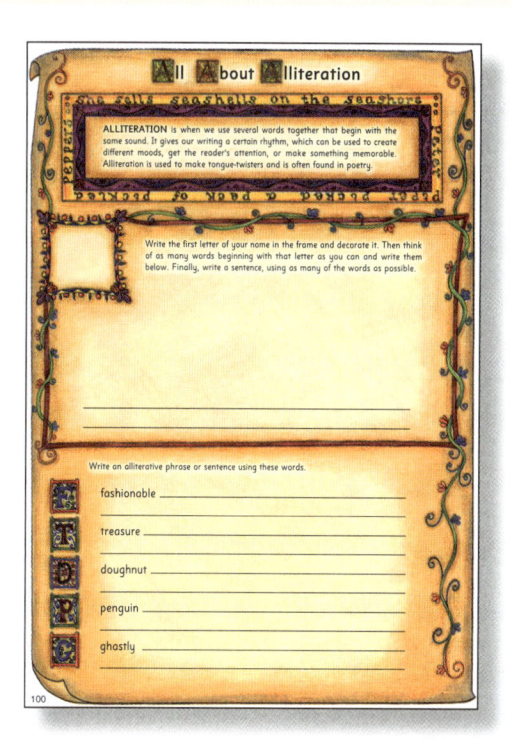

Activity Page
- The children write the first letter of their name in the frame and decorate it.
- They then think of as many words beginning with that letter as they can and write them in the box below. (If a child's name starts with a particularly difficult letter, like ‹x›, they can choose another one).
- Then they use as many of these words as possible to make an alliterative sentence.
- Finally, they write alliterative sentences or phrases for the five words underneath.

Extension Activity
- Ask the children to think back to the previous two lessons (see pages 97 and 99) and the names they gave to their inventions. Working in pairs or small groups, they decide whether these names are alliterative or not and, if not, think of alliterative names that they could use instead to make them catchy and memorable.
- The children could also be encouraged to write down alliterative idioms and short phrases in their Spelling Word Books or to collect real-life examples for a class project.

Rounding Off
- Go over the activity page with the children, discussing their sentences and phrases.
- If they have done the extension activity, ask some of the children to read out the names of their inventions.

Spelling: ‹-ly›

Spelling Test
- The children turn to the backs of their books and find the column labelled *Spelling Test 33*.
- Call out the spelling words learnt last week.

Revision
- Write *breath* and *breathe* on the board and discuss the different pronunciations of ‹ea› in each one.
- Ask the class to suggest other words in this word family (such as *breathable, breathless, breathing, breathtaking* and *breathy*) and identify their part(s) of speech.

Spelling Point
- Remind the class that the suffix ‹-ly› is added to an adjective to make an adverb. Because ‹-ly› begins with a consonant, it is usually just added to the root word, so *actual, frequent, sincere, physical* and *accidental* become *actually, frequently, sincerely, physically* and *accidentally*.
- However, there are some exceptions that the children should be familiar with:
  – If the word ends in a consonant plus ‹y›, *shy ‹i›* replaces *toughy ‹y›* before the ‹-ly› is added, so *hearty* and *necessary* become *heartily* and *necessarily*.
  – If a word ends in ‹le›, the ‹le› is removed before adding ‹-ly›, so *probable* becomes *probably*.
  – If a word ends in ‹ic›, the suffix ‹-ally› is added instead of ‹-ly›, so *symbolic* and *systematic* become *symbolically* and *systematically*.
- Go through the other words in the spelling list and identify the adjective root each time.

Spelling List
- Go through the list, asking the class to find and highlight the ‹-ly› suffix each time. Also discuss the meaning of any unfamiliar words.
- Point out other spelling features, such as the soft ‹c› in *centrally, excellently, sincerely, necessarily* and *accidentally*, the ‹ear› saying /ar/ in *heartily*, the vowel saying its long sound in *frequently, immediately* and *environmentally*, the alternative /f/ spelling and ‹s› saying /z/ in *physically*, the ‹y› saying /i/ in *physically, symbolically* and *systematically*, the way /ear/ is spelt in *sincerely*, the ‹ie› saying /i/ in *mischievously*, and the ‹e› saying /i/ in *environmentally*.
- It is a good idea to blend and sound out the spelling words quickly every day with the class. Where appropriate, use the *say it as it sounds* strategy, stressing, for example, the pure sound of any schwas (as in *fre-*

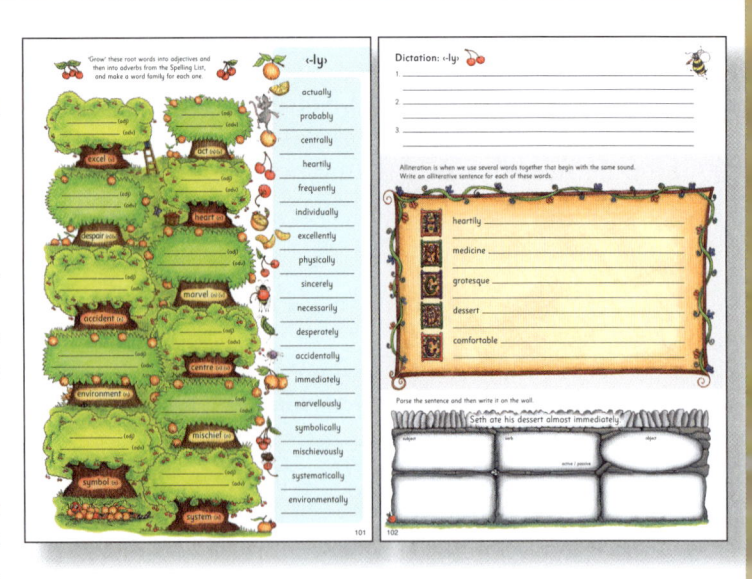

actually
probably
centrally
heartily
frequently
individually
excellently
physically
sincerely
necessarily
desperately
accidentally
immediately
marvellously
symbolically
mischievously
systematically
environmentally

quently, individually and *excellently*) or any syllables that are almost swallowed, (as in *actually, physically, desperately* and *marvellously*).

Activity Page 1
- The children split each word into syllables to help remember the spelling (*ac/tu/al/ly, prob/a/bly, cen/tral/ly, heart/i/ly, fre/quent/ly, in/di/vid/u/ally, ex/cel/lent/ly, phys/i/cal/ly, sin/cere/ly, nec/es/sar/i/ly, des/per/ate/ly, ac/ci/den/tal/ly, im/me/di/ate/ly, mar/vel/lous/ly, sym/bol/ic/al/ly, mis/chie/vous/ly, sys/tem/at/ic/al/ly, en/vi/ron/men/tal/ly*).
- They then complete the *word family* trees, writing the correct adjective and spelling list adverb each time (*act: actual/ly; excel: excellent/ly; heart: hearty/heartily; despair: desperate/ly; marvel: marvellous/ly; accident: accidental/ly; centre: central/ly; environment: environmental/ly; mischief: mischievous/ly; symbol: symbolic/ally; system: systematic/ally*).

Activity Page 2
- The children write an alliterative sentence for each word.
- Then they parse the sentence and complete the wall:
Seth ate his dessert almost immediately.
Top: Seth - ate - dessert
Bottom: [blank] - immediately (almost) - his
Verb: active
  – The adverb *almost* modifies the adverb *immediately*.

Dictation
- Dictate the following sentences:

  1. Her parents visit Ireland quite frequently.
  2. Their products are environmentally friendly.
  3. "I have probably passed my test," I replied.

- Remind the class to use speech marks with the correct punctuation in Sentence 3. *Ireland* is a proper noun and needs a capital letter.

Grammar: Homophone Mix-Ups

Aim
- Reinforce the children's understanding of homophones and develop their ability to choose between similar-sounding words in their writing.

Introduction
- Ask the children to call out some homophones that they know. The most commonly confused ones usually include parts of the verb *to be*, possessive adjectives or contractions, as in the following:
  - *Our, hour* and *are*
  - *Their, there* and *they're*
  - *Your* and *you're*
  - *Its* and *it's*
  - *Where, wear* and *were*
- *Our* is more properly pronounced /ou-r/ to sound like *hour*, but in practice it is often pronounced /ar/ and can be confused with *are*.
- *Were* is not strictly a homophone of *where* either, but it looks and sounds similar enough to cause confusion. Remind the children that words like this are called near homophones.
- Some numbers are also homophones: one *(won)*, two *(to, too)*, four *(for)* and eight *(ate)*.
- Quickly go through these words, as well as any others that the children called out, and make sure that they know which meanings go with which spellings.

Main Point
- Remind the children that it is important to use the correct spelling when writing homophones, otherwise their writing will not make sense.
- They need to pause before writing a homophone, decide which meaning is needed, and think how the word with that meaning is spelt.
- Write the homophones from the activity page on the board, look at the spellings, and check that the class know what they mean: *herd/heard, who's/whose, serial/cereal, ascent/assent, father/farther, dissent/descent, draft/draught, principle/principal*.
- If the children are unsure of any meanings, ask them to look up the words in the dictionary and see who can find them first.
- Remind the children that they can sometimes use their existing knowledge to help them choose the correct homophone. For example:
  - *Heard* is the simple past tense and past participle of the verb *to hear*, so if the homophone needed is the verb, they should use this spelling.
  - *Whose* is either a question word or a relative pronoun, whereas *who's* is a contraction of either *who is* or *who has*.
  - *Serial* is an adjective meaning *forming part of a series*.
  - *Farther* is a comparative meaning *more far*.
- Ask the class to think of a sentence for some of the homophones and discuss which spellings they would use.

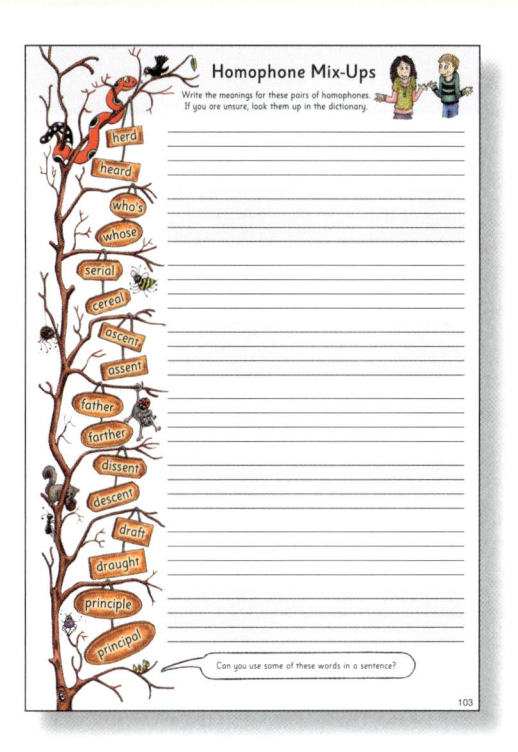

Activity Page
- The children write the meaning for each homophone. Encourage them to use a dictionary, if needed, to look up the meaning or to check the spelling.
- Writing on a separate sheet of paper, they then use each homophone in a sentence. (Alternatively, this could be done as part of the extension activity.)

Extension Activity
- The children can work in pairs, dictating one of their sentences to their partner, and then checking whether the correct spelling has been used.

Rounding Off
- Go over the activity page with the children, discussing their answers.
- If they have done the extension activity, ask some of the children to read out their sentences and check that they have used the correct spelling.

GRAMMAR 6 PUPIL BOOK: PAGES 104 & 105

Spelling: ‹ere› and /oa/

Spelling Test
- The children turn to the backs of their books and find the column labelled *Spelling Test 34*.
- Call out the spelling words learnt last week.

Revision
- Write *individually* on the board and discuss how the suffix ‹-ly› has been added to the adjective *individual* to make an adverb.
- Explain that these words are in the same word family as *divide* and ask the class to think of some others (such as *(un)divided, (in)divisible, division, divisive(ly)* and *individuality*).
- Identify the part(s) of speech for each word.

Spelling Point
- The most common spellings for /oa/ are ‹oa›, ‹ow› and ‹o_e›, but ‹o› can also say its long vowel sound, as in *soldier*.
- There are other less common spellings too, as found in *toe, brooch, sewn* and *mauve*. Remind the class that ‹oe› usually says /oa/ in plurals like *potatoes* and *tomatoes*.
- Now revise ‹ere›, which is an alternative spelling of both the /ear/ and /air/ sounds, as in *here* and *there*.
- See if the children can think of any other words with this spelling and write them on the board (such as those from the spelling list, as well as *sphere, cereal, mere, coherence, atmosphere, somewhere, wherewithal* and *elsewhere*).
- Point out that the word *werewolf* can be pronounced with either the /air/ or /ear/ sound.

Spelling List
- Go through the list, asking the class to find and highlight the ‹ere› or /oa/ spelling each time. Also discuss the meaning of any unfamiliar words.
- Point out other spelling features, such as the ‹e› saying /i/ in *severe, revere* and *persevere*, the ‹di› saying /j/ in *soldier*, the silent ‹e› in *mauve* and *therefore*, the ‹o› saying /oo/ in *werewolf*, the ‹a› saying /e/ and ‹y› saying /ee/ in *anywhere*, the ‹wh› spelling in the compound words *anywhere, wherever, whereupon* and *whereabouts*, the way the middle ‹e› in *wherever* belongs to both *where* and *ever*, the soft ‹c› in *sincere*, and the prefix in *interfere*.
- It is a good idea to blend and sound out the spelling words quickly every day with the class. Where appropriate, use the *say it as it sounds* strategy, stressing, for example, the pure sound of any schwas (as in *shoulder, soldier, interfere, whereupon* and *whereabouts*).

toe
brooch
sewn
severe
revere
cashmere
shoulder
soldier
mauve
werewolf
anywhere
wherever
sincere
therefore
interfere
persevere
whereupon
whereabouts

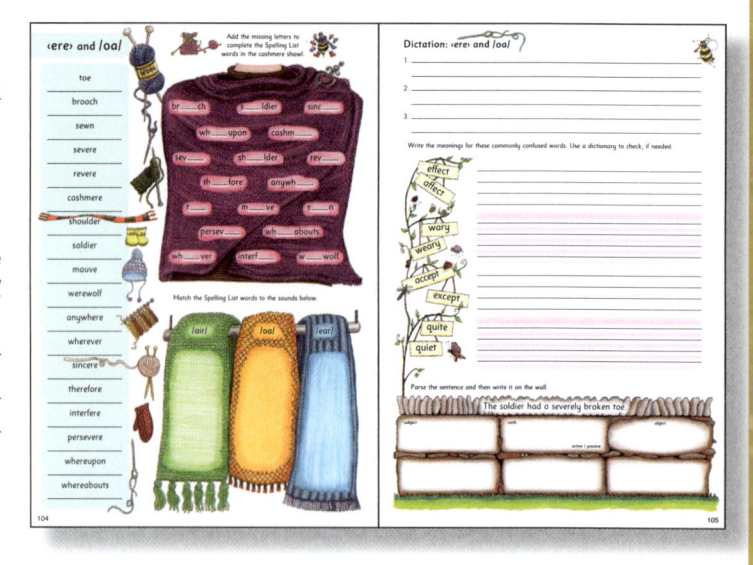

Activity Page 1
- The children split each word into syllables to help remember the spelling (*toe, brooch, sewn, se/vere, re/vere, cash/mere, shoul/der, sol/dier, mauve, were/wolf, an/y/where, wher/ev/er, sin/cere, there/fore, in/ter/fere, per/se/vere, where/up/on, where/a/bouts*).
- They then add the missing letters in the shawl (*brooch, soldier, sincere; whereupon, cashmere; severe, shoulder, revere; therefore, anywhere; toe, mauve, sewn; persevere, whereabouts; wherever, interfere, werewolf*).
- Then they sort the spelling list words by sound and write them in the correct scarf (/air/: *werewolf, anywhere, wherever, therefore, whereupon, whereabouts*; /oa/: *toe, brooch, sewn, shoulder, soldier, mauve*; /ear/: *severe, revere, cashmere, (werewolf), sincere, interfere, persevere*).

Activity Page 2
- The children write the meanings for each pair of commonly confused words, using a dictionary to help them if needed.
- Then they parse the sentence and complete the wall: The soldier had a severely broken toe.
Top: soldier - had - toe
Bottom: The - [blank] - a severely broken
Verb: active
  – The adverb *severely* modifies the adjective *broken* (which is the past participle of *to break*).

Dictation
- Dictate the following sentences:

1. The mauve buttons had been sewn on securely.
2. "I cannot find my brooch anywhere," I admitted.
3. She draped the cashmere scarf over her shoulders.

- Remind the class to use speech marks with the correct punctuation in Sentence 2.

Grammar: Antonyms and Synonyms

Aim
- Reinforce the children's understanding of antonyms and synonyms and develop their ability to use a wider variety of words in their writing.

Introduction
- Briefly revise dictionaries and thesauruses. Remind the children of the following:
  - We use a **dictionary** to check a word's meaning or its spelling.
  - We use a **thesaurus** to help us find synonyms and antonyms for a particular word.
- Make sure that the children know the difference between synonyms and antonyms, both of which are words with a Greek origin:
  - The word **synonym** means *with name* and is used for words with the same or similar meanings.
  - The word **antonym** means *opposite name* and is used for words with opposite meanings.
- Make sure that everyone in the class has access to either a dictionary or a thesaurus and call out some words. The children race to look up each one and whoever finds it first can read out its meaning in the dictionary or call out some of its synonyms and antonyms from the thesaurus.
- This is a good opportunity to look again at this week's (or other recent) spelling list words.

Main Point
- Remind the children that using a more varied vocabulary will help them avoid overusing certain words and can make their writing more interesting.
- Write some overused words on the board (possible words include *big, small, nice, nasty, good, bad, hot, cold, happy, sad, angry, dirty, run, go, pretty, fun* and *say*). Then ask the children to do the following:
  - Think of other words (synonyms) that they could use instead.
  - Think of any words that mean the opposite of these words (antonyms).
- Also remind the children that:
  - Many prefixes and some suffixes can be used to make antonyms, as in **un**happy, **dis**like, **mis**understand, **il**legal, **im**possible, **in**capable, **ir**relevant, **non**sense, **de**activate and **anti**social.
  - Some prefixes have opposite meanings so that when they are added to the same root word, they create pairs of antonyms, as in **pre**-war and **post**-war, **super**script and **sub**script, **in**clude and **ex**clude, **in**flate and **de**flate.
  - The suffixes ‹-less› and ‹-ful› can also create pairs of antonyms, as in *thoughtful* and *thoughtless*, *fearful* and *fearless*, *hopeful* and *hopeless*.

Activity Page
- The children read each group of words and cross out the one that is not a synonym of the word in the web (*Top: reliable, constant, ignore; Middle: decorated, retreat, hobby; Bottom: eventually, carefully, politely*).
- They then match the pairs of antonyms and synonyms with the correct word in the drawers (**weird**: *bizarre, strange/ordinary, normal*; **enjoyable**: *fun, amusing/unpleasant, boring*; **jovial**: *jolly, cheerful/miserable, gloomy*; **antique**: *old, ancient/new, modern*; **grotesque**: *ugly, hideous/beautiful, gorgeous*; **bygone**: *past, former/present, recent*; **genuine**: *real, true/fake, insincere*; **frequently**: *regularly, often/occasionally, rarely*; **valuable**: *precious, expensive/cheap, worthless*). The children may want to use a thesaurus or dictionary to check whether they are correct.

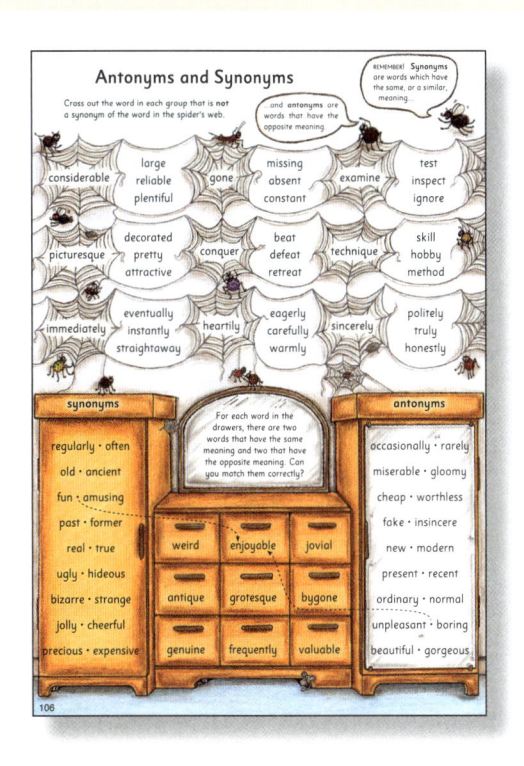

Extension Activity
- The children choose some words from the drawers on the activity page and write a sentence for each one.
- Then they rewrite each sentence twice, first using one of the synonyms and then using one of the antonyms.

Rounding Off
- Go over the activity page with the children, discussing their answers.
- If they have done the extension activity, ask some children to read out their sentences.

GRAMMAR 6 PUPIL BOOK: PAGES 107 & 108

Spelling: The Schwa

Spelling Test
- The children turn to the backs of their books and find the column labelled *Spelling Test 35*.
- Call out the spelling words learnt last week.

Revision
- Write *sincere* on the board and point out the soft ‹c› and the ‹ere› spelling of /ear/.
- Ask the class to think of some other words in this word family (such as *insincere, (in)sincerer, (in)sincerest, (in)sincerely* and *(in)sincerity*) and identify their part(s) of speech.

Spelling Point
- Revise syllables, which are units of sound that contain a vowel sound.
- In spoken English, if a word has two or more syllables, we stress one of them by saying it a little louder and lengthening the vowel slightly, which keeps the vowel sound pure.
- However, the vowel in an unstressed syllable is often swallowed and becomes – most commonly – a neutral *schwa*, sounding something like /uh/, but it can sometimes change to an /i/ sound instead.
- Go through the spelling list words with the class and listen for these swallowed vowels. (Letters in bold indicate a schwa; underlined letters say /i/; underlined letters in bold can say either: barg**ai**n, cert**ai**n, per**ha**ps, d**e**velop, c**o**ntinue, r**e**memb**e**r, d**e**cide, rel**e**vant, am**a**teur, cat**e**gory, strength**e**n, diction**a**ry, veg**e**table, stom**a**ch, crit**i**cize, cem**e**tery, rest**au**rant; there is also a schwa sound in the ‹le› in *vegetable* and *vehicle*.)

Spelling List
- Go through the list, asking the class to find and highlight the swallowed vowel(s) each time. Also discuss the meaning of any unfamiliar words.
- Point out other spelling features, such as the soft ‹c› in *certain, decide, criticise* and *cemetery*, the ‹t› saying either its own sound or /ch/ in *amateur*, the /ng/ in *strength*, the ‹tion› saying /shun/ in *dictionary*, the soft ‹g› in *vegetable*, the ‹o› saying /u/ and ‹ch› spelling of /k/ in *stomach*, the ‹s› saying /z/ in *criticise*, the silent ‹h› and ‹e› saying its long vowel in *vehicle*, and the ‹a› saying /o/ in *restaurant*.
- It is a good idea to blend and sound out the spelling words quickly every day with the class. Where appropriate, use the *say it as it sounds* strategy, stressing, for example, the pure sound of any swallowed syllables (as in *vegetable* and *cemetery*) or syllables that are almost swallowed (as in *cat**e**gory* and *diction**a**ry*).

bargain
certain
perhaps
develop
continue
remember
decide
relevant
amateur
category
strengthen
dictionary
vegetable
stomach
criticise
vehicle
cemetery
restaurant

Activity Page 1
- The children split each word into syllables to help remember the spelling (bar/gain, cer/tain, per/haps, de/vel/op, con/tin/ue, re/mem/ber, de/cide, rel/e/vant, am/a/teur, cat/e/go/ry, strength/en, dic/tion/a/ry, vege/ta/ble, stom/ach, crit/i/cise, ve/hi/cle, cem/e/tery, res/tau/rant).
- They then unscramble the letters in the dinner plates to make some of the spelling words (Left-hand column: continue, perhaps, amateur, relevant, strengthen, stomach, vegetable / Right-hand column: certain, remember, dictionary, category, vehicle, criticise, restaurant).

Activity Page 2
- The children try to write down a fruit or vegetable that starts with each alphabet letter (for example: apple, beans, carrot, date, endive, fig, grape, horseradish, iceberg lettuce, Jerusalem artichoke, kiwi fruit, leek, melon, nectarine, onion, potato, quince, radish, spinach, turnip, ugli fruit, vine leaves, watercress, xigua, yam, zucchini).
- Then they parse the sentence and complete the wall:
  The cashmere shawl was a bargain.
  Top: shawl - was \ bargain (a) - [blank]
  Bottom: The cashmere - [blank] - [blank]
  Verb: linking
  – The verb *was* links the complement noun *bargain* to the subject *shawl*, which it defines.

Dictation
- Dictate the following sentences:

  1. "Do you remember that restaurant?" asked Dad.
  2. They sorted the books into certain categories.
  3. We must continue to develop our dictionary skills.

- Remind the class to use speech marks with the correct punctuation in Sentence 1. *Dad* is a proper noun and needs a capital letter.

Grammar: 'Grammar Consequences' Game

Aim
- Have fun revising the different parts of speech. Play *Grammar Action Sentences* and a new game called *Grammar Consequences*.

Introduction
- Briefly revise the different parts of speech and the nine verb tenses (see pages 6 to 16):
  - Do the grammar actions with the children and ask them which parts of speech they represent.
  - Revise the colour associated with each one: nouns, pronouns, adjectives, verbs, adverbs, prepositions and conjunctions.
  If action cards were used in earlier lessons (see pages 45, 55 and 61), these could be held up each time.
- Remind the children of the actions for the definite and indefinite articles, which are a special kind of adjective, and discuss the different ways to write the past, present and future tenses (simple, continuous and perfect).
- Also remind the class that many words can act as more than one part of speech, depending on how they are used in a sentence.

Main Point
- Play *Grammar Action Sentences,* either by doing the actions or using action cards:
  - The actions should be ordered in a sequence, following the pattern of a simple sentence (see below).
  - The children think of a suitable word for each part of speech and create a sentence.
- Try to use a different sequence each time, perhaps from the following examples, and specify which article and tense should be used:
  - article / adjective / common noun / verb / adverb
  - article / adjective / adjective / common noun / verb
  - pronoun / verb / preposition / article / common noun
  - proper noun / conjunction / proper noun / verb / adverb
  - article / common noun / verb / adverb / conjunction / adverb
  - proper noun / verb / preposition / article / adjective / common noun
- As you create each sentence, it may be necessary to rethink some of the words used in order for it to make sense; the verb chosen, for example, may not work if it precedes a preposition. However, it can also be fun to see how more random choices affect the meaning.
- Play the game again but this time ask a different child to think of the word each time, without revealing what it is. At the end of the sequence, the children call out their words and see if the sentence makes any sense. This game is called *Grammar Consequences*.

Activity Page
- The children trace over the three articles *a, an* and *the* and then think of five words for each part of speech, writing them in the appropriate boxes. Remind the children to use examples of both common and proper nouns.
- The children then play *Grammar Consequences*. They look at the sequence of grammar actions at the bottom of the page and create a sentence, choosing a word from each of the lists. The children should try to use a word that will make sense grammatically, but this may not always be possible, resulting in a rather silly sentence!

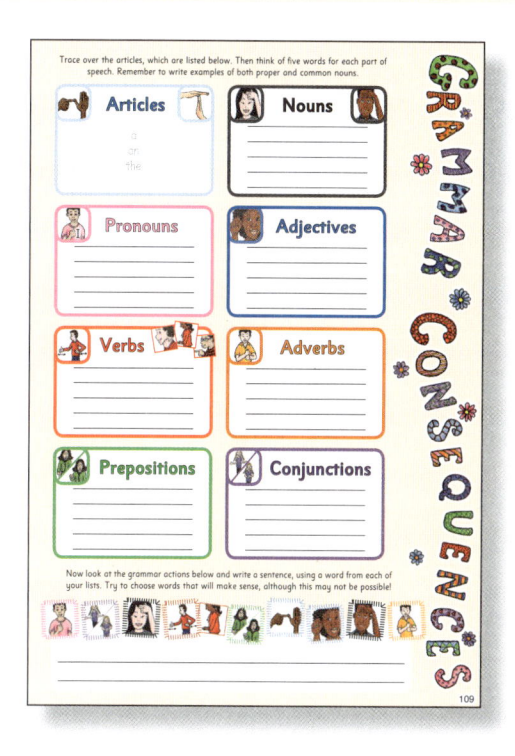

Extension Activity
- The children can play *Grammar Consequences* as a class. Give each child a sheet of paper; then hold up the first card in a sentence sequence (or do the action) and ask the children to think of a suitable word. Without telling anyone what it is, they write the word at the top of their sheet, using the appropriate colour, and fold the paper over so that it cannot be seen. They then pass the sheet to their right-hand neighbour and continue the game. At the end of the sequence, the children unfold their sheets of paper and read their 'silly' sentence.
- The children could also draw a picture to illustrate their *Grammar Consequences* sentence.

Rounding Off
- Go over the activity page with the children and ask some of them to read out their sentence to the rest of the class.

The Grammar 1 to 6 Pupil and Teacher's Books

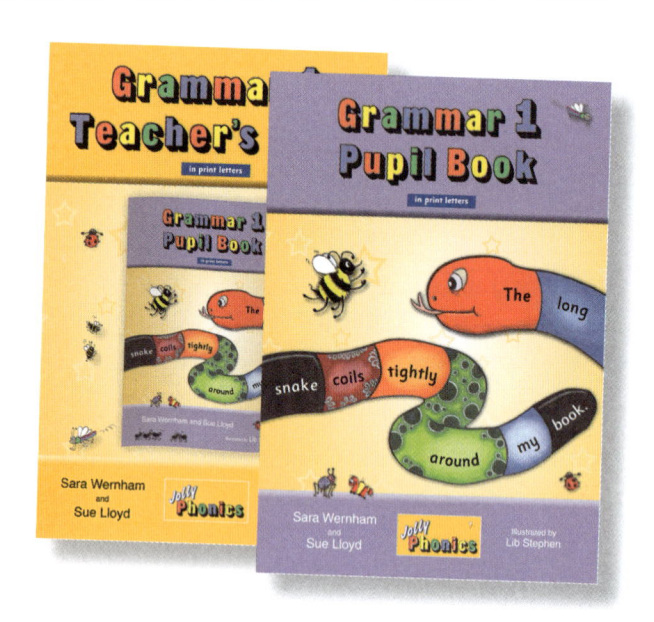

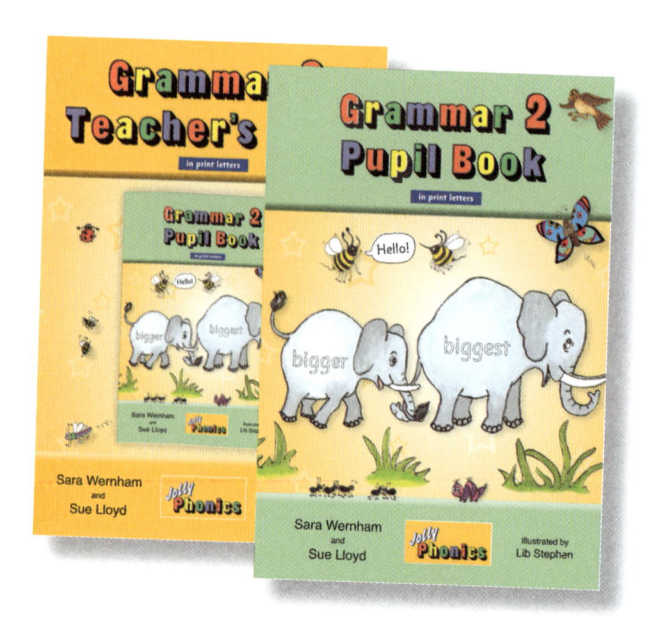

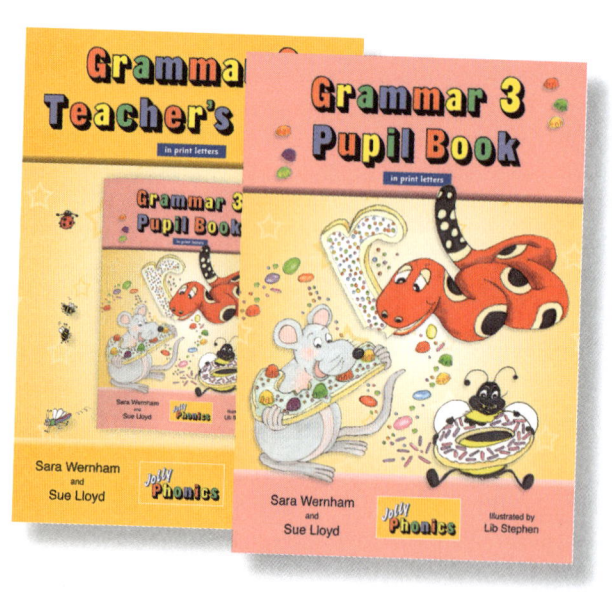

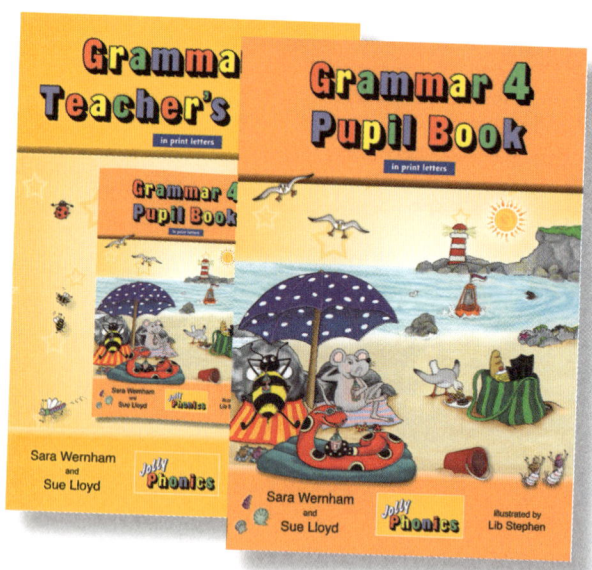

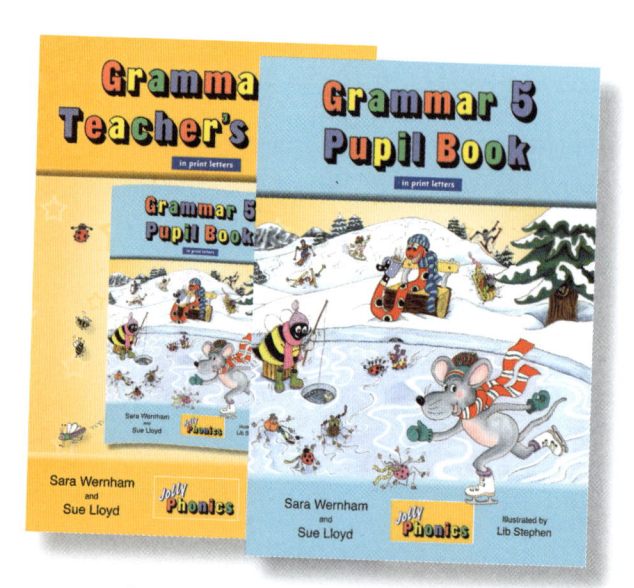

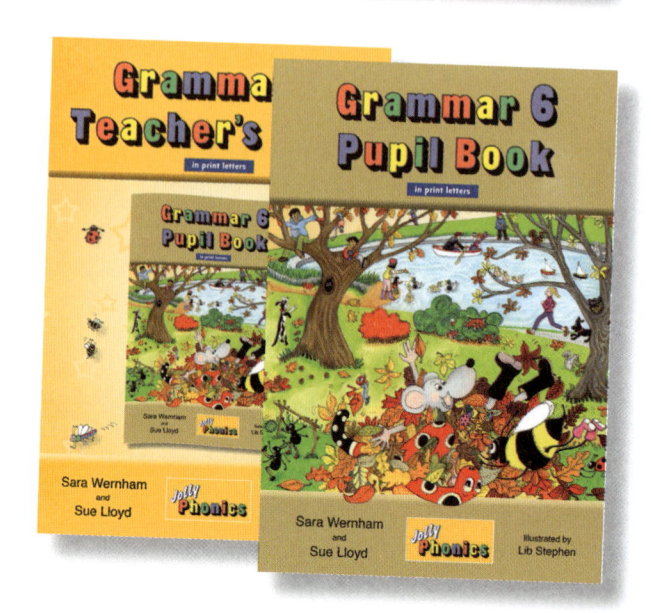